THE LIBRARY YEARS
1892 – 1992

THE LIBRARY YEARS
1892 – 1992

Richard Dodge Whittemore

Port Washington Public Library

Port Washington, New York

Port Washington Public Library
One Library Drive
Port Washington, New York 11050

Designed by Joseph P. Ascherl

ISBN 0-9615059-3-1 (Casebound edition)
ISBN 0-9615059-4-X (Paperbound edition)

DEDICATION

This book is dedicated to the
many devoted individuals—
volunteers, librarians, and staff—
who for 100 years have labored and
continue to labor to make the Port
Washington Public Library the finest
community resource.

Foreword

The Library Years is the result of a meeting among Joan Kent, Edward de Sciora, Henry Salomon and myself in 1989 to start planning for the 100th anniversary celebration of the Port Washington Public Library.

Among many decisions concerning the Centennial celebration, perhaps the most ambitious was, quite logically, a book—a chronicle of the events from 1892 to 1992 in the development of this library from a few books on a shelf in the front hall of Charles W. Mitchell's home to this modern library and cultural center which has been selected as one of the fifty outstanding public libraries in the country.

Throughout the life of any institution there are a few devoted individuals who carefully record and preserve the story of that institution. The Port Washington Library is no exception. Without the beautifully handwritten minutes of the first few years in the life of the Port Washington Woman's Club, sponsor of the library, there would be no recorded history.

Of equal importance in developing *The Library Years* were the many members of today's library staff whose enthusiastic support from the beginning made the research a pleasure instead of a chore:

Priscilla Ciccariello, head of Information Services, who with her associates, Vera Fiddler, Lina Coffey, Hinde Fertig and Trudy Friedman, opened many doors in research; Janet West, keeper of the keys to Special Collections, unfailing in her ability to find the right archival material; Richard Hausdorff in Periodicals and Jerry Sears whose willingness to copy from microfilm hundreds of pages of *Port Washington News* articles lessened that burden immeasurably.

From the outset of this project many members of Friends of the Library contributed hours of their time in identifying articles about the library in *Port Washington News* on the microfilm records. I am genuinely appreciative of all their help.

Special thanks are due Debbie Jaszcar who taught a complete neophyte in the daunting world of word processing how to cope and in the process to produce a manuscript.

Without the valuable editorial comment and copy editing by Amy Pett, a seasoned journalist, the final product would be far less acceptable.

Jacqueline Maldonado and Sheldon Tarakan, with their photo files, saved the day more than once.

To Ann Pellaton and Ruth Feingold, my gratitude for sorting out the complexities of, respectively, the Art Advisory Council and the Music Advisory Council.

My thanks to Joe Scrofani and his staff who searched out and brought to light many cartons of old records and memorabilia which have enriched the book.

To Virginia Parker, Ellie Sewell, Elly Shodel, and Debbie Wanna, thank you for so many kindnesses.

There has to be a "without whom." His name is Joe Ascherl, long time friend and peerless book designer without whom this book would still be in manuscript.

Finally, to my wife, Wilda, who shared this long journey and emerged as a dedicated proofreader, my thanks and my love.

A grave danger lurks in the compiling of a list such as this: someone's contribution may have been overlooked inadvertently.

In that event I apologize sincerely.

Richard D. Whittemore
Port Washington, N.Y.
July 1992

ABOUT THE AUTHOR

A graduate of Harvard and a retired Doubleday publisher, Richard Whittemore is a founding member of the Friends of the Library, a former president of Friends, and former president of the Library's Board of Trustees. He received the Friends of the Library Award for outstanding service to the library in 1991. He is also a former chairman of the Port Washington Continuing and Community Education Advisory Council, and with his wife, Wilda, was honored by the Community Chest of Port Washington with its Citizen of the Year Award in 1985.

Contents

Prologue

During the first years of the 1800s about 200 people lived in Cow Neck, a small peninsula jutting out into Long Island Sound between Great Neck and Cow Bay to the west and Hempstead Harbor and Glen Head to the east.

Cow Neck was a prosperous farming community, growing garden produce for New York City residents and hay for their horses, all of which was shipped by packet sloops through Hell Gate and down the East River. Returning vessels often carried manure from the city streets to be used as fertilizer on the farms.

A new enterprise for Cow Neck developed out of the successful planting and growing of seed oysters in Cow Bay during the 1830s. At mid-century Andrew Van Pelt and A.J.N. Thatcher put oystering on a profitable basis when they brought experienced baymen from Staten Island with their families to settle near the shore. In time more and more workers were attracted to town to share in the fruitful harvests of this new industry.

Charles W. Mitchell 1816–1902

In 1857 two prominent citizens, Thomas McKee and Elbert Mackey, went to Albany to get the town's name changed from Cow Neck to the more impressive Port Washington.

One of the oldest and much respected families in Cow Neck, the Mitchells, had been large land owners since before 1700. Their holdings covered over 1,100 acres. One of the heirs to this property was Charles W. Mitchell whose 100 acres along the Cow Bay waterfront were adjacent to another parcel owned by his wife, Sarah Covert Mitchell. Although Charles Mitchell started out as a farmer, he found far greater satisfaction in owning and operating the Port Washington Stage, a two-horse coach from Cow Bay to Sands Point.

There were other satisfactions as well. The Mitchells became land developers, selling more than sixty parcels over a twenty-five year period to baymen and oyster entrepreneurs. Their home was an inherited 36-room mansion near the bay originally called "Manhasset Hall." Of their seven children those best remembered today are Samuel, Commissioner of Highways for the Town of North Hempstead, and Wilhelmina around whom much of the history of the Port Washington Library revolves.

Following the oyster boom came an even more spectacular boost to the economy in the sand and gravel industry around 1868. Gradually the hills on the shoreline of Cow Bay, later Manhasset Bay, and along Hempstead Harbor would disappear as the sand on the Cow

Hannah Covert Mitchell 1816–1902

Manhasset Hall, built in 1769, later called the Anchorage, home of the Mitchell family until 1889.

Dr. D. Preston Wysong (1853–1924), one of Port's first doctors called on his patients in a "doctor's wagon" similar to the one below.

Neck peninsula turned out to be the finest in the world for making the concrete for building New York's skyscrapers.

Even the Mitchells did well in this new initiative. The Murray and Reid sand bank, part of the Mitchell's holdings, was among the first to be mined.

In 1892, when this history begins, the shoreline of Manhasset Bay had already changed in character from wooded hills and a winding road to a level stretch of land where houses were rapidly appearing.

At the junction of Shore Road and Flower Hill Avenue (later lower Main Street) was Bayles Drug Store, for many years the only one in town, and the site of the first telephone in town—1893. If you needed Dr. Wysong in a hurry, you wrote your name on a slate at A.P. Baxter & Company's emporium opposite the drug store. When Dr. Wysong called there at 2 P.M. each day, he came to see you in your turn.

Port Washington was a quietly beautiful village where everyone knew everyone's name.

CHAPTER I

The Early Years 1892–1903

Mitchell and Baxter Homesteads

The day dawned bright, clear and cold on January 27, 1892, a typical winter day in Port Washington. At her home, "Old House" on Sands Point, Miss Caroline Hicks anticipated an exciting day ahead for she had planned a very special meeting for that afternoon. As a matter of fact she had submitted a news item which appeared in the January 27th *Roslyn News* concerning the organization on that day of a Woman's Club whose "members will devote themselves to mutual entertainment and improvement, and to philanthropic work. Their first efforts will be made towards establishing a circulating library for the village."

And that is just what they did! There was much discussion among the ladies who had responded to Miss Hicks' invitation about entertainment, self-improvement and philanthropy. One prospective member, Miss Wilhelmina Mitchell, in her forthright manner, made it clear that she would join the Woman's Club "only after she was promised that *there actually would be a library.*"

At the same meeting the following charter members elected their officers:

CHARTER MEMBERS OF THE
PORT WASHINGTON WOMAN'S CLUB
Founders of the Library

Miss Caroline Hicks, *President*
Mrs. J. H. Tredwell, *Vice-President*
Mrs. Walter Cornwell, *Treasurer*
Miss L. P. Onderdonk, *Secretary*
Miss Wilhelmina Mitchell, *Librarian*

Miss Phebe Burtis	Mrs. Annie Mott
Miss Searing	Mrs. W. I. Cocks
Miss Mattie Tredwell	Mrs. Messenger
Mrs. A. H. Baxter	Mrs. M. U. Onderdonk
Mrs. D. P. Wysong	Mrs. William Cornwell
Mrs. Samuel Mitchell	

The "Old House" at Cowneck, home of Caroline Hicks, 1892

An 1873 map of Cow Neck, later Port Washington and Sands Point, identifies many of the homes of the ladies who attended that meeting. Miss Hicks lived in "Old House" on Old House Lane; the

Map of Sands Point (c. 1873) showing the homes of some of the charter members of the Port Washington Woman's Club in 1892.

Tredwell family, just west of there near Sands Point Road; the Cornwells, further west; the Onderdonks, on old Middleneck Road not far from the Willets home (now Sands-Willets House, on Port Washington Boulevard).

Nearer the village center, considered then to be the Mill Pond area and southward up Shore Road to Flower Hill Road, lived the Baxters and the Cocks.

Distances which have shrunk in this day of the automobile were far greater to the ladies in 1892, whether they walked or, if fortunate, drove a horse and carriage. They were hardy, however, and quite accustomed to the rigors of a Long Island winter.

In 1892 the village of Port Washington was inhabited by 800 residents, mostly oystermen, farmers, local merchants and workers in the sand banks. A few of the large estates on Sands Point were occupied year round, but many of the homes were summer places only for city people from Queens, Brooklyn and Manhattan.

The Mill Pond and Tom McKee's General Store—the center of town in the late 1800s.

1892 *Woman's Club establishes circulating library—Members and townspeople donate books—Miss Wilhelmina Mitchell first Librarian*

Wilhelmina Mitchell lived with her father and mother, Charles W. Mitchell and Hannah Covert Mitchell, on a forty acre farm (part of which property is now occupied by Thomson Industries) at the corner of Shore Road and Pleasant Avenue. The Mitchells purchased this home after selling "Manhasset Hall" further south on Shore Road in 1889.*

Just two busy weeks of preparation after the organizational meeting, the Port Washington Circulating Library opened officially on February 10, 1892, in the front hall of the Mitchell home with 125 volumes, all having been covered and marked by club members. Each of the members had contributed at least two books, other townspeople gave generously from their libraries. Mr. Henry Onderdonk's valuable histories of Long Island were donated by Mrs. Adrian Onderdonk; Mrs. Benjamin Mott also presented books dating back to 1777. Most important of all, Wilhelmina Mitchell was appointed Librarian, assisted by her sister-in-law, Mrs. Samuel Mitchell.

As the official newspaper of Port Washington, the *Roslyn News* was eager to publish reports of the big event and carried what appears to be all the notices submitted, presumably, by Miss Hicks:

*For further information about the Mitchell family, see *Historic Mitchell Farms,* by George L. Williams, published by the Landmarks Committee of Cow Neck Peninsula Historical Society

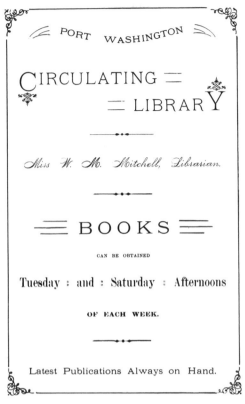

Flyer announcing opening of library at Mitchell home.

"The library is open for procuring books Tuesday and Saturday afternoons of each week. The latest publications constantly on hand and the Library contains some rare old books and histories interesting to students and bibliographers. Yearly subscription for one book taken at a time, $1.50; two books taken at a time, $2.00."

Within days flyers were printed and circulated throughout the village by the proud ladies of the Woman's Club, and new members were joining the Club weekly. Miss Hicks set the pace for activities of the Woman's Club by selecting committees responsible for entertainment at monthly meetings. Such diversions as reading amusing newspaper clippings, musical renditions, and story-telling were prepared, and every meeting ended with tea and cake (or cookies). In addition there were committees to bring the food, serve, and wash up.

Since raising money to keep the Library running was by far the most important function of the club at that time, a series of "Entertainments" was planned for the Spring starting with a program on March 16 at Liberty Hall on Carlton Avenue, home of the Atlantic Hook and Ladder Fire Company, organized in the late '80s. Liberty Hall had a fine auditorium which was rented to clubs, fraternal organizations, and frequently to the Woman's Club. The name *Entertainment* became attached to the Club's public performances and remained for years.

On Wednesday Evening March 16, an impressive group of townspeople headed by Miss Caroline Hicks and Mr. I.A. Willets (an amateur violinist of some local fame), Mrs. Albert Messenger, Mrs. Samuel C. Mott and others performed musical numbers, followed

Liberty Hall, scene of many Woman's Club/Library "Entertainments" and home of Atlantic Hook and Ladder Company.

ENTERTAINMENT

GIVEN BY THE

Woman's Club of Port Washington

AT LIBERTY HALL,

Wednesday Evening, March 16, 1892

PROGRAMME.

PART FIRST.

Duett, Violin and Piano, Overture from Stradella.................Flotow
Miss Caroline Hicks and Mr. I. A. Willets.

Reading........ ....Selected
Mrs. Albert Messenger.

Soprano Solo, "Last Greeting".......................Levi
Mrs. Samuel C. Mott.

Duett, Piano, "La Malle des Gardes"................ George LaMootie
Mrs. C. A. Remsen and Mrs. D. Orr.

Recitation.....................................Selected
Mrs. Charles Sperry.

Soprano Solo, "Love's Sorrow".....................Shelly
Mrs. Anna L. Peck.

Duett, Violin and Piano, "La Ingenue"..............Arditti
Miss Caroline Hicks and Mr. I. A. Willets.

PART SECOND.
Social Tableaux From Life

And Popular Advertisements.

F. M. Eldredge, Steam Printer, 330 Grand Street, Brooklyn.

⊛ENTERTAINMENT⊛

IN AID OF THE

Port Washington Circulating Library

UNDER THE AUSPICES OF THE WOMAN'S CLUB,

Consisting of Music, Readings and Tableaux.
AT LIBRARY HALL, PORT WASHINGTON,

Wednesday Evening, March 16th, 1892

TICKETS, 35 CTS.   RESERVED SEATS, 50 CTS

Doors open at 7 30.   Entertainment to commence at 8 o'clock.

Flyer and ticket for the first "Entertainment" to raise money for the new library.

by comic strip tableaux—all of which was presented with gusto and good humor.

1892 *Library outgrows Mitchell home—Baxter House parlors rented— Gala opening celebration*

The new library in the Mitchell's front hall was a success, in fact, too great a success. On March 23rd, not quite two months after the library opened, "it was decided by unanimous vote to rent Mr. Allen J. Baxter's parlors for club rooms" and the library.

For an unexplained reason the *Roslyn News* published on March 25 the following notice:

"The officers of the Woman's Club and Miss W.M. Mitchell, Librarian, wish to be understood that the circulating library of Port Washington has not been organized merely for the use of club members, but for the use and benefit of all residents of Port Washington and neighborhood. New books to suit the tastes of all readers are constantly on hand and everyone is cordially invited to take books from the library."

Miss Caroline Hicks was a true leader. It was through her continuing prodding and cajoling, that each new project was undertaken. As soon as the library's new home was announced, she made certain that the rooms would be properly appointed, and consequently sent to the clubrooms "three large carved oaken chairs, formerly belonging to an Odd Fellows' Lodge. The rooms will be furnished comfortably and artistically and will make a delightful meeting place for the members."

The second Entertainment for the benefit of the Reading Room and Woman's Exchange was presented at Liberty Hall on April 18th featuring a banjo quartette, vocal solos, and the piano and violin duo of Miss Hicks and I.A. Willets, followed by *The Trials of A Chaperone*, An Original Farce Comedy by Miss Hicks, a fund raiser at Liberty Hall, Tuesday, May 2nd.

OPENING OF THE NEW LIBRARY
The Baxter House—May 11, 1892

Friends of club members received invitations to the opening of their new quarters at the corner of Shore Road and Central Drive, the entrance to Baxter Estates.

Welcoming Door to the Library at Baxter House

Baxter House from Shore Road

View of Baxter House looking North

Engravings of Baxter House and the first Library (Roslyn News, May 15, 1892)

At that time...

Grover Cleveland elected 24th
    President

Secretary Onderdonk's minutes of the meeting mirrored the heartfelt spirit of the occasion:

"The formal opening of the Club Rooms of the Woman's Club of Port Washington which took place on Wed. afternoon May 11th was a happy and auspicious event, a 'red letter day' to be remembered with pride and pleasure. The meeting was called to order by the president, and the secretary called the roll...twenty-two members present. An able and eminently appropriate paper was then read by our gifted and popular president. In well chosen words she voiced the feeling of the entire membership in regard to the almost phenomenal success of the club and the kindly feeling and perfect harmony that prevail amid its members. She called attention to the good work already done, and that yet to be accomplished by the club, particularly in the leveling of artificial social barriers that tend to make us forget that we are a common family, and sisters in the truest sense of the word. The music furnished by Miss Hicks, Miss McLean, Miss Jackson and Mr. Willets was most heartily enjoyed. Mr. Willets was deservedly applauded for his kindness in playing and his bravery in venturing unprotected into a woman's club room."

Miss Onderdonk also announced that the library had been enriched by a very generous donation by Mr. Martin Joost of Sands Point, and "has been enabled thereby to purchase an assortment of books for young people which were greatly needed."

The *Roslyn News* carried a three-column report of the Port Washington Library's opening ceremonies just *one* day after the event.

Thus began a new era of service to the readers and browsers and borrowers of this town in the spacious quarters of the Baxter Homestead, and also to those who enjoyed the pastries and other delicacies delivered to and on sale at the newly opened Woman's Exchange, another popular amenity of the Woman's Club.

Many men in town "had kindly helped at our Entertainments" and received invitations to a reception in their honor. "It was a happy and friendly event)...and about fifty friends were present in the club rooms."

A summer fund-raising sale took place at the Exchange "respectfully soliciting patronage of local industry." One of those who received an invitation was Mr. Bloodgood H. Cutter who "had become owner of practically all of what in 1929 would become the incorporated Village of Plandome Heights."..."a more colorful character in Long Island would be hard to find...a simple-minded honest, old-fashioned farmer with a strange proclivity for writing rhymes," wrote his friend, Mark Twain, in his notes for *Innocents Abroad*.

Mr. Cutter's hand-written RSVP to the ladies' invitation arrived in the following form:

LONG ISLAND FARMER
To the Woman's Club of Port Washington

Your Invitation did receive
To not meet with you make me grieve
Tis pleasant to nice Ladies meet
It is to me a pleasing treat
(To such distinguished ladies meet)
To join with you in what you've done
For the good of Port Washington
I trust you'll have a pleasant time
With speeches both in prose and rhyme.
In haste to you these lines have pened
And in my place to you them send,
With them I'll send my thanks to thee
For the invitation you did send.

So ladies, will you congratulate
On your pleasing and prosperous state
In each good house, may Club succeed
In your labors by word and deed.
*Bloodgood H. Cutter**

Little Neck June 29 1892

Bloodgood Cutter

During the following months the Woman's Club forged ahead with their fundraising projects:

In September a Loan Exhibition of antiques from Port Washington homes was on display at the Baxter House rooms—some for sale. "A good number attended and a good sum was realized."

A musical and literary recital at "Old House" combined with a sale of Woman's Exchange home-made foods and "fancy articles too numerous to mention were offered for sale and found ready purchasers."

While far from prosperous financially, the club had weathered the first year successfully.

1893   *Woman's Club inaugurates own news journal—woman's suffrage major topic of discussion—"gentlemen" permitted limited membership*

As the second year of the Woman's Club commenced, Caroline Hicks, Mrs. Tredwell and Mrs. Walter Cornwell remained in their elected positions and Mrs. D.P. (Rebecca) Wysong became Recording Secretary. The club established a newspaper, *The Club Record*, which would include "Editorials—Essays—Short Stories—Comedy department for original conundrums—and any convivial incident

*For a detailed biographical sketch on this colorful gentleman, see "Bloodgood Haviland Cutter, The Long Island Farmer Poet," by Richard A. Winsche, *The Nassau County Historical Society Journal*, Vol. XLV, 1990

Tennis, anyone?

Theatre bound.

happening to members—Fashion Department, not fashions that are, but fashions that ought to be: a continual protest against *tight clothing, big theater hats, hoop skirts.* All contributions must be sent by mail, unsigned, to the Editor (Miss Hicks)."*

The Annual Report of the Woman's Club prepared by retiring secretary, Miss Onderdonk, glowingly reviewed the past year's accomplishments: "Club started with 10 members, now numbers 64…27 regular and 4 special meetings…Five public entertainments have been given, three at the Hall, one at our club rooms, and one at the home of our President…An informal reception to our gentlemen friends…the removal of our Library and the formal opening of our club rooms and Woman's Exchange."

The minutes of subsequent meetings reflect the growing concern among club members as to just where they stood on this matter of *woman's right to suffrage.* Mrs. Wysong did not hesitate to make her position clear: "This correspondent expressed herself as thinking woman's proper sphere was in her home, and to utilize her influence upon the male sex rather than frequenting the poles [sic]."

For some time there had been no mention of Miss Mitchell until the February meeting when Mrs. Wysong wrote: "It has been one year…since the opening of the Library, which fact was called to our attention by our Librarian, whose presence in our midst was a real pleasure, after an absence of many weeks. Her (Miss Mitchell's) report was encouraging, although the Library is worthy of better support, and it would be well if each member should feel it her duty to endeavor to procure at least one new subscriber."

Ever alert to ideas which would benefit the community as well as the financial status of the Club, the members voted to "include gentlemen as associate and honorary members with the regular annual two dollar ($2.00) fee, and to rent another upstairs room at an additional $2.00 monthly to be used as a reading room for the men and youths of the village, to be opened every night. The officers and members (of the Woman's Club) earnestly desire that the boys' club-room will meet with a cordial response from the gentlemen of Port Washington and neighborhood as it is a broad field for beneficial work."

A musical recital in October by Miss Hicks, Arthur Prince and Percy Hicks must have been a consummate success. The *Roslyn News* reported: "The entertainment given at the 'Old House'…for the benefit of the Port Washington Library brought in much needed funds, and an encyclopedia, and a number of new books have been added to the library which is constantly increasing in usefulness."

On October 20th an organizational meeting "took place at the

*It is regrettable that after much research into the archives no copies of the *Club Record* still exist.

handsome new club rooms. William Carpenter, Frank Smith, Percy Baxter and Gordon Stevens were elected officers."

The sixty-first regular meeting of the Woman's Club ended the year 1893 on a high note: the Editor of the Club Record read an anonymous poetical contribution entitled "Adam Never Was A Boy"...Miss Onderdonk read an original article upon "Freedom versus Bondage" concerning the much discussed *woman* question.

1894   *Blackballing by members outlawed — Suffrage gaining — Port Washington League offshoot of Woman's Club*

At no time in the Minutes of the club meetings over the years did a complete list of members at any one time appear. In the winter of '94 membership totaled seventy, including three just-elected members whose family names are still familiar to the town a century later: Hults, Seaman and Dodge.

During the spring, at Miss Hicks' behest, the membership voted unanimously to erase the clause in their Constitution "concerning blackballing which was voted upon and the 'ayes' carried the day, hence that doubtful privilege is of the past." The decision came about as the result of a negative vote for a prospective member at an earlier meeting Caroline Hicks was unable to attend.

News of the library itself during the early part of the year is meager, only a fund-raising Entertainment in the club rooms, "Six Cups of Chocolate," for which an unsung member prepared the programs in handsome calligraphy (see pages 14 and 15).

Woman's Suffrage was again the topic of discussion during April: visiting lecturers as well as Miss Hicks addressed the club. Her contribution was part of a lecture delivered by her great aunt, Lucretia Mott, a pioneer in the cause. Mrs. Wysong wrote in the minutes: "the lecture, though written in 1837, fully met the requirements of women's life today,"—a step forward from her position the previous year.

In the club minutes and in the *Roslyn News,* the accomplishments of Miss Mitchell and Miss McKee in maintaining high standards of library service to the community were rarely mentioned. This was due perhaps to the split-up of the club into the Port Washington League and the Woman's Philanthropic Club, an idea to better define that part of the club (League) where members were more concerned with *issues.* In contrast to the Philanthropic branch whose interests were library, woman's exchange and welfare, the League sponsored instructive programs on the advancement of women, the new duties of woman in carrying her influence into public life, and temperance.

Not quite a year later, and with no explanation in club minutes or in the *Roslyn News,* the then Woman's Club president, Mrs. Annie Mott, "proposed that the members of the Port Washington League

—The first of a series of entertainments for the benefit of the Port Washington Circulating Library and Exchange for womens work will take place in the club rooms Wednesday afternoon, December 7th at 2:30 p. m. The entertainment will consist of readings with musical preludes, entitled a "Quaker Pastoral" The stories will be read by Mrs. Charles Newbold and the preludes will be played by Miss Hicks. The programme will contain the following selections:

Piano Prelude   A Pastoral   Beethoven.
Reading,   A Story of an Old Country House
Prelude,
     The Quiet Rioulet in the Forest, Jungman.
Reading,   The Silent Man.
Prelude,   A Horse Medley, Arranged.
Reading,   A Comical Revenge
Prelude.   A Curious Story,   Heller
Reading, "A Curious Story of Brotherly Love"
Prelude,   Happiness Enough   Schuman
Reading.   "The Satisfaction of Sarah Atwater

Roslyn News, *Dec. 2, 1893.*

—The entertainment given by the Woman's Club, of this village, on Wednesday afternoon last, was largely attended.

Entertainment Program

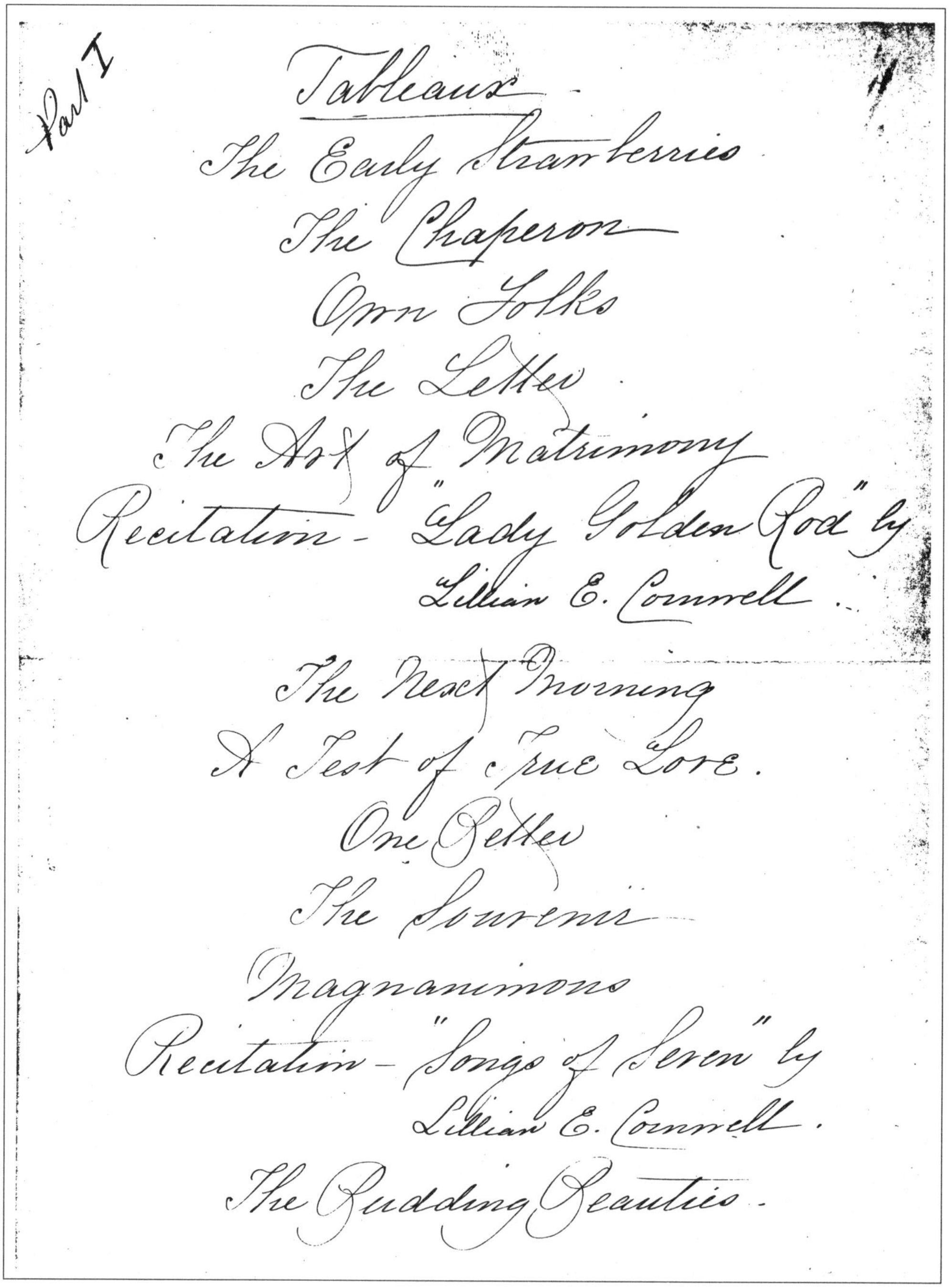

Part I

Tableaux

The Early Strawberries

The Chaperon

Own Folks

The Letter

The Art of Matrimony

Recitation - "Lady Golden Rod" by
Lillian E. Connrell.

The Next Morning

A Test of True Love.

One Better

The Souvenir

Magnanimous

Recitation - "Songs of Seven" by
Lillian E. Connrell.

The Pudding Beauties.

which was recently dissolved should be invited to join the (P.W.W.) club."

The one deep bow to the Mitchell family, whose members were constantly making contributions to the successful operation of the library, appeared, somewhat tersely, in the December minutes: "It was decided that a vote of thanks be sent to Mr. C.W. Mitchell for carrying packages for Library and Exchange free of charge."

Part II "Farce" April 2nd/16
"Six Cups of Chocolate"
Scene — A college town in New England
Time — Early Spring
Characters

Miss Adeline Van Lindau (A German Girl)
　　Miss Martha Dodge Tredwell

Miss Marion Lee — (A Southern girl)
　　Miss Julia Estelle Lawrence

Miss Dorothy Green — (A New Englander)
　　Miss Charlotte Pearsall Onderdonk

Miss Hester Beacon — (A Bostonian)
　　Miss Florence Estelle Hutts

Miss Beatrice Van Kortlandt (A New Yorker)
　　Miss Jennie Praulse Hutts.

Miss Janette Durand (A French girl)
　　Miss Margaret Udall Tredwell.

Note — One of the many joys in digging into the past history of Port Washington is reaching out to people who can fill in details on their ancestors. On the following page is a letter received from Dr. Edson L. Stannard who practiced medicine in Port Washington at 458 Main Street from 1949 to 1980. His grandmother, Ellen B. Stannard, was active in the Woman's Club from 1894 and continued her interest in the Library as a Trustee until 1916.

He wrote:

"Ellen B. Stannard was my Grandmother, second wife of Elbert B. Stannard, a retired sea captain (who) moved to P.W. with their three children, Edson, Dan, Mable about 1895 from Westbrook, Conn. At that time he bought the Old Mitchell farm which ran from the MBYC boatyard to (the site of) the R.R. station. They remodeled the old farm house by raising it entirely and building a new ground floor and a new wing (32 rooms).

"Grandfather returned to business, frustrated by retirement, demolishing U.S. Naval Vessels for their scrap metal value. These vessels were towed usually from the Norfolk, Va. Naval Yard to P.W. and grounded mid Manhasset Bay then moved toward shore as they were lightened by burning. Divers picked up the brass and bronze from the bay bottom (then clear enough to see). He leased all of the beach property from Louie's Restaurant to the P.W. Yacht Club for this activity, about 1895 to 1908 when he died.

"The house (458 Main Street) my office was located in was built by his men as was the duplicate next door during slack work periods. My Grandmother moved there with Mable and Dan after he died. The former home (Mitchell Farm) became the "Anchorage," a summer hotel operated by a Mrs. Haskell who also ran another site known as the Haskell House across from Louie's (where the Community Chest building is located).

"Ellen, my grandmother, was born in Saybrook, Conn. She was soon orphaned and raised with her brother, John Molyneux, by a family named Brown. I believe she was directly descended from Priscilla Mullens who got involved with a guy named Miles Standish. I think she (grandmother) was a teacher when she met Grandfather.

"In the early days of their marriage she made several trips by clipper ship from N.Y. around the Horn to Japan and China with her husband as Captain, and as I grew up she would keep me entertained by tales of her adventures at sea. In fact she was there (Japan) on one of the first merchant ships when Admiral Perry opened trade between the U.S. and Japan. Later he was to sell the Japanese Government their first warship (one that he patched up). During later years he was known as 'the Father of the Japanese Navy.'

"Your letter was the first time I'd heard she was a Trustee of the library. She was active in the Methodist Church. Grandfather was a quiet benefactor of many community activities and I suspect that he might have made a contribution to the origin of the library.

"I remember her fondly as a small, very deaf, kindly old lady, wearing those tiny, round gold-rimmed glasses, and white hair. She died about 1937 and is buried in the family plot in Westbrook, Conn."

Edson L. Stannard

House built by Captain Stannard at 458 Main Street before porch was removed.

The Anchorage. Port Washington, N. Y.

The Anchorage

Summering on Long Island and wintering in one of the boroughs of New York was common practice among many Sands Point residents. Except for the occasional meeting in Port Washington, during the winter Caroline Hicks lived at #191 Amity Street, Flushing, where in January, 1885, she entertained both the Port Washington Woman's Club and the Port Washington League along with delegates from all the Long Island clubs from Port Jefferson to Bensonhurst. "The object of the reception (was) to arrange a convention for Long Island women's clubs, and to introduce Long Island club women to each other."

Mrs. M.K. Wetmore, cousin of Mrs. Jacob Wetmore.

Mrs. Annie Mott was now President of the Woman's Club, Mrs. Albert Messenger, V.P., Mrs. Ellen Stannard, 2nd V.P., Mrs. Walter (M. Eleanor) Smull, Recording Sec'y., Mrs. Walter Cornwell, Corres. Sec'y., and Miss Margie Treadwell, Treas. At the Annual Meeting the redoubtable Miss Hicks was elected Honorary President of the club. It was also announced that a number of new books were added to the library, and the Christmas sales of the Exchange ran the amount of sales, since the Exchange was opened, to $1,200.

An infrequent listing of new members appeared in the March 6th minutes: "the names of four candidates were presented, passed by the executive committee, and announced by the Secretary to the membership—Mrs. Jacob Wetmore, Mrs. Isaac Allen, Mrs. Timothy Bird and Miss Frances Fay."

1895   *Idea of Free Library advanced—Trustees appointed—refreshments give rise to problems—First Library report submitted to State Department of Education—Bloomers!*

At the following meeting of the club, Honorary President, Caroline Hicks, according to the minutes, "introduced the subject of a Free Library. Among the many useful schemes which she entertains for the improvement of our village and to which she devotes so much of her valuable time, this is one of the most cherished, and she received hearty cooperation from the club members who one and all expressed their interest in the enterprise, and their willingness to aid Miss H. in collecting the necessary amount for its establishment which if not exceeding $200. will be duplicated by the state *under the present law of educational improvement.*"

The minutes continue:

"The following members of the club and of the Port Washington League were appointed Trustees [of the proposed free library] Miss Caroline Hicks, Miss Mina Mitchell, Mrs. Stannard, Mrs. E. Weeks, Mrs. Ella Davis, Mrs. Nostrand and Miss Onderdonk. It is hoped that an excellent library may be formed for the use of the people of Port Washington and it will be a lasting monument to the indefatigable energy and perseverance of Miss Hicks and the generous bestowal of her time and labor for the improvement of our village.

"This important matter being disposed of, Miss Hicks with her usual forethought declared her intention of formally transferring to the Woman's Exchange the articles of furniture, etc., which she so generously tendered for the use of the club at its first occupancy of its present rooms. It is impossible in these minutes to more than touch upon the work accomplished by Miss Hicks for our benefit. She has advanced the club to its present almost phenomenal position and through her efforts it is recognized among other clubs and favorably noticed by them."

Mrs. Smull ended this tribute to the founder by writing, "All honor to the lady who has labored so nobly in our behalf. A sincere vote of thanks but feebly expresses our appreciation of her services."

At the March 20, 1895 meeting the subject of a Free Library was aired again. Miss Mitchell stated the formalities to be observed in its formation which consisted of applying to the New York State Department of Education and certifying that the library had raised $200 to be matched by the state.

Few references have been made to the club's refreshments following each meeting. "After tea and cake were served the meeting adjourned" was the usual ending for the minutes. However, at the meeting in March, Mrs. Smull, whose sense of humor pervades the minutes, wrote, following the musical session, "Our attention was then called by Mrs. McLean to a most disreputable tin pail in which the water is boiled for our tea and after giving the price of different kinds of kettles including possibly the one that Polly is so frequently enjoined to use, Mrs. McLean suggested that for the respectability of the club, and the satisfaction each member would derive from the use of a clean looking utensil, that we purchase a new one. This was approved and it was decided that the club indulge in the luxury of a kettle, pail and tea strainer."

With the exception of an Entertainment in Liberty Hall on June 29th, and a Peach Festival in August, the club was inactive during the summer months. The Peach Festival raised about $10.00.

Total Volumes	370	Payment for books	$42.70
Circulation	855	Payment for serials	11.15
Hours open per week	9		$53.85

Received from State Aid	$100 (?)
Received from Gifts	30
	$130

Miss Mitchell at times called for help from her fellow club members. At a September meeting she "invited any of the members who were disposed to do so to attend the club rooms on Saturday afternoon to assist her in arranging and classifying the library books."

Although the exorbitant rent ($65.00 per year) of the Baxter rooms rankled with the membership, it was decided to remain in those quarters until April, 1896. However, the idea of moving continued and during September discussion took place about how "A Library Building in which the club could hold their meetings would be most desirable and it is hoped we may have one in the near future." Miss Mitchell, always with an eye to adding to the fund for a new library, reported, in her position as head of the Exchange, a profit of over $35.00 realized from a special sale.

ENTERTAINMENT.

Under the Auspices of Woman's Club, for Benefit of Relief Fund.

LIBERTY HALL, Port Washington,

Saturday Evening, June 29, 1895.

DOORS OPEN 7:30.   CURTAIN 8:15.

Admission 25 cents.   Reserved Seats 50 cents.

PROGRAM.

1st Farce.   **" MAN PROPOSES."**

CHARACTERS:

CAPT. HUNTINGTON,	Mr. Stephen Robbins Hewlett.
DORA,	Mrs. Anna Nostrand Mott.
BELL HUNTINGTON,	Miss Martha Dodge Tredwell.

2nd Farce.   **" OUTWITTED."**

CHARACTERS:

HAROLD FOSTER, (Nephew of General Foster)
                                        Mr. Samuel Lewis Hewlett.
BERTHA STEWART, (Niece to Miss Euphrasia Singleton)
                                        Miss May Eliza Hooper.
JANE, (Miss Singleton's Maid)   Mrs. Anna Nostrand Mott.

3rd Farce.   **" THE MARBLE ARCH. "**

CHARACTERS:

JACK MEREWETHER,		Mr. Charles H. Hungerford.
CAPT. TRENTHAM, (Bachelor)		Mr. Stephen Robbins Hewlett.
CONSTANCE CAMERON, (Widow)		Miss Maude Gladis Jackson.
MARION MEREWETHER, (Jack's Wife)		Miss Martha Dodge Tredwell.

. ENTRACTE.

Vocal and Instrumental Music by the Misses Titus.

ROSLYN NEWS JOB PRINT.

News clipping, June 27, 1895 and program for Liberty Hall Entertainment

An entertainment under the auspices of the Woman's Club, for the benefit of the relief fund, will be given at Liberty hall, on Saturday evening, June 29. The program will consist of three farces, "Man Proposes," "Outwitted" and "The Marble Arch," interspered with vocal and instrumental music by the Misses Titus. This will no doubt be one of the most pleasing entertainments ever given in this place.

The world of fashion was aired from time to time and at a November meeting Mrs. Smull noted: "Lizzie Jones favored the club with a pretty song, after which the subject of "Bloomers" was taken up. None of the members expressed a very decided opinion preferring to give the views of distinguished ladies about them.

"Many of these agreed in calling them hideous, but Mrs. Elizabeth Cady Stanton* speaks boldly in their favor. Mrs. Messenger read an article in point from a newspaper and Mrs. Tredwell read an acrostic upon Bloomers, but it remained for Mrs. Walter Cornwell to illustrate her subject by exhibiting a paper pattern of this much discussed 'reform.'"

Poor attendance on the part of members plagued the officers of the Woman's Club. On November 24th, though the day was fair and the parlors thanks to Miss Mitchell warm and bright, only six members attended. Mrs. Smull pointed out that "since many members are away for the winter those who remain should keep up their interest in the club by attending as often as possible."

FIRST LIBRARY CHARTER

Eleven members attended the December 4th meeting at which time Miss Mitchell presented the Library Charter from the State Department of Education "which was read to the club by Mrs. Stannard. The Library was incorporated Nov. 21st, 1895 and embraces a period of five years. It is to be hoped that sufficient interest will be taken in the library by the people of Port Washington to make it an object of pride to the village and a help to those who patronize it."

Thus one more step forward toward the goal of a true public library.

1896 *Exceeding inclement weather—Heat in library daily problem—
Members still yearning for own library building—Long Island
Rail Road, so near but so far*

At the Annual Meeting Mrs. Stannard wished to resign her office but "her proposal was met with such determined opposition that she was induced to remain as 2nd Vice President." The library and the town would have lost the services of a strong leader and genial trustee had they accepted her resignation. She was continuously active in the library until 1916!

The weather in the winter of 1896 was "exceeding inclement" (much snow and very cold) and the need for constantly refilling the wood bin was eased somewhat when Mr. A.H. Baxter "whose generosity is well known offered the club as much wood as one man could cut in two days, and as an immediate acceptance Miss Mitchell had already engaged a man for the work thus ensuring us protection

*Mrs. Stanton along with Lucretia Mott called the first women's rights convention in Seneca Falls, N.Y. in 1848. Amelia Jenks Bloomer, for whom the famous 'Turkish Pantaloons' were named, was also an upstate New Yorker, ardent supporter of women's rights and temperance reformer.

At that time...

William McKinley
elected 25th President

against the inclemency of the season." Mr. L.B. Smull also received his share of thanks for a load of wood sent to the Baxter House for the club.

Warmth in the club rooms was always a Mitchell family concern. In February Mrs. Smull wrote, "The room was delightfully cheerful and warm thanks to Miss Mitchell in having a stove put up and Mrs. Mitchell's exertions to always have a fire ready." Average attendance was down to five to eight members at each winter meeting, although they did attract a large number of guests for a Five O'Clock Tea—net proceeds $3.75.

Miss Mitchell again introduced the subject of a library building and proposed a birthday box, and also suggested that each member "might by some sacrifice add her quota to the building fund." Friends of members were solicited for contributions for the library either as a birthday offering or "an equivalent number of days in the month that the natal day occurs." Fund-raising ever calls for innovative stratagems.

At the August meeting great excitement erupted over the most discussed topic on the North Shore: the Long Island Rail Road's greatly anticipated and frequently postponed extension from Great Neck to Port Washington.

Minutes of Club Meeting, August 18, 1986:

"Someone had suggested to Mrs. Walter Cornwell that the present delay and uncertainty with regard to the extension of the L.I. Railroad to Port Washington would be entirely done away with and the railroad would come through with flying colors and a speed of no one knows how many miles an hour, if some of the fair members of the Woman's Club would exert their fascinations, and favor with their conversation the superintendent of the road, and in such an event The Woman's Club would have the glory of being the means of bringing this much needed improvement to our village. Mrs. Cornwell and Mrs. Messenger were appointed to find out all they could on the subject and report in September."

Sadly, there is no record of a follow-up or a response from the superintendent.

At times Mrs. Smull, the Recording Secretary, expressed her opinions somewhat obliquely and with humor. Following a long harangue to the club members about how great the Chicago Woman's Club had become, the guest speaker at the August meeting, Mrs. Craigie, President of the Brooklyn Library Association, then touched on woman's suffrage opening once again a favorite avenue of discussion. Another guest, Mrs. Chapman (of Roslyn, a strong local advocate of woman's suffrage) picked up the topic quickly.

Mrs. Smull reported: "Everyone knows it (suffrage) is one dear to her heart and so favorable an opportunity of making proselytes was not to be neglected, and before the club fairly realized it, a committee had been appointed to establish a suffrage league. The ladies forming it are Mrs. Mott, Miss Mitchell, Mrs. Stannard, Miss Annie Maclean, Mrs. Wysong and Mrs. Newbold. They are to meet Mrs.

Chapman on Oct. 16th. All hail to the new woman! May she flourish like the proverbial bay tree, and never say die!"

Attendance at meetings was again waning. President Mott remarked on Oct. 11th that "It is most unfortunate for the stability and improvement of the club that many of its members should show little interest in it." Nevertheless the club officers kept charging ahead following the lead set for them by Miss Hicks.

Winter was on its way. Miss Mitchell was having stoves repaired. Two barrels of kindling were donated by Mrs. Stannard.

The fifth anniversary of the founding of the Woman's Club and the library was duly celebrated on January 26th, 1897, at a Birthday Party held at the Library Rooms. The Roslyn News reported that over 300 invitations were issued and "the occasion bids fair to be the leading social event of the season." The Entertainment Committee took good advantage of the oversized tickets by printing on the back of each a poem asking for financial help in their endeavor to have a building of their own.

The Port Washington Woman's Club

Present their compliments, and cordially invite you

to attend a

Birthday Party,

——— AT THE ———

LIBRARY ROOMS, TUESDAY, JAN. 26, 1897,

FROM 2 TO 5 P. M.

Contributions received by Mrs. Albert Messenger, Chairman of Committee, Sands Point, Long Island.

BIRTHDAY PARTY.

~~~~~~

The Woman's Club is now just five years old,
Of its work, much has been written and told,
But if you would really know just what we do,
Attend our reception, 'tis given for you.
Sweet music you'll hear, and have something to eat,
While your presence will furnish the Club's social treat.
A Library building we'd like much to own,
And take this occasion to make our want known.
As nothing accomplished can be without friends,
And the kindly assistance each one of them lends,
These dainty receptacles here we enclose.
Please put within yours, just as much as you choose,
And return when you come, or else kindly send it,
Let the contents be large and your good will attend it.
While the members will meet you with greetings most hearty
And hope you will come to the Club's Birthday Party.

Invitation to Fifth Birthday Party, January 26, 1897.

The Port Washington Woman's Club tender their friends, through the columns of the "News," their sincere thanks for the generous response to the invitation to their Birthday Party. It is a source of great gratification to the Club, to find that the project of a Library building should meet the cordial approbation of their friends as shown by the donations received. At the same time the Club deeply regrets that anyone should have been omitted in the invitations issued. Great care was taken by the committee that every one should be remembered, and if any one has been overlooked, the Club sincerely hope that the omission will kindly be pardoned.

Note of thanks from the Woman's Club, Roslyn News, February 12, 1897.

The Port Washington Woman's club, of which I have written before, is one of the most progressive. The Port Washington women have done great things, but yet are not content. They look for more work and find it. Their latest scheme is to build up their library. They have a number of books now, but not enough to satisfy them, for these women are not easily satisfied. They want lots of things and the best of everything, and the most encouraging thing about it all is that they never rest until they get what they want.

Now that they are determined to increase their library, these women are devising all sorts of plans to raise money for this object.

Columnist "Polyanthus" wrote of the Library in her Brooklyn Times *column, January, 1897.*

The Port Washington Woman's Club, will give an afternoon tea, at their club rooms on Friday, Oct. 22d, commencing at 2.30. Mrs. M. E. Craigie, President of the Brooklyn Board of Education will deliver an address. Mrs. Craigie's charming manners and eloquence as a speaker are universally acknowledged. Those who have heard her, will not lose this opportunity of repeating the pleasure, and those who have not, will do well to avail themselves of this intellectual treat. Admission 15 cents.

Notice of afternoon tea, October 15, 1897.

Five years after the original officers were elected many of the same names appear on the roster:

Mrs. Annie Mott, *President*
Mrs. A.A. Messenger, *1st Vice President*
Miss Wilhelmina Mitchell, *2nd Vice President*
Mrs. M.E. Smull, *Recording Secretary*
Miss Florence Fay, *Corres. Secretary*
Mrs. Walter Cornwell, *Treasurer*

Miss Mitchell had two favorable reports in February, first, that there had been a most satisfactory increase in the number of books loaned each month, and that the Library Building Fund had reached "the encouraging sum of $132.40." Another $7.60 was added following a very successful Children's Matinee on Washington's Birthday which included a magic lantern exhibition and pin-the-tail-on-the-donkey contest.

Mrs. Smull, through the minutes of meetings, continued to berate the membership about attendance. She wrote, "Atmospheric or some other influence not known to science conspired to prevent a large attendance at the 204th meeting of the Women's Club held March 3rd, and guests there were none." Nor did the officers get by without a scolding, for she wrote in May, "A meeting of the executive board was called for Saturday, May 8th at 4 P.M., but a quorum of officers not being present, *nothing was done.*"

No meetings were held and little fundraising activity took place throughout the summer.

Mrs. Mary E. Craigie, President of the Brooklyn Library Association, again addressed the members of the club in October on "The Ideal Woman," exhorting them to "make their ideals real and the reality ideal." Shortly thereafter Mrs. Mott provoked a lively discussion upon female suffrage: "One member being a decided anti-suffragist gave the opposition required to bring out the views on that side: the debate was both entertaining and instructive."

FAVORITE BOOKS 1892–1897

Tess of the D'Urbervilles by Thomas Hardy
History of David Grieve by Mrs. Humphrey Ward
Treasure Island by Robert Louis Stevenson
Trilby by George du Maurier
The Other Wise Man by Henry Van Dyke
Soldiers of Fortune by Richard Harding Davis

On November 8, 1897, the Brooklyn Times, in its Long Island
News section ran an article that put joy and gladness into the hearts
of all residents of Port Washington. It read in part:

THE PORT WASHINGTON RAILROAD

Progress of the Work of Building the Extension
What Must be Done in Order to Carry Passengers To and From
Port Washington — The Work of the Engineers

"Every year for the past thirty years something has been done
toward constructing an extension of the Long Island Railroad from
Great Neck to Port Washington, but as the expense attached was
something far above reasonable, the idea has always been given up,
but under the new management of the Long Island Railroad it has
taken another start and the people are at last satisfied of better
accomodations in the near future, as under the eye of Chief Engi-
neer Cattel the contracting firm of Holmes and Cogan are pushing
the work as rapidly as possible but it is said even now that the work
cannot be completed before next April or May.

"The bridgework on the road will be furnished by Carnegie Steel
Company, and will cost nearly $30,000, while the entire sum for
complete construction will be between $175,000 to $200,000."

1898   *Piano makes money for building fund — Ralph Waldo Emerson
disrupts January meeting — Endless fund-raising — Long Island
Council of Women's Clubs in Garden City — June 23rd Celebration
of LIRR extension to Port*

Miss Phebe Burtis, a charter member of the Woman's Club in
1892, was the first to resign. She lived some distance from the Baxter House (on Middleneck Road not far from the E. Willets Farm —
now the Sands-Willets House) and pleaded distance as the principal
reason for her withdrawal.

Music was very much a part of the Woman's Club meetings as well
as their Entertainments. Miss Mitchell, not overlooking any small
source of income for the building fund, was given permission to
loan out the piano for a fee (and the borrowers paid for moving
both ways!). Her mother, Mrs. Mitchell, however, suggested that in
the case of the St. Stephens Chapel no fee should be charged inasmuch as "the Chapel people are obliging and twice during the past
year their chairs have been loaned to the club."

Mrs. Mott had been a popular President but declined reelection
and was succeeded by Mrs. Kittie C. Messenger who promptly set
about to do something about those members who failed to pay their
dues but did not resign. It was agreed by the members present at
the January 26th meeting that after delinquents were sent the customary notice and did not pay "they should be quietly dropped as
the only thing to be done."

Not only did the Woman's Club run a successful library and a very popular Woman's Exchange, but that part of their charter calling for "improvement" was observed assiduously. Their weekly meetings were planned around current events, famous authors and philosophers, musicians, and any other topics that were agreed upon weeks in advance. For example, at the meeting in January, each member present was required to answer the roll call with a quotation from Ralph Waldo Emerson. Secretary Smull responded with his *Essay on Love,* which to the dismay of the membership did not mention *charity* or, as she wrote in the minutes, *"love for thy neighbor,* not to speak of *loving our enemies,* (so) the members hardly knew where they were at. A short but not very animated discussion followed, the subject of marriage being too sacred for public debate, and the pride of the ladies would not allow them to admit their early mistakes in the matrimonial venture before they learned how to manage that package of contradictions called man."

Fund-raising continued to absorb the attention of club members. On the first of January they held an Exhibition of Ancestral Portraits in Liberty Hall with a $.25 admission. (No record of proceeds).

On the 14th at Liberty Hall an Entertainment consisting of Vocal and Instrumental Solos was a great success according to the always congratulatory reviews in the *Roslyn News,* and best of all the net was $19.55. "Not liking odd numbers, Mrs. Mott generously contributed the remainder to make an even $20.00. Miss Mitchell as Chairman of the 'Library board' extended a vote of thanks to the Woman's Club for the donation."

Miss Mitchell found that a stage (coach) could be provided at $5.00 to carry the club ladies to Garden City for a L.I. Council of Women's Clubs meeting "if enough members would avail themselves of it to cover the expenses." Later she reported that "the stage engaged from Mr. Cornwell arrived on time at the club rooms and after a delightful drive brought the occupants in good season to the Casino in Garden City which gave them the choice of the best seats. After the conclusion of the Council, Mr. Cornwell very kindly drove to Camp Black (an Army staging camp—the Spanish-American War was imminent) on the outskirts of Garden City giving the visitors a full view of the encampment and adding much to the pleasure of the day." All this for just $5.00 each!

A Minstrel Show planned for April 30 was cancelled because on April 25, 1898, war against Spain was officially declared. In the May 22nd minutes, Mrs. Smull recorded:

"$1.00 should be paid out of the treasury towards defraying the expenses of printing, etc. for the Minstrel Show that *we did not have.* Thus the cost of the war falls upon the Woman's Club as well as on other organizations."

By all measures the extension of the L.I.R.R. to Port Washington was the major event of the year 1898! During the winter and spring

Admission Ticket to Liberty Hall Exhibition.

there were weekly reports of progress. Everyone in town seemingly joined in planning and working toward a common goal—making the arrival of the railroad the biggest celebration in the village's history. The Woman's Club participated with the gift of a large U.S. Flag, and Mrs. McLean was on the refreshment committee which "provided 3,000 visitors with something to eat, introducing their famous chowder."

Bloodgood H. Cutter, Long Island's farmer poet, wrote an epic poem, said to have had 28 stanzas. Here is a sample:

Port Washington is too nice a place
To be shut off from city race.
For summer boarders 'tis the place
So safe it is for city race.
Manhasset has a lovely bay
With splendid scenery all the way.
Cars running here will be so nice
That many ladies 'twill entice
To city go, to shop and buy
Things that do most attract the eye;
To get a new hat or a shawl
Or cloak to wear on over
In winter evenings they can go
To theatres or public show.
The advantages be so great,
Too many to enumerate.
Some now may think this wild in me,
Many will live to all this see;
I suppose in fifty year
There will be a great city here,
With trolley car and electric light
To illuminate it well at night.
So I will say to friends, each one:
O, prize this place, Port Washington.

Handwritten (by Miss Mitchell) "Library Card."

To promote as extensively as possible the joys and rewards of living in Port Washington since the advent of easy travel to New York City, the real estate firm of Jenks and Baxter published *The Port Washington Review*. To the credit of Editor Jenks, this little publication describes the town in 1898 as well and, possibly as accurately, as any other. The last chapter, titled "Of Feminine Interest" chronicles the first six years of the Woman's Club and library in glowing terms and ends with "Port Washington is very proud of this brilliant organization of its ladies."

During the 1880's the *Roslyn News* commenced a regular column about happenings in Port Washington which usually was one-half a column. By November, 1898, because of normal growth and the

Long Island Rail Road, William M. Hyde, correspondent and authorized agent for that newspaper, was awarded a large-type, two-column heading and relatively unlimited space for his weekly column about this town. In his first column under the new format, Hyde wrote, "There is reason to believe that the recognition thus given to our village (which the *Brooklyn Times* not long ago announced 'had jumped into the world') will be appreciated by the many readers of the *News* and the public in general."

A severe storm at the end of November, 1898, presaged a winter of exceptionally merciless weather. "If this is the real beginning of winter," Hyde wrote, "and a good sample of what we may expect for the next three months, it would seem that many hardships will have to be endured before it is over." He was right.

LEGAL ANNOUNCEMENT—January 1, 1899

Nassau County, formerly a portion of Queens County, becomes an incorporated municipality, encompassing 274 square miles. Three towns comprise the new county: North Hempstead, Hempstead, and Oyster Bay.

The annual election of officers, took place at a meeting of the Port Washington Woman's club, held Wednesday, Jan. 18th, at which the following ladies were elected for the year 1899. President, Mrs. Kittie C. Messenger; vice president. Miss W. M. Mitchell; recording secretary, Mrs. M. Eleanor Smull; corresponding secretary, Miss Frances E. Fay; treasurer, Mrs. Walter Cornwell. Lay members of the executive board, Mrs. L. B. Smull and Mrs. I. H. Cornwell. Board of trustees, Miss Mitchell, Mrs. Messenger and Mrs. Nostrand. Members of the relief fund, Mrs. A. H. Baxter, M⁺⁺ Walter Cornwell and Miss Mitchell.

Roslyn News, *January 22, 1899*

During January the Woman's Club was experiencing the same poor attendance that seemed to have plagued the officers for many months. The annual meeting notes were not too optimistic, yet the officers and few members who did attend meetings continued planning and holding meetings to augment the Building Fund.

To add to their problems they were the victims of vandalism as reported in the *Roslyn News*: "It is a pity that the person or persons who tore down the Free Library sign of the Woman's Club, and threw it into the bay where it was picked up, were not caught in the act. One would imagine the woman's club which is noted for its liberality and kindly offices, to be the last place in the village to suffer the annoyance of a miscreant."

The prediction of bad weather for 1899 was more than fulfilled in February. The combination of high tides, blizzard conditions, overflowing cellars, Shore Road impassible because of foot-deep waters all together brought traffic, business, school and home life to a standstill.

1900   *Mild threat to dissolution of Library—efforts to raise money, by all means, redoubled—"Vast improvements" in village not realized by arrival of railroad*

Mrs. Smull's report at the annual meeting in January again reflected the status of attendance at meetings. "Abatement in interest," "indifference," "enthusiasm which first existed is no longer felt," are a few of the comments leading up to her very strong caution to club members. She wrote:

"It remains therefor for those who can come to do so. I am sure that every member…would regret its dissolution, and if it is thought for a moment that it would mean the end of the Woman's Exchange and possibly the Free Library, I am sure every member would sacrifice something for the club's existence, both Exchange and Library. I know that the Exchange has been and is a help to our village, and the Library is so firmly established in the regards of the people that its close would be almost a public calamity."

At least four Euchre Parties were held during the spring and fall to raise money for the library. Entertainments by Miss Libby Mott, Mrs. Baker and others also helped, but the real pressure was put on in September when Miss Mitchell made a motion which was immediately carried "that a thorough canvass of the village be made to gather subscriptions for the library fund. Mrs. Smull was requested to write an appropriate heading to the subscription papers."

Simultaneously, Miss Lillian Flower, newly elected Corresponding Secretary, sent a letter to the *Roslyn News,* briefly describing the work the library had already done and its urgent need of money.

The September meeting minutes reflected the urgency:

"Miss Nostrand and Miss Lawrence at once offered to canvass the block nearest their residence, Mrs. W. Cornwell will take the residents about Sands Point, Mrs. McLean will take a portion of the village and Mrs. Smull a few in Manhasset and vicinity. Miss Mitchell, who hesitates to profer a request even in a cause when all are interested, modestly requested that those members having conveyances should offer them to the ladies who are to solicit subscriptions. Mrs. Messenger, Mrs. J. Cornwell and Mrs. Smull responded."

Miss Libby Mott gave her own "entertainment," a steamboat excursion on the steam launch to Glen Island, a popular amusement park across Long Island Sound on the Westchester Shore, which brought in $12.75. A total of $28.75 was collected for the library fund in just one week during September. In November Miss Mitchell announced the good news that the Library Building Fund stood at $890.70.

Two and one half years had elapsed since the arrival of the railroad. But to *Roslyn News* correspondent for Port, William Hyde, things were not quite as had been anticipated by Bloodgood Cutter in his poem to the town. He wrote in the *News:*

"Port Washington *is* a beautiful place, but undoubtedly Mr. Cutter looked for vast improvements in keeping with the picturesque surroundings. He no doubt predicted an established system of village improvement. An improvement in everything essential to an enterprising community. Good streets; a sprinkling system; a lighting district, and above all things sidewalks with no dangerous pitfalls…but the average resident knows that it has made very little progress since that memorable day of 1898.

Wilhelmina Mitchell as she appeared at the turn of the century.

In view of the imperative necessity which
exists, that the Port Washington Free Library should be
worth the sum of one thousand dollars, by November next
in order to retain its Charter, and avail itself of the
assistence given under the Educational Laws of the
State of New York, the trustees, in connection with the
P. W. Woman's Club, have decided to appeal to the generosity of the residents of Port Washington and its vicinity, to raise the necessary amount, feeling that they fully
realize its value, and are willing to save it from going
out of existence. You are therefore respectfully requested
to set opposite your name any amount you desire to give
to this important institution.

A Friend	$ 1.00
Mrs. J. Cocks	1.00
Mrs. G. Smith	.20
Hatch	.25
Mrs. Miller	.25
Mrs. O.	.25
	.25
	.50
Nelsen	.10
Mrs.	.25
Mrs.	1.00
	2.00
Mrs.	.25
Mrs.	
	.50

Mrs. Smull's renowned Spencerian hand embellished all the subscription papers.

THE EARLY YEARS

"Can nothing be done to remedy the present condition of things in that direction? Take for illustration the walk extending from A.C. Bayles' corner to what is known as Baxter's bridge (across from Baxter House on Shore Road). Is it not time that something was done toward putting the sidewalk at this particular point in reasonable shape? Likewise the walk from the depot to the village. All too horrible to think of and too dangerous to pass over especially at night. The village of Port Washington is all right; the people are all right, no better in the world; but they must get together, incorporate if necessary, and make the place what it should be: the ideal spot on the North side."

One year had gone by in this proud new Twentieth Century. But many in Port Washington felt that the feet of Progress were still mired in the Nineteenth. William Hyde expressed only a few of the villagers' needs and desires.

Miss Mitchell's own efforts to expand and upgrade the quality of the library were equaled by her zealousness in raising money for the dreamed-of library. During the summer of 1891 she arranged for catalogers from the New York State Library Division to classify the entire collection according to the Dewey Decimal System. The cost for the fifteen-day task was $110.00. One of the rare *Roslyn News* items about the library that year tells of the event.

The new slate of officers elected at the January 15, 1902 annual meeting included:

Mrs. M.E. McLean, *President*
Miss Wilhelmina Mitchell, *Vice President*
Mrs. M.E. Smull, *Recording Secretary*
Miss Lawrence, *Corresponding Secretary*
Mrs. Walter Cornwall, *Treasurer*

The Womans' club of this village held a progressive euchre on Wednesday afternoon. A very pleasant time was spent among those present.

The librarian and some of the ladies have been working hard to get the cataloging of the Free Library finished. There was much work to be done, after the professional catalogers were through. There will be a full report in the columns of the NEWS soon. By another week the library will again be open to the public.

A "Rubbage Sale" will be held for the benefit of the Port Washington Free Library, on Nov. 1 and 2. Friends of the library and Woman's Club have offered to send articles, and all are solicited to send what they can. Articles can be sent to the library rooms on Tuesday, Wednesday and Saturday afternoons. Future notice of place will be given.

News of library activities in Port Washington appeared in the Roslyn News *almost weekly in 1901.*

Lilian Flowers' Letter to the Editor, Sept. 14, 1900.

PORT WASHINGTON FREE LIBRARY.

Dear Mr. Editor:—As so many summer visitors and new residents are appreciating our library this summer and are asking as to its source of support, perhaps a little sketch of its past, present and future may be interesting reading to these anxious enquirers. The library is an offspring of the woman's club. It is cared for, worked for, and partially supported by her. It was opened eight years ago with twenty-five books, but was not then a "free" library, and consequently its circulation was limited. Five years ago the woman's club president together with the librarian and other workers conceived the idea of making the library free, and of also putting it under the supervision of the State, and so making it a state library. The initiatory steps were taken, the State inspector of libraries came here, inspected the books, and in November, 1895 a provisional charter was granted for five years, a permanent charter to be granted at the expiration of that time, providing the requirements under the state act concerning libraries were met. These requirements refer mostly to the number of books purchased and the increase in the number of readers, and are fulfilled, but there is one requirement which is a nightmare to the woman's club just at present, it haunts her asleep and awake, it is simply this; that by November this present year, the library must be worth in money "one thousand dollars" in order to secure its permanent charter. The advantages of being a state library are many, one of them being that whatever amount of money is raised to buy new books, the state adds the same amount to it, thereby doubling the number of books. The books in the library to-day number more than one thousand, and who can estimate the amount of pleasure and instruction this means to the town, how many sick ones are cheered, how many new thoughts and pleasant hours are thus given the young people. There is nothing self centered about this, it is a far reaching, ever widening work. Now the philosophy of the Sunshine Club comes into effect, and we say, "Have you had a kindness shown? Pass it on." The woman's club and others have worked hard and kept the current expenses paid, bought new books from time to time, and a small portion of the thousand dollars is already in the bank, but two thirds has now to be raised. The librarian is perfectly devoted to the work and has confidence that the amount will be raised in time. Any amount will be received with thanks by the committee, who will subsequently canvass from house to house. As this is the first appeal made to the public it is hoped no one will fail to respond, but that all will feel they have a part in this store house of pleasure.

LILIAN FLOWER,
Corresponding Secretary Woman's Club.

Mrs. Caroline Hicks-Phillips

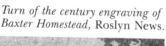

Turn of the century engraving of Baxter Homestead, Roslyn News.

While many townspeople may have had legitimate gripes about the slow pace of moving into the new century, the members of the Woman's Club surely must have been pleased and deservedly proud on January 25, 1902 to read a flattering article in the *Brooklyn Times* (on the following page) about their achievements over the previous ten years.

Miss Caroline Hicks, about whom nothing had been reported either in the *Roslyn News* or minutes of club meetings since 1896, meanwhile had married a Mr. Phillips. Quite in character, she had retained her maiden name through hyphenation: *Mrs. Caroline Hicks-Phillips.**

1903   *William M. Hyde starts* Port Washington News...*Down payment for library building culmination of endless fundraising...Library moves to Main Street*

In December, 1902 and January, 1903 townspeople and members of the Woman's Club and the Free Library grieved over the deaths of two well-loved ladies, Mrs. Mary E. Smull, wife of Charles G. Smull, and Mrs. Kittie C. Messenger, wife of A.A. Messenger. Both were early members of the club, the former serving for many years as Recording Secretary, and Mrs. Messenger as President during 1888 and 1899.

After many years as correspondent in Port Washington for the *Roslyn News,* William M. Hyde opened the *Port Washington News.* His former editor in Roslyn wrote of him, "Mr. Hyde is well known as an energetic and hustling news gatherer, and with his ability and experience at the helm the Port Washington *News* will find easy sailing upon the troubled waters of local journalism."

Thanks to innumerable fund-raising events over a period of eleven years such as Entertainments at Liberty Hall and at their own club rooms, Euchre Parties at the homes of generous members, Woman's Exchange sales, golden opportunities seized by Miss Mitchell to "pass the hat," and finally the untiring efforts by club members who carried solicitations (or petitions) throughout the town, $1,000 was raised.

"In 1903, in the winter months before they were able to announce with triumph that they had bought Burtis' store for the library's home, the club minutes show from one to five members only present. 'No meeting. Very stormy.' Perhaps the roads from Sands Point, Roslyn and Manhasset were drifted over and the horses could not get through. Miss Phebe Burtis perhaps couldn't dash around so freely in her little trap."—Ruth Bornn, *Port News,* 1941

*The engraving of her portrait on the front page of the *Brooklyn Times* is the only picture of this gracious and ubiquitous lady found in Woman's Club files or in local newspapers.

The following statement appeared in the January, 1903, library's account book:

"We have selected and secured by contract for property, a building (title to be passed May, 1903) and are to pay $1000 and give mortgages for $4000, the latter we are to pay off when we will have the income from (the) building to help meet our annual expenses."

Thus the third home of the Port Washington Library came into being in a three-story frame structure on one-fifth of an acre at the top of lower Main Street (now the parking area for St. Stephens Church and almost directly opposite the library today). Originally the building had been a late nineteenth century general store owned by John Burtis whose daughter, Phebe Burtis, was a charter member of the Woman's Club.

The library moved into its new quarters in June, 1903. At that time the book collection had grown to 1,162 volumes and circulation for the year was 2,133 books, but the library was still open only nine hours per week. It occupied one half of the first floor and rented out the other half to the Bank of North Hempstead, fulfilling the goal of making the property income producing. At a later time rooms in the upper two floors would be rented to "suitable individuals."

FAVORITE BOOKS 1899–1903

Richard Carvel by Winston Churchill
In His Steps by Charles M. Sheldon
David Harum by E. N. Westcott
Lavender and Old Lace by Myrtle Reed
The Virginian by Owen Wister
Rebecca of Sunnybrook Farm by Kate Douglas Wiggin
The Little Shepherd of Kingdom Come by John Fox

Port Washington Free Library, occupied June, 1903.   *Burtis Store, in the 1880s.*

*Early 20th century commuters arrived at the L.I.R.R. station on foot, by the local hack
or by their own horse-drawn vehicle.*

View from the tracks of the station and Flower Hill Avenue (Main Street) beyond.

CHAPTER II

A New Home on Main Street
1904–1912

Burtis House

1904   *New Library a busy place, but fortunes of Woman's Club dwindle —*
       Miss Mitchell expands floor space — Trolley cars arrive at front
       door

At that time...

**Theodore Roosevelt elected 26th
   President**

In spite of the slowing of Woman's Club activities, a few members
who in great part had been responsible for continuing the library
fund-raising maintained their interest and efforts. Among them
was Mrs. Mary Elizabeth McLean who served as President for many
years and was Secretary Pro Tem much of the time. Her Annual
Report on January 6, 1904 was the last full report for many years.

At that time she wrote:
    "The year just closed has been a very important one in the history
of the club. It has seen us in a new home of our own, the goal we
have been working for steadily since our organization about 12
years ago, a permanent place for our library, which in these years
has grown to such magnificent proportions, and is now filling a long
felt need in the community. The satisfaction it must give to all our
members, and those who have been willing to give us a helping
hand in our work, can hardly be estimated."
    A few months later Mrs. McLean's daughter, Annie McLean, now
Secretary of the club, recorded in the minutes:
    "On Wed. Nov. 2, 1904 the library room was opened for the regu-
lar meeting of the P.W.W.C. The day being beautiful and balmy a
large attendance was anticipated—but Alas! for human hopes.
    "Five members were all that were interested enough to come—the
five faithful ones. Verily their names should be engraved in letters
of fire in the halls of philanthropy!"

THE FAITHFUL

Mrs. McLean	Miss Lillian Cornwell
Miss Mitchell	Miss Annie McLean
Mrs. W. J. Cornwell	

The dwindling fortunes of the Woman's Club were dramatized by very skimpy balance sheets for 1904, 1905, and 1906, culminating in one cryptic message for January 1907: *Balance on hand, $1.06.*

Aside from these devastating statistics, no news has come down about the final demise of the Woman's Club aside from a few almost illegibly scribbled meeting notes. Nor do the pages of the *Port News* yield any vital information about the library during those early years of the twentieth century.

After opening shop as the *Port Washington News* William Hyde carried almost no library news until 1913, possibly owing to his total immersion in local politics and town improvement projects, or just that no one at the library was sending him information.

By 1906 the constantly increasing use of the library put demands on the trustees (still members of the Woman's Club) to make major changes. The Bank of North Hempstead had departed to new quarters "uptown" leaving Miss Mitchell the needed area to expand to twice the floor space. A little income was derived from renters who occupied rooms on the second and third floors.

In 1903 a company calling itself the Mineola, Roslyn and Port Washington Traction Company applied to the authorities for a "certificate of consent and of public necessity to build a trolley road from Mineola to and through Roslyn to Port Washington." A little over four years later, January 1, 1908, the first trolley arrived in Port Washington which terminated near the Manhasset Bay Yacht Club. Although a list of the trolley stops in Port Washington is not available, it is more than just a possibility that there was one close to the top of lower Main Street (Flower Hill Avenue) near the library.

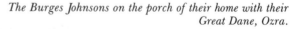

Flower Hill Avenue (Main Street) at the corner of Irma Avenue as it appeared in 1912 showing trolley car tracks.

The Burges Johnsons on the porch of their home with their Great Dane, Ozra.

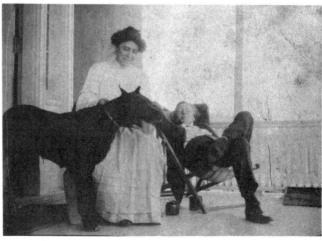

House at 24 North Washington Street built in 1906 by Constance and Burges Johnson.

1906   *The Burges Johnsons, Mrs. Mary McLean, Mr. John S. Witmer become strong leaders in library and community activities*

An event of considerable significance for the town and for the library took place in January, 1906, when Burges Johnson and his wife, Constance, Manhattanites for many years, moved into their new home, a house they had built at 24 North Washington Street, across the street and up a short hill from the library.

Successively Burges Johnson was an editor at Harper Brothers, E.P. Dutton, and later Editor-in-Chief of *Judge Magazine*. When the Johnsons moved from Port Washington over ten years later, he became a college professor.

The Johnsons selected this town over many within commuting distance of Manhattan—"Too long to Jersey Shore; south shore of L.I., crowded beaches and Sunday mobs; Hudson River, swimming not good; just North Shore of L.I. remained," he wrote in his autobiography, *As Much As I Dare*. He continued:

"In those days, Long Island's north shore had not been thoroughly suburbanized because of the Long Island Rail Road. Fares

Burges Johnson in his Atlantic Hook and Ladder Company uniform with motorcycling friend.

One of the most imposing homes on Carlton Avenue (#39) was owned by Mrs. Mary E. McLean where she, her daughter, Annie and son, David, lived until the '20s.

were too high, the trains were too few and too dirty. Port Washington, at the head of Cow Bay, then beginning to be called Manhasset Bay, was a fishing village with only a few commuting residents."

Years later he wrote:

"Port Washington suggests a bundle of memories so varied and intimate that it is hard to determine what I am justified in recording. Our ten years ran the whole gamut of suburban life."

The Johnsons, as will be seen, literally threw themselves into community activities, made a very wide circle of friends, and both took with them and left behind warm memories of this town.

Mrs. Mary E. McLean became President of the Woman's Club in 1900 and, as far as is known, remained in that position until the library was reorganized in 1913, after which she continued on the Board of Trustees until 1921. Her contributions to the library through good, and not so good, years were outstanding. Mrs. McLean, along with Miss Mitchell, were the backbone of that institution through the first twelve years of the century.

Mary McLean and her family had lived in their home at 39 Carlton Avenue for six years when Mr. John S. Witmer, Jr., of 23 Bayview Avenue, a noted photographer and later member and president of the Library Board, took the accompanying photos at Mrs. McLean's home in 1906. Throughout her years of service to the library Mrs. McLean's charming home was the scene of library board meetings and fund-raising affairs for both the library and the Methodist Church.

In October, 1906, John S. Witmer took this photo in the McLean home. Although no caption was found, it is reasonable to assume that Mrs. McLean is to the right, with Annie and David to the left.

View from the McLean's front porch overlooking Manhasset Bay, July, 1906.

*1911   *Week-long* Carnival *helps put town on map—*Plain Talk *competes with* Port News *and lauds library in every issue*

Two major events in 1911 had a most salutary effect on the entire population of Port Washington. The first was an "all-town" Carnival spearheaded by Burges Johnson, plans for which commenced in May with W. Bourke Cockran, local U.S. Congressman, as President (Honorary) and a most distinguished group of citizens on the committees. The feature of the Carnival was a production of Gilbert and Sullivan's *"H.M.S. Pinafore"* staged on a floating barge moored just south of the Manhasset Bay Yacht Club. A grandstand with a capacity of over a thousand was erected at the site of the barge. Townspeople took leading roles and were members of the chorus. Parades, a balloon ascension, band concert, fireworks were just a few of the fabulous events which everyone felt took one more giant step forward in putting Port Washington on the map.**

The other event was *Plain Talk,* a biweekly newspaper in magazine form, edited and published by H. K. Landis, a bachelor who lived at 24 Fifth Avenue and founded the North Shore Publishing Company just to publish *Plain Talk.* From the first issue of *Plain Talk,* it was obvious that a spirited, if not always friendly, rivalry

*From 1907 to 1911 minutes of Woman's Club meetings are non-existent.
**In spite of its great success, publicity-wise, the Carnival closed with many unpaid bills necessitating fund-raising concerts during 1912, all with Burges Johnson as master of ceremonies.

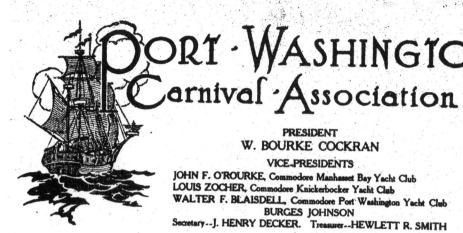

PORT·WASHINGTON Carnival·Association

PRESIDENT
W. BOURKE COCKRAN

VICE-PRESIDENTS
JOHN F. O'ROURKE, Commodore Manhasset Bay Yacht Club
LOUIS ZOCHER, Commodore Knickerbocker Yacht Club
WALTER F. BLAISDELL, Commodore Port Washington Yacht Club
BURGES JOHNSON
Secretary--J. HENRY DECKER.   Treasurer--HEWLETT R. SMITH

Committees

Finance
Henry B. Ranken, Chairman
Charles N. Wysong
Geo. E. Bauer
C. H. Perry
J. H. Decker
James F. Dinn
A. P. Baxter
John W. Mitchell
J. Drummond
E. J. West

Reception
A. T. Vance, Chairman
C. E. Hyde
C. Ross

Production
George Thomas, Chairman
George Bowles

Automobile
R. B. Hults, Chairman
Earl Milliken
Geo. O. Linkletter
E. C. Davis

Publicity
J. Floherty, Chairman
Wm. M. Hyde
O. A. Marsh

Construction
J. H. Decker, Chairman
T. B. Taylor

Law and Order
C. R. Weeks, Chairman
C. N. Wysong
A. P. Baxter

Boat Carnival
A committee from the Knickerbocker
Yacht Club.

Transportation
J. A. McIlhiney

Parade
Chief T. J. Bird, Chairman
Fire Board

Information
H. K. Landis, Chairman
C. H. Perry
Frank B. Smith

Water Sports
H. T. Huntting, Chairman
Port Washington Yacht Club

Fireworks and Concert
Burges Johnson, Chairman
The Italian Society

Illumination
John Sarano, Chairman
A. T. Witherell

Title page of the printed program distributed at the Port Washington Carnival, July 11 through July 15, 1911.

H. M. S. PINAFORE AT COW BAY

IN SIGHT OF THE HEIGHTS OF M. E. CHURCH HILL.

A Feature of the Port Washington Carnival Association's Several Big Days— Government Vessel to Guard the Bay —An Aeronaut Much Out of Sorts.

Despite the fact that Fritz Williams, Sally Fisher, George Bowles and a whole colony of regular actor folk have cottages in that high part of Port Washington L. I., known officially as First Methodist Episcopal Church Hill, overlooking Cow Bay—Manhasset Bay of late, but for about two centuries Cow Bay—the town and the Port Washington Carnival Association passed up the professional troupers when opening the village's five days of high jinks last night with a production of "H. M. S. Pinafore." Local talent carolled from the deck of a regular boat pinned securely to the mud of Cow Bay a few feet away from the boatanding of the Manhasset Yacht Club.

Port Washington is just splitting herself wide open this week. What with Undertaker Austin Knowles neglecting all his clients to give his entire time to singing Bill Bobsta'ys part at three performances of the operetta this week; all the Bauer Building, in Flower Hill avenue, the town's skyscraper, swathed with flags from the street level clear to the roof of the two story office building; red, white and blue harness on Charley's Hewett's hack horse, not only when the 6:03 gets in each evening but all day; balloon ascensions, water sports, fireworks, Burges Johnson, poet and publisher, heading committees; automobile parades, band concerts—take it on the word of a volunteer fireman, it's some week along the north shore.

From the first flash one gets of Charley Hewett's red, white and blue harness trappings waiting at the station the eye jumps straight to the two flags on Joe Giner's bakery across from the station. From this point on out past Du Bois's Model Laundry, George Johnson's lawn, wrapped in American, English and Irish flags; Doc Neuman's residence a little beyond and so on westward it's a riot. Even though to-day is Orangeman's day, George Johnson says that not a green flag on his lawn is coming down.

And when one gets to the top of First Methodist Episcopal Church Hill near Burges Johnson's house and starts down toward Main street all of a sudden while rounding the turn on Baxter's Hill Main street itself is disclosed exploding westward to the shores of beautiful Cow Bay. The sandlot near the foot of the sandbank at the head of Main street brings one back to coronation week itself. Attraction after attraction after attraction, three of them, have erected tents at the foot of the sandbank, with Joe Wood, the Living Skeleton's attraction, looming even higher than Charley Schwartz's carousel or the other show in the third tent where a gent suspends a lady frind in the air and walks under, in front of and back of her to show that there is no deception.

Well may President W. Bourke Cockran of the Carnival Association feel proud, along with Vice-Presidents John F. O'Rourke, Burges Johnson, Walter Blaisdell, the coal man; Louis Zocher, commodore of the Knickerbocker Yacht Club, and District Attorney Charley Wysong, Editor A. T. Vance of the Pictorial Review, Jack Floherty, the artist; O. A. Marsh of Tammany Hall, Postman Hults, Editor Bill Hyde of the Port Washington News, Plumber George Bauer, Doc Ferry, hotel man and veterinarian; Congressman Martin Littleton—every officer of the various committees has a right to grow chesty over the way Port Washington does things when she does them.

One of Leo Stevens's aeronauts was to have opened the celebra——but wait a moment; the Government of the United States of North America is represented also. Out in Cow Bay yesterday forenoon along comes the United States revenue cutter Mohawk, seven officers and a crew of about fifty men, to keep the aisles of Cow Bay clear of standees while the operetta performances are on. Some one on the committee asked the Government to send a launch to keep things straight around the good ship Pinafore each night and Washington drops all work and sends the big Mohawk for a week. What d'you know about that? Bad, what?

As we were saying when interrupted, one of Leo Stevens's areonauts was to have started the week's high jinks yesterday afternoon by racing with a motor boat across Cow Bay in a balloon—one on the water and the other in the air—and then the aeronaut was to have made a triple parachute jump without missing Long Island.

Into the carnival headquarters in the Hyde & Baxter building in Main street yesterday walked heatedly one of the flossiest dressers up, or down, that Port Washington ever has seen. He was crusted with diamonds and while he spoke he continued to snap impatiently a stout rubber band that circled a roll that conservatively was estimated at $10,000,000.

"Do you know who I am?" he demanded.

Not a soul did.

"Well, I'm the aeronaut," he explained. "Why didn't a committee meet me? Do you know what I'm going to do? I'm going to get right on the next train out of here and leave Long Island flat."

He did. Consequently there was no balloon ascension yesterday, but as the commttiee have a contract with Leo Stevens there's going to be some parachute jumping to-day, you can bet your sweet life, so the balloon committee announced while moppi g its brow last night.

The cast of "Pinafore" last night was one of the finest casts in all Port Washington. Have a look:

The Right Hon. Sir Joseph Porter, K. C. B.
Justice of the Peace Charley Weeks
Capt. Corcoran............Artist Jack J. Floherty
Ralph Rackstraw......Man About Town Art Jones
Dick Deadeye.........Lithographer George Thomas
Bill Bobstay............Undertaker Austin Knowles
Bob Becket......Man About Town Fred Farmer

The characters of *Josephine, Little Buttercup* and *Hebe* were sung very well by Flora M. Engel, Agatha Shields and Ethel Allen. The "sisters and the cousins and the aunts" and the able seaman chorus were sung by all that part of the North Shore which wasn't necessary to make up the audience that filled the long and high tiers of seats facing the good old British frigate.

Article in Brooklyn Evening Sun *during Carnival week in Port Washington.*

Postcard promoting the Carnival, 1911.

between Hyde of the *Port News* and Landis would ensue. The week after the first issue appeared, Hyde carried a mildly sarcastic column about that first issue of his new-found competition. Landis' reply in *his* second issue started "We are glad to see that *News* is pleased with our modest efforts and agrees that we 'will supply a need which is self-evident.' The editor finds our cartoon 'real funny' and our editorial 'too funny for words.' "

H. K. Landis became one of the town's leading boosters. In issue after issue he wrote warmly and convincingly about the virtues of Port Washington, constantly exhorting his fellow townspeople and merchants and Board of Trade to better publicize this "ideal community." No area of possible improvement within the town was exempt from his efforts to improve it, for example, he advocated "free delivery of mail, street signs, houses numbered and all streets

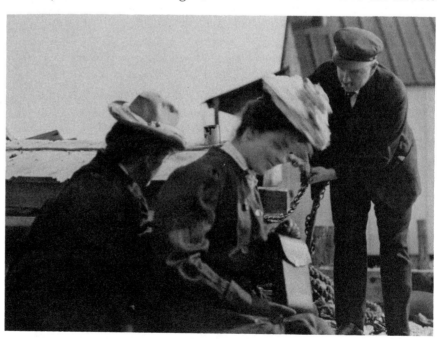

May, 1907—(l. to r.) Miss Virginia Spencer who later became Mrs. John S. Witmer, Sr., Miss Annie McLean and Mr. H.K. Landis on Mackey's Beach.

named, a first-class steam laundry, more system in garbage collection and disposal; also of ash disposal." Just a short list during 1912!

His greatest contribution from Wilhelmina Mitchell's point of view, however, was his continuing efforts to publicize the library and good books. Although the minutes of library meetings for almost eight years were not recorded, *Plain Talk* has supplied much information for at least one of those years, 1912.

In the February 3rd issue, Mr. Landis devoted a page and a half to "Our Library" summarizing its history and bringing his readers right up to date:

"At the present time, about $500 are needed to keep the library running...Miss Mitchell's annual report for fiscal year ending June 30, 1911 gives a total expenditure of $425.67, which includes $200 for interest on bonds, $7.70 for fuel and light, $8.00 for services of janitress, $2.30 for permanent improvements, and $94.73 for books."

Dues from associate members, $2.00 per year, and $1.00 additional to those who "also desire to contribute to the book fund" was a major source of income, also rent of the upstairs rooms and of the barn, overdue book fines, a charge to summer residents of 50 cents, and donations made up the total.

Mr. Landis did not hesitate to chide the public about using the library more fully:

"The number of volumes in the library June 30, 1911, were 2,280, and 4081 were loaned that year, as compared with 430 books in the library February 10, 1893 and 37 readers. This shows growth, but not as much as one might expect. It is just possible that our public-spirited citizens have overlooked the library as an enterprise deserving encouragement. There must be a large number who have books stored away which should be on the shelves of the library doing good. Certainly there are many who have stacks of magazines of no use to them, and which the library would be glad to have. The Young Women's Recreation League could take upon themselves the collecting of such reading matter. A card dropped to Miss W. M. Mitchell would be sufficient to set the donation in motion."

Thus commenced a firm and enduring friendship between the library and *Plain Talk*.

FAVORITE BOOKS 1904–1911

Story of the Bible by J. L. Hurlbut
Freckles by Gene Stratton Porter
The Trail of the Lonesome Pine by John Fox
Girl of the Limberlost by Gene Stratton Porter
The Rosary by Florence Barclay
The Winning of Barbara Worth by Harold Bell Wright
The Harvester by Gene Stratton Porter

At that time...

Woodrow Wilson becomes 28th President

Progress Amid Controversy
1913

Charles N. Wysong, District Attorney of Nassau County, was a member of Library Board of Trustees (1913 to 1917) and President for four years.

Twice a year for 29 years Miss Mitchell made an interest payment of $100 on the library mortgage held by the Monforts.

1913   *Library Association organized—Prominent men new Trustees— Public Reading Room opened—Constitution and By-laws adopted*

To many of those who founded the Woman's Club, it was saddening to see the slow demise of that organization which over the years had received such accolades from the citizens of Port Washington and the surrounding towns—accolades for their vigorous and enduring efforts in starting and continuing a library and for their services to women in the village whose culinary and needlework skills brought them additional income from the Woman's Exchange.

Time was moving on, however, and a new Library Association separate from the Woman's Club was organized. The members of a new Board of Trustees, including five from the Woman's Club Board, met on January 19, 1913.* The meeting was governed by the constitution of the Woman's Club "until such time as necessary for the final adoption of a new constitution." The members of the Board included:

Mr. E.W. Gaillard, ("one of our citizens who is connected with the New York Public Library")

Mr. Charles N. Wysong   Mrs. Mary E. Baxter
Mrs. Ellen Stannard   Mrs. Mary E. McLean
Miss W. M. Mitchell   Miss Florence McKee

*First meeting since 1907 in which formal minutes were taken.

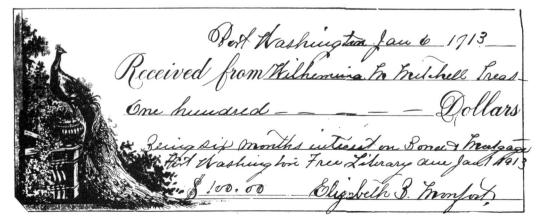

Principal business discussed at this meeting was "the best method for renting to suitable persons the apartment above the Library room, and also the Barn. Mrs. McLean was appointed a committee of one, with power, for having Hyde & Baxter's TO LET signs placed on these properties."

A motion was passed to invite the Board of Trade (a forerunner of the Chamber of Commerce), the Board of Education, the Village Welfare Society and the Young Woman's Recreation League to a joint meeting to consider ways and means of bringing about a considerable enlargement and improvement of the Library and its work.

From the January 19, 1913 minutes it is obvious that considerable activity had been going on with members of the community, well before the joint meeting above was planned, in an effort to bring more townspeople into the library.

As a consequence Miss Mitchell reported that a new Public Reading Room in the library would be opened on January 21, just two days after the regular board meeting. The Reading Room was to be under the auspices of the joint committee of the Village Welfare Society and the Young Woman's Recreation League, Mrs. Burges Johnson, Chairman. One other piece of business at that meeting:

"On motion, Mrs. Johnson was given permission to have lettered on the window of the Library, without expense to the Library, the following: *Port Washington Free Library*."

Finally, a committee on Constitution was appointed: Mrs. Stannard, Mr. Wysong, Mr. Gaillard.

Sixty people attended the ceremonies opening the Public Reading Room on January 21 with John Mitchell representing the Board of Trade. He told how the Library Association had carefully cast about for someone to head up the Public Library Association who was trained in library work. Fortunately they found Edwin White Gaillard "who was connected with the New York Public Library and a resident of Port Washington." He was immediately elected Chairman of the Library Association.

When called upon Mr. Gaillard spoke about the future of the Port Washington Free Library, "how National and State Libraries helped local libraries, for young people a separate room and special books...this library is deficient in juvenile literature and is something to work up."

Plain Talk reported that "After looking over the equipment we might suggest that a dictionary of the English language be donated, likewise some boys' books and periodicals. 'Youth's Companion' is the only boys' paper received."

The Reading Room was under the charge of Mr. Griffiths, supervising principal of the Manhasset Schools, and Mr. Gardiner of the Sands Point School. In February the 21st birthday of the library was celebrated by lending books for home use every evening from 7 to 10 o'clock.

Mr. Gaillard, in one of his first official actions as Chairman of the Board of Trustees called in Mr. Asa Wynkoop, Inspector of Libraries for the State of New York, who, after visiting Port Washington, wrote the following letter:

"You certainly have a very interesting proposition before you. The time ought to be ripe for some very decided advances in that community and we do not believe that you will have any great difficulty in putting the library on a very solid basis. My advice would be: do not attempt to create a new kind of library, let everything be a development from the present library. Make the Constitution broad, liberal, democratic, permitting everyone in the community to become a member on easy terms and giving everyone who becomes a member a voice in the selection of trustees and in shaping the general policy of the library."

Mr. Wynkoop promised on behalf of the State Education Department every possible form of help, and to give excellent advice leading to the better establishment of the library, and perhaps to the obtaining of a new and thoroughly modern library.

The editor of *Plain Talk* echoed Mr. Wynkoop's sentiments: "Let those who believe in increasing our general intelligence and raising the standard of our community, help along this library by joining the association, contributing books and funds, and saying the good word whenever opportunity offers."

One event was piling on top of another: To publicize the new Reading Room, Mr. William Patten and Mr. Burges Johnson were requested to give a public reading in the library rooms on February 10; the Chairman was authorized to prepare and distribute posters announcing the opening of the library both as a reading room and a circulating library; he also was instructed to arrange with the telephone company for the installation of a pay station in the library; and finally Miss Mitchell reported the gift from William Mullon of a handsome new sign-board for the library. Not to overlook the fact that the rooms above the library had been rented for $12.00 a month!

Mrs. Mary McLean generously opened her home month after month for regular and special meetings of the association. She and her daughter, Anne, had devoted many years to library work so it was fitting that the March 4th, 1913, meeting should have been held at her house. For it was that evening when "in the absence of Mr. Wysong, Chairman of the Committee on Constitution, Mrs. Stannard presented the report of the committee in the form of a proposed constitution and by-laws. These were read and after considerable discussion, Mrs. Stannard moved their adoption. The motion was seconded by Miss Mitchell and was carried without objection. Miss Mitchell as Chairman of a Committee on Rules moved the adoption of a new set of library rules governing the issue of books which was seconded and carried.

Whether by chance or the influence of Mr. Landis, the gift of a *dictionary* from Mr. Dalton and also one from Mr. William Patten was announced.

The new Reading Room, opened just twenty-three nights, had scored an attendance of 227, and 81 books had been loaned. An official library organizer was scheduled by the State Education Department to start in April on "completing the classification and cataloging of the books and the making of an inventory of all of the books in the library. (This) work will very greatly aid in rounding out the work of the librarians."

Mr. Gaillard, just before closing the meeting, made the long-awaited announcement that he had received a "Certificate of Approved Circulation" from N.Y. State Department:

"This certifies that Port Washington Free Library is subject to the inspection of the Regents and registered by them as maintaining a proper standard; that its system of recording the circulation of books and the character of the books so circulated have been officially inspected; that its trustees have reported year ending June 30, 1912, and that in the judgement of the authorized inspector this Library has circulated for the free use of the public during said year three thousand, eight hundred volumes of such a character as to merit a grant of public money."

Signed, A.S. Draper, Commissioner of Education

"This Certificate will entitle you to ask your school district at its next meeting for as much as $380."

Signed, Asa Wynkoop, Inspector, Public Libraries

1913   *Benefits held to pay 1911 Carnival debts—First meeting of Library Association, April 1—Trustees increased to nine members—Officers named*

The 1911 Carnival, such a success in publicizing Port Washington, still had outstanding debts which were slowly being paid off. *Too Many Husbands*, a farce-comedy "featuring many of the people who were in *Pinafore*, was produced for two nights at the High School (Main Street School) with such (then) well-known townspeople as Charles R. Weeks, Mr. & Mrs. Arthur Jones, Mr. & Mrs. Burges Johnson, Austin Knowles, Jack Floherty, Miss Ethel Allen, and Miss Kathleen Willis. They expect to have a clean slate before the end of the year."

As part of a general plan for the continuing development of the library, the new Association held its first annual meeting on April 1, 1913, at Mrs. McLean's home for the purpose of electing a Board of

LIBRARY NOTES

At a joint meeting of delegates representing the various civic organizations of Port Washinington, held at the home of Mrs. McLean on Carlton avenue last Sunday, some important business was accomplished.

The Library Trustees reported that a complete reorganization had been made in its affairs, that a new constitution and by-laws, and a new set of library rules had been adopted and ratified. According to the new program, any resident may now become a member of the Library Association upon payment of one dollar, and may vote and hold office. This, in effect, places the management of the library in the hands of the citizens of the town, as it will, through the Library Association, elect the trustees at the annual library meeting in April, as provided in the new constitution.

The further development of the library was discussed at length. In the end, it was decided that the School District be asked to set apart a small portion of the high school campus for a site for a new and thoroughly modern library building, and to ask Mr. Carnegie to donate a sum of money for the erection of such a building.

It is the intention of the library trustees, if such a building is erected to use it, not only as a library for adults, but also to furnish an excellent room and books for children. In the basement it is expected that a lecture room can be arranged, and this room will be intended for the free use of any organization for civic purposes. In addition to letting the various organizations have the free use of this room, it will be used also for a series of free lectures.

At the Board of Trade meeting on Monday night, Mr. John Mitchell and Mr. Gaillard reported this suggested program. After talking over the prospects for getting a new library, it was voted that the Library Trustees be tendered the approval, sympathy and support of the Board of Trade.

It would seem that the library is making every effort to obtain as good library facilities as has any other town in the State. Even if the gift from Mr. Carnegie should not be obtained, it would be an excellent plan to let the library use a part of the high school campus for a building which it would undoubtedly manage to get in some other way. Its own property would be a first rate beginning for a building fund, if placed on the market.

Port News, *March 15, 1913.*

Trustees, increasing the number from seven to nine. The minutes state that "This election will be held in accordance with the provisions of the new Constitution, by which final control of the Library, and of its general policies, are placed in the hands of the members." A Nominating Committee was appointed and notice was given that nominations could be made from the floor, without previous notice. In other words the trustees were making every effort to assure the public that operating the Library was a truly democratic affair.

Trustees were named as follows:

For three years	Mrs. Mary E. McLean
	Miss Wilhelmina Mitchell
	Mr. E. W. Gaillard
For two years	Miss Florence I. McKee
	Mr. John S. Witmer, Jr.
	Mr. Mason Trowbridge
For one year	Mr. Charles N. Wysong
	Mrs. Mary E. Baxter
	Mrs. Ellen B. Stannard

As might be expected the officers elected were President, Mr. Gaillard; Vice President, Mrs. Stannard; Treasurer, Miss Mitchell; Secretary, Mr. Witmer. The real innovation of the new Board was to have three working committees in Finance, Book Selection and Administration.

Immediately after the April 1st meeting the Library Trustees met to petition the Regents of the State of New York to grant a new charter changing the number of trustees from seven to nine.

After ten years in their own library building the Trustees of the new association started discussing the question of obtaining and maintaining a *new library building*. Mr. Gaillard sparked interest in the idea and started the ball rolling by suggesting a petition asking the school district for a site for a proposed building, and for a yearly appropriation for support of a suitable library.

Later he wrote a lengthy letter which was printed in the *Port News*, April 19th issue. Its clarity of presentation of a very complex subject foretells the "selling exercise" always required in community improvements, sometimes successfully, frequently not. In this case a 100′ × 100′ piece of land at the Northeast corner of the High School (Main Street School) property, which today is directly opposite Finn MacCool's Restaurant, was requested of the School Board in the petition, along with a request for $1,000 for the maintenance of the Library each year. (The library trustees, in their appropriation request, purposely went well beyond the guidelines suggested in Mr. Wynkoop's addition to Commissioner Draper's letter, from $380 to $1,000.)

In the week following Mr. Gaillard's letter to the *News*, Mr. Hyde wrote an editorial praising the plans and ending:

"In our opinion the resolutions to be voted on at the annual school meeting on May 6, one to set aside a plot of land 100 × 100, the other to appropriate one thousand dollars each year toward the maintenance of a library, should appeal to the honest thinking people of the district. The land should be granted and the library be made an actuality. It will pay for itself ten times over, as have the public schools."

Mr. Landis in *Plain Talk,* however, branched out on a slightly different tack. He came up with the idea of building an addition onto the High School, combining two projects, expansion of the High School which was badly in need of more classrooms *and* the library. In the same issue he quoted an extensive article on *Using The Library* from the New York Public Library, just one more effort to promote the idea of libraries. The cover of the May 10 *Plain Talk,* displaying an elf-like character with books, and a caption, "Everybody Works for the Library," accented his enthusiasm.

Plain Talk *did its part for the library graphically as well as editorially.*

EVERYBODY WORKS FOR THE LIBRARY.

Soon, however, opposition developed—strong, articulate and quite in character with this growing town. In a Communication to the *Port News,* Mr. J. F. Dinn expressed with great passion his hostility toward:

"...a proposition to donate to the Library Association a piece of the High School property, as I understand it, 100′ × 100′ to be taken from the children's playground and baseball field. It may be to the youngster's benefit to take candy from the child, but it certainly is not conducive to his moral or physical welfare to confiscate his playground and deprive him of the opportunity of letting off a little excess energy in a healthful and legitimate environment.
"...not only will the running track be irreparably spoiled, but...a baseball field will be an absolute impossibility...Do you imagine for a moment that the people of Port Washington will turn their children into the streets to find recreation in order to give valuable property to an institution which already has a location, *and the future of which is not without some little uncertainty?*
"It is in the opinion of the writer, and numerous others to whom he has spoken, the plain duty of every mother, father and taxpayer to attend the school meeting on Tuesday, May 6th, and vote this proposition down. Don't leave it to someone else."

The conflict grew hotter when, during an evening lecture at the High School on how other libraries worked, a minor riot broke out, led mainly by local athletes. In the same *Port News* as Mr. Dinn's letter the following appeared:

Editor of the *News,*
Dear Sir:
I would like to enter my protest against the behavior of some of the boys who were present at the lecture given by Mr. Edwin W. Gaillard at the High School. They did their best to interfere with the lecture by noise and ill-timed applause and altogether acted in a most childish and unsportsmanlike manner. Even if the boys do not like the idea of using school ground for library purposes, they have other ways of showing their disapproval. Let us hope that the boys who do so well in baseball, will not in the future disgrace their school and their village by their rudeness in the lecture room.

Yours truly, *Constance W. Johnson*

Additional Letters to the Editor followed including another from Mrs. Johnson which ended:
"No matter what we believe in regard to a proper site for a new library, and there is room for an honest and friendly difference, we want some kind of a library and we have got to support it. Twenty-five or fifty cents a year from each taxpayer will do the business. Keep your library where it is, or put one on a small corner of the

Dear Sir and Dear Lady:

Please come to the High School on Tuesday night, May 6, and vote against the proposition to take part of our playground away from us. Thank you.

The School Children of Port Washington.

How to "rig" an election!

school land, or buy the Folwell property and set your library on a hill. Put it where you want—but vote for the thousand dollar appropriation or you may not have any library at all."

The opposition did not let up, however, and just before election day a card with the appearance of engraving was distributed to (it is assumed) all the voters of Port Washington. Whether or not it was the *coup de grace* to the Resolution on the school site for the library on May 6th was never determined.

Mr. Landis reported in *Plain Talk* on May 10th:
"Meeting in the High School auditorium on the evening of May 6, and standing in the aisles, was the largest school district gathering seen here for some time. The occasion was a demonstration in electing school trustees and an antilibrary site agitation worked up through the school children. We regret to record these facts, and trust that a more fair-minded after-judgement will make the participants anything but proud of their achievement...the library resolutions were taken up, and we will say that the dignified and skillful way in which a difficult situation was adjusted won our admiration. The resolution to place the library upon the school campus was withdrawn when presented by Mr. Gaillard, chairman of the library trustees, in a clear and accurate statement which showed that they (the trustees) had every reason to think that *the people approved of the proposition at the time the resolution was advertised.*"

The motion to withdraw the library site resolution was seconded by Charles N. Wysong who then took the opportunity to speak for the second proposition (to raise by taxation $1,000 toward maintaining the library annually), to praise highly Mr. Gaillard's ability and "the faithful service of Miss Mitchell, the librarian, for twenty-one years without compensation." Other speakers from the floor were Mr. Jack Floherty and Mrs. William R. P. Benet.

With the site proposition withdrawn, 340 votes were cast *for* the $1,000 appropriation, and only 114 *against*.

1913   *As some in town wrangled, others kept the fund-raising torch aflame—Miss Mitchell finally receives more than just praise— Library now open six days, 2 P.M. to 8:30 P.M.—Generous book donations, furniture and a house heating furnace welcome gifts— LIRR Port Washington branch electrified*

While the debate over the library site was going on, preparations for two library benefits were afoot. The Board of Trustees announced that Messrs. Newman and Filan had offered to donate the Nassau Open Air Theatre* on Monday, June 9th, for a benefit, the entire receipts of which would be used to establish a children's department in the Free Library.

*Nassau Open Air Theatre was located on the north side of Main Street opposite Crooker Street (no longer open to Main St). This steep property ran from Main Street down to Locust Avenue.

Advertising card and admission ticket sent to prospective patrons of a library benefit given at the Nassau Open Theatre, June 9, 1913.

PORT WASHINGTON FREE LIBRARY

The Board of Trustees of the Port Washington Free Library wish to announce that Messrs. Newman and Filan have donated the **Nassau Open Air Theatre**, on **Monday June 9th, 1913, for a benefit.** The **entire receipts** of which will be used to establish a Children's Department in the Public Library.

On that occasion high-class moving pictures will be given and some of our professional neighbors have kindly consented to **"do something,"** in other words, it will be a **"big night"** which you can't afford to miss. We have taken the liberty of sending you_____ tickets which we trust you will dispose of, as the cause is such a worthy one.

Kindly return check or tickets to

J. S. WITMER, Jr., Secretary,

Port Washington, L. I.

---

411   NASSAU OPEN AIR THEATRE

MONDAY, JUNE 9TH. 1913

Monster Benefit for Children's Department

PORT WASHINGTON FREE LIBRARY

ADMISSION - - 15 CENTS

Victoria Hall (far left) connected to Victoria Hotel at the corner of Main Street and Haven Avenue (now the Plaza Building), which was the setting for The Grand Parada *presented for the benefit of the library, May 19–22, 1913.*

At the same time literally hundreds of townspeople were happily and productively occupied in rehearsing a *Grand Parada and Fiesta* which included incidental solos, choruses, stage dancing and marching, "accompanied by orchestra and lighted by stage effects," also for the benefit of the library, to be produced at the Victoria Theatre* for four nights, May 19 through May 22, 1913.

In June the Joint Committees of Village Welfare and Recreation League asked the Library Trustees to assume responsibility for the Reading Room which they had been running for six months very successfully. No reasons are given in the minutes, but as a result of this major change in responsibility, the Trustees made new arrangements to keep the library open daily from 6 to 8:30 and on Tuesday, Thursday and Saturday afternoons beginning at 2 o'clock.

On June 9 Mr. Witmer reported that the proceeds from the Open Air Theatre, to date, were $138.15 and in July an additional $15.30 was added. The *Port News* reported that the library had benefited by over $200 from *The Grand Parada*.

Still aware that the library was searching for land for a new library, in August Mr. and Mrs. Charles Tuxhill, owners of considerable acreage on Beacon Hill, offered one-half acre of ground for a library site. The land was triangular in shape close to the Tuxhill real estate development and valued at $3.000. After full discussion of advantages and disadvantages the Trustees reluctantly declined the Tuxhill offer, "as it was felt that the location was not near enough to the center of population."

To Wilhelmina Mitchell perhaps the most gratifying event of the year was a vote taken at the July 1st Board Meeting—Resolved: that Miss Mitchell and Miss McKee are to keep the library open six days

*Victoria Hall was on Haven Avenue just behind the Victoria Hotel which was at the corner of Flower Hill Avenue (Main Street and Haven Avenue).

THE GRAND PARADA

COPYRIGHT

FOR THE BENEFIT OF

Port Washington Free Library, at Victoria Hall

Monday, Tuesday, Wednesday and Thursday, May 19, 20, 21, 22, 1913

Patrons and Patronesses

Phoebe A. Underhill
Mr. and Mrs. Leo D. Chase
Mr. and Mrs. A. Valentine Fraser
Miss Frances Elenda Fay
A. C. Bayles
Julia A. Lawton
The Misses Fraser
Mr. and Mrs. R. W. France
A. A. Kilduff
Dr. and Mrs. Charles A. Steurer
Mr. and Mrs. E. T. Keyser
John C. Drummond
Mr. and Mrs. E. J. Evans
Florence I. McKee
Frank J. Cornell
J. S. Witmer Jr.
Mrs. J. S. Witmer Jr.
Mr. and Mrs. Frank B. Smith
Mr. and Mrs. Isaac A. Willets
Wm. I. Cocke M. D.
George Wansor
N. H. Vanderwall
Mrs. Sarah A. Thurber
Mrs. B. A. Mackinnon
Mrs. and Mrs. Lyndon Connett
Alfred F. Gray
Ida M. Harris
Mr. Mrs. Jacob Wetmore
Mrs. and Mrs. J. L. Salg
Mr. and Mrs. Wm. H. Taylor
Mr. and Mrs. John W. Mitchell
Charles R. Weeks
Mr. and Mrs. Charles E. Tuxill
Mrs. Hugh B. Van Deventer
M. Alice Gedney
Charlotte E. Gedney
Mrs. M. E. McLean
Mrs. E. Stannard
Mr. and Mrs. Charles S. Fallows
Frank S. Smith
Mr. and Mrs. William Patten
Mrs. Irene S. Anderson
W. E. Cummings
Thomas O'Connell
Mr. and Mrs. Maurice J. Engel
Mr. J. Oliver Sinkinson
Mrs. J. Oliver Sinkinson

PROGRAMME
PART ONE

BABYLAND
Soloist   Miss Marjorie Townsend

FLOWERS AND BEES
The Lily and the Rose
Soloist   Miss Lena Townsend

JAPANESE
Fleur-de-Lis
Soloist   Miss Sophie Hickock

PARASOL GIRLS
Soloist   Mrs. Flora M. Engel

NEWS-BOYS
Soloists   Herman Jacobs
                rant Townsend

PROM GIRLS
Soloist   Arthur W. Jones

PART TWO

Ring-ting-a-ling
        Eulalie Hayden and Chorus
Jane from Maine, Miss Jessie Holbrook
Indian Song,   Carl Smith and
        Clifford Varney

INDIAN DANCE

PART THREE

GRECIAN POSINGS WITH SONG
Soloist   Mrs. Flora M. Engel

DANCE OF THE BIRDS
Vanity Fair
Soloist   Miss Elizabeth Crawford
You're Just the Girl I'm Looking For
        Miss Sophie Hickok and Chorus

MANDY
Soloist   Mr. E. C. Davis

HUSSARS
Soloist   Miss Julia Lawrence

BABYLAND No. I
Edward Varney   Albert Varney
Christine Walters   Frances Wetmore
Anita Smith   Helen Rice
        Alva Marie Merritt

Continued Second Page

STEAMER

MARY E. GORDON

will run from

PORT WASHINGTON

TO

NEW YORK

For Freight From June 1st.

N. Y. Freighting by Water

Randall Clark
TEACHER OF SINGING
29 Carlton Avenue,   Port Washington

Program for The Grand Parada.

a week *"at a combined salary of $600. per year."* Miss Mitchell had worked for 21 years without pay!

In September the Book Committee reported to other Trustees that receipts from the "moving picture performance (plus other funds) amounting to a total of $154.00 had been expended for children's books which were selected from those found most popular in New York City libraries."

After the voters indicated their willingness to support the library through a form of taxation, it took on a new and brighter life. October attendance during the evenings was 483, a gain of 269 over the previous month; 10 per cent more books were loaned.

When the work of Miss Phelps from the State Education Department in classifying and cataloging the library's collection had been completed, book search was far easier. The added advantage was that the library could now be open every day from 2 P.M. to 8:30 P.M. except Sundays and holidays.

Good will and generosity toward the library was widespread. The Village Welfare Society (whose home was at 81 Webster Ave.) presented to the library the tables they had loaned for use in the Reading Room. Also Mrs. John W. Mitchell donated a table she had loaned earlier.

Other donations to the library included all the sod needed for the library lawn from Miss Vandeventer, and from Jacob Cocks sufficient top soil to complete the grading and sodding.

Book donations also continued at a good pace: the Trowbridges donated 30 volumes which included mostly non-fiction while Mrs. Laidlaw of Sands Point gave 53 books of fiction. When townspeople moved from Port Washington they frequently left their personal libraries to Miss Mitchell who could pick and choose books for her shelves.

The list of books selected for the children's room appeared in *Plain Talk* and Mr. Landis' comments accompanying the list show his enthusiasm for the project:

"Some (of these books) all children should read—all of them some children will read. The books are not cheap editions but are handsomely bound, printed and illustrated."

Providing new magazines for the reading room was a necessity, and with the help of a number of persons well qualified to select magazines, the Book Committee chose twenty which were on the tables in October. In the same vein the Trustees authorized Mr. Gaillard to consult librarians in the area. He obtained a list of 107 recent works of fiction, 27 of which were already on the shelves. The remaining were purchased soon thereafter.

The forerunner of *Robert's Rules of Order* was *New Cushings Manual of Parliamentary Practice* which had been used by the Woman's Club throughout its existence; a copy was donated by the Johnsons. Also in November Austin Knowles contributed a set of *Chambers*

Encyclopedia, Collier Edition, 1888, in 8 volumes. To add to the growing magazine collection, Kathleen Norris (who had moved to Port Washington two years earlier) donated a dozen recent numbers of magazines. George E. Bauer, whose store and shop occupied the building now the home of Finn MacCool's Restaurant, made a substantial offer of a house heating furnace as a donation for heating the library, costing the library only the labor to install it.

On October 25, 1913, the town and the Long Island Rail Road celebrated the completion of electrification of the Port Washington Branch. "Nothing is as vital to any suburban community as transportation," wrote Mr. Landis, "The electric coaches will carry the pleasure seeker and home hunter to our doors. We are ready to greet the newcomer the electric will bring."

1913 was a year of both controversy and progress, rounded out with a small but extremely significant check—$100—from the Department of Education in Albany, the largest paid out to a small library in New York State. Surely this was further proof that the Port Washington Free Library, under Miss Mitchell's guiding hand, had become a state-wide leader in library service.

CHAPTER IV

A Literary and Artistic Community

*"One of the most delightful hamlets
of the entire world"*—Kathleen Norris

In 1914 this village of 5,500 residents at the end of a branch of the
Long Island Rail Road was slowly becoming a suburb of New York
City while retaining all the charms of a summer resort. Hotels such
as the *Renwick* (later *Gildo's* and a whole succession of restaurants)
on Shore Road near the Mill Pond, the *Victoria* across from the railroad station, and John Bradley's famous Hotel and Restaurant close
to the town dock were among the favorites of summer visitors.

Summer boarding or rooming houses were also popular, one in
particular being Mrs. A.H. Haskell's "The Anchorage," former
home of the Mitchell family, later owned by Captain and Mrs. Stannard. Mrs. Haskell rented "The Anchorage" from the Stannards
and ran it for summer visitors through the 1920s.

Merchants lined Main Street and new buildings were going up
from Middleneck Road (Port Washington Boulevard) to the shore.
Editor Landis wrote of lower Main Street:

*Burges Johnson, Toastmaster of the First
Annual Banquet of the Alumni Association of
Port Washington High School.*

*Mrs. A.H. Haskell's summer boarding house,
"The Anchorage" in 1915.*

Bayles Building at Main Street and Shore Road.

"The new stores in the Bayles Building [still standing at the northwest corner of Main Street and Shore Road] are what we may expect in the Port Washington of tomorrow. The top floor is an excellent ballroom and should be very popular. The first dance in this hall was under the auspices of the Nemo Club. Those who become thirsty while dancing may either patronize the soda fountain or step across the street."

The Burges Johnsons were responsible in part for attracting members of the artistic and literary community to Port Washington. Their energy and their generous spirit went far toward making the town a "better place to live."

A few of the writers and artists who made their homes in Port Washington included:

Charles G. and Kathleen Norris

In 1910 the Norrises, he, a "glorified man-of-all work" on the staff of the *American Magazine,* later to become prominent in the field of controversial novels of protest, and she, a budding novelist, already recognized by Doubleday, Page & Company, had been living in Manhattan for a few years, but began hungering for a home in the country.

In her biography, *Family Gathering,* Kathleen Norris writes about their house-hunting:

"Some literary folk we loved, the Burges Johnsons, lived in Port Washington at the end of one of the Long Island lines, and gradually the charms of Port Washington seemed to eclipse the others, and it was decided that the country home was to be there.

"We rented a house (at No. 20 Vandeventer Avenue), an unusual house, as sound as a little fortress, set in a meadow that ran down to

The house at 20 Vandeventer Avenue, in succession home to the Norrises, the Lewises and the Foxes.

Rear view of 20 Vandeventer Avenue.

Kathleen and Charles Norris on the steps of their California home about 1926.

Grace and Sinclair Lewis with James Branch Cabell.

a pond, and only a straggling block or two from the station. We loved it, and after us the Sinclair Lewises took it, and after that the Fontaine Foxes, so we felt a proprietary interest in it for many years. After a year of trying out what was then, and may still be *one of the most delightful hamlets of the entire world,* we bought a home across the village, on Bayview Avenue (on the south side of the dogleg) which stood in a spacious garden, had a garage, even a chicken yard, and when we had the blinds painted we named it 'Green Blinds.' "

A year later the Norrises and Kathleen's younger sister, Teresa, and her husband, the poet William Rose Benet, were rejoined when the Benets bought a house not far away on South Maryland Avenue. Mrs. Norris continues:

"By this golden summertime we were members of the Port Washington Beach Club, and Teresa and I learned to swim...we lived in the water, and when our first new social advantages developed to include the freedom of beaches out at Sands Point, we were never at a loss for Sunday Plans."

Two miles away, in Plandome, lived a very good friend of the Norrises, Frances Hodgson Burnett, the author of *Little Lord Fauntleroy* and *The Secret Garden,* whose own garden "stretched to the shores of the Bay, and in the comfortable rambling house tea was of course served daily, and we and the small children could come in for tea when we would."

Sinclair and Grace (Hegger) Lewis

In her delightful autobiography, *With Love from Gracie,* Grace Lewis writes as charmingly as her predecessor, Kathleen Norris, about *the same house* at 20 Vandeventer Avenue:

"It may have been on a visit to William Rose Benet, who had married Teresa, sister of Kathleen Norris, and who was living in Port Washington, that we found—not the Little White House of his poems but the Little Brown Bungalow on the estate of Miss Maude Vandeventer. Charles and Kathleen Norris had lived in it until they moved to a larger house on the *right* side of the tracks...But the Vandeventer property was a large one and the bungalow, rental $50 a month, was set on a hill which sloped to an orchard and open fields and distant woods.

"When we began to be invited to parties on distant Sands Point, in Roslyn we acquired two bicycles when bicycles were as unfamiliar as the horse and buggy. Our neighbors thought it quaint when we arrived at garden parties on large estates with manor houses imported stone by stone from the British Isles, Hal in white flannels and me in ruffled organdy and a floppy hat, both astride our bicycles. " 'He's a writer, they're newlyweds,' the hostess would whisper to the questioning eyebrows, as an excuse."

Grace Lewis got her first taste of community life through membership in the Village Welfare, Campfire Girls, local elections and woman suffrage. Hal, as Lewis was called, cared little for small-town activities, "except suffrage, for which we both worked, and in that he was interested only because he hated prohibition of any kind. Hal was applaudingly proud when I read 'An Appeal to Liberty' between reels at the Nassau motion picture theater on the night of July 5th; and I glowed when from the back of roadsters he made provocative speeches in which he said that if a human being who was a man had the right to vote, a human being who was a woman had the same right."

The Lewises remained in Port Washington until Christmas, 1914, at which time Fontaine Fox, the cartoonist and creator of *Toonerville Trolley,* rented the same bungalow. The Lewises were leaving for Charleston, S.C., and before they left Grace wrote rather poignantly:

"A real family, with excited children sleeping in the upstairs room, would be celebrating Christmas there. 'You won't regret the little brown house and the garden and the Village Welfare?' Hal asked me, sounding a little frightened now at the thought of the step we were taking. But I reassured him, and we shook hands like two men signing a business agreement. I wished we could start that very night."

Sinclair Lewis in a rare smiling pose.

Fontaine Fox

Famous throughout the country for his wryly humorous cartoon series, *Toonerville Trolley,* Fontaine Fox was a resident of Port Washington for many years, first on Vandeventer Avenue, then later he purchased the large house at 45 Carlton Avenue. This handsome Georgian Colonial home looks out over the Bay at the top of Third Avenue.

Fontaine Fox and his family lived in this house at 45 Carlton Avenue for over 20 years.

A favorite cartoon, 1911, at the time of the famous Port Washington Carnival.

Tradition has it that Fox got many of his ideas, if not the original inspiration, from the trolley line that ran from the "Anchorage" up Main Street to the Boulevard, thence to Roslyn and Mineola. J. S. Otruba, in the 1985 issue of the Cow Neck Peninsula Historical Society's *Journal* wrote: "…from his window the artist could see Manhasset Bay, especially in the wintertime, as that strange contraption, his beloved trolley, was visible from this vantage point."

Fontaine Fox, with his wife and daughters, Betty and Mary, lived here through the 1920's.

Arthur T. Vance

Editor of *Pictorial Review,* Arthur T. Vance had been one of the first to recognize Kathleen Norris's writing talents and he published many of her early stories. He built the house at 68 Carlton Avenue in 1905. For a short period of time he became a member of the Library Board of Trustees, filling the unexpired term of Mrs. Baxter in 1914. Mr. Vance also served as President of the Board of Education and Commodore of the Port Washington Yacht Club.

William Rose Benet and Teresa Benet

The Norrises and the Benets quite naturally were very close. Together they went house hunting and spent much time on the beaches of Manhasset Bay. Somewhat overshadowed by his younger brother, Stephen Vincent Benet, William nevertheless became an

Arthur Vance built this home at 68 Carlton Avenue around 1905.

editor of *Saturday Review of Literature,* and he received a Pulitzer Prize in 1942 for *The Dust Which Is God,* a verse novel. Teresa Benet was very active in both the Village Welfare Society and the Young Women's Recreation Society. She is credited with starting a cooking school in her home and advocating the establishment of a cooking class in the High School. Even Editor Landis supported the idea of domestic science: "(Parents) be practical and get some of your school tax back by having your children taught how to cook and make clothing."

Addison Mizner

Although not a literary personage, Addison Mizner was one of the most distinguished architects and land developers in the country. In 1907 he spent a weekend at the estate of former Congressman W. Bourke Cockran and during his visit he discovered the Baxter Homestead four years after the library had moved to its new home on Main Street.

D. W. Curl in his biography of Addison Mizner, *Mizner's Florida,* writes:

"Although the house had neither central heating nor indoor plumbing, and needed much work, it faced on Manhasset Bay with Baxter Pond to the south. Mizner leased the house, probably with the understanding that he might purchase it, and added bathrooms and central heating. In the spring of 1914 he bought the house from Mrs. Elizabeth Perry and spent $5,000 for further renovations and the addition of a new kitchen wing."

Mizner named his new home "Chateau Myscene" and entertained not only the cream of Port Washington society, but also international celebrities.

William Rose Benet

Dining Room in the Baxter House at the time Addison Mizner lived there.

Author Curl continues:

"Mizner was very friendly with H.K. Landis, publisher of *Plain Talk,* who at times seemed to act as the architect's press agent within the columns of his newspaper. Almost every issue contained a story of Mizner's latest commission or a fanciful account of the activities at the 'Chateau Mizner.' "

John J. Floherty

Best known for his twenty-five books on careers for young people, Jack Floherty, "The Star Reporter for American Youth," was very much a part of life in Port Washington for over fifty years. Newspaperman, artist, public relations director for Helena Rubenstein, he became a victim of the early Depression years. Undaunted by financial reverses, he set out to learn photography, worked with Charlie Miller, a Port resident who had a photography studio in New York. Soon he had his own studio at 5th Avenue and 45th Street where his clients included Chesterfield cigarettes, Borden's, a bathing suit company and advertising agencies.

An accident in the early '30s forced him to remove his New York studio to his home at 9 Shoreview Road, Baxter Estates. Having discovered that the photographs he took of the various activities of the Atlantic Hook and Ladder Company were in great demand by young people in town, Jack Floherty conceived the idea of writing a book about fire companies which was later reprinted as *Five Alarm: The Story of Fire Fighting.* Books on careers from Coast Guard to FBI and from news cameramen to radio and television broadcasters found ready markets throughout the world.

Ernie Simon, in one of his *Port Remembered* columns, recalled that Jack Floherty "who was one of my most intimate friends" was instrumental in getting the Manhasset Bay Sportsmen's Club started at the old Custom House, a shack situated where the town dock is today.

Herbert Bayard Swope

Somewhat distant from the modest homes of those who lived near the village of Port Washington was the fabled Sands Point mansion of another reporter-editor who climbed to the heights in newspaper publishing, Herbert Bayard Swope. Variously called "the star turn in the American journalistic world" and the "crusading New York editor," Swope counted among his many friends here and abroad Bernard Baruch for whom, legend has it, Swope coined the phrase "cold war."

Designed by Stanford White and decorated by Lady Mendl, Swope's home for many years was the scene of lavish living and entertaining on a grand scale.

CHAPTER V

1914—
Start of A Twelve Year Quest:
A Modern Library Building

1914   *Over 90% of library books available for circulation—Burges John-*
son replaces E.W. Gaillard—Old documents sought for library safe-
*keeping—*Plain Talk *ceases publication—Mrs. Stannard retires*
from Board after 22 years

Mrs. Stannard, Mrs. McLean and Mr. Trowbridge were appointed
by the Board to come up with a plan for increasing membership in
the Library Association. One of their recommendations was to send
out a mailing to a large list of townspeople asking:
"Do you know the free public library in your neighborhood?

"Are you a member of it?

    "If not, visit it as soon as possible and see what advantages it
offers you.

    "There are books for the student who wishes to educate himself;
for the worker anxious to qualify for a better position; for the
housekeeper or home-maker; for one who wishes to read or study
books in foreign languages; and, finally, for every man or woman
who loves the entertaining company of a good book.

    "*You* are one of these; the library is for you; come and make use
of it."

    Boy Scout books were in particular demand, perhaps because
Board members, J.S. Witmer, Jr. and Burges Johnson, were officers
of the Boy Scout Council, and looking out for Scouts' interests.

    A campaign to pay off or reduce the mortgage was voted down
by the library's Finance Committee who felt that the Board of
Trustees must first determine whether the property they occupied
should be sold or retained for library purposes. If retained, reducing the principal would be advisable. If a new library were to be
build on another site, it would be·unwise to pay off the mortgage at
that time.

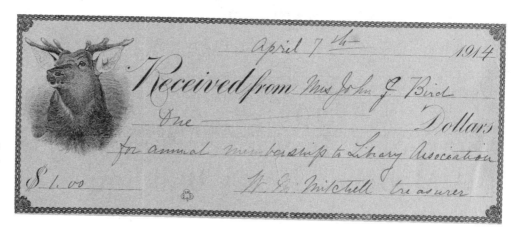

Receipt for annual library dues from Mrs. John J. Bird.

In early 1914, of the 3,740 books in the library, 3,500 were available for circulation. Reference books, always more costly than popular fiction and non-fiction, were restricted to use only in the library. Miss Mitchell and Miss Florence McKee, with occasional help from the State Department of Education, were running the library efficiently and profitably in terms of the number of patrons and the volume of books circulated. And even more important to recall is that neither of these ladies had professional library training.

The budget for the year 1914 included substantial increases for books and magazines. Constant efforts on the part of the trustees and the librarians to bring in new members of the Association, along with weekly reminders in both newspapers kept a very steady stream of book requests in front of the librarians.

Changes in the Board of Trustees were inevitable. Mrs. Mary E. Baxter resigned; her position was filled by Arthur T. Vance. The library's very strong leader, Edwin W. Gaillard, who had helped put the library on a firm and modern footing, resigned from the board as he was moving out of Port Washington. A resolution by the Trustees stated in part:..."the present prosperity and usefulness of the Port Washington Free Library is due in large part to the enthusiasm and energy of Mr. Edwin W. Gaillard."

Mr. Burges Johnson was elected to fill Mr. Gaillard's unexpired term.

In the June 13 issue of *Port News,* Editor Hyde announced a Public Library Benefit at the Nassau Theater on Main Street for the following Monday evening:

"The library deserves public support, and it is hoped that everyone will buy tickets, whether or not they are able to attend. Admission is only 25 cents and reserved seats are ten cents extra. Among the features on the program are the following: Piano solos by Miss Young and Miss Bird; vocal solos by Mr. Floherty and Mrs. Dan Stannard; violin solo by Miss Murphy; selections by Mr. Langer's Orchestra; selections by the Nassau Quartette; sleight of hand performances by an expert; moving pictures by Messers. Newman and Filan. The entertainment begins at 8:30. Don't miss it!"

Over 450 people attended the program and net receipts were more than $92. The money was used to pay immediate expenses of the library *until the school appropriation became available.* The Trustees were constantly besieging the School Board for payment of the $333.33 due the Library every four months. The School Board was often behind by two payments, creating mild fiscal havoc for the Library Trustees. Many library trustees over the years questioned the reasoning behind this laggardly approach to paying legitimate obligations voted on by taxpayers of the school district.

201

ENTERTAINMENT
FOR THE BENEFIT OF THE
Port Washington Free Library
NASSAU THEATRE
Monday Evening, June 15, 1914
AT 8.30 O'CLOCK
ADULTS 35 CENTS   CHILDREN 25 CENTS

Ticket for Nassau Theatre benefit.

In one of his last issues of *Plain Talk,* H.K. Landis made an urgent plea which has resounded through the years (and is as true in 1992 as it was in 1914 and will be in the 2000's):

"We earnestly solicit for the library old documents, papers, maps, clippings or other matter concerning the former days in Port Washington. All old residents have matter of this kind which is in danger of being burned or thrown out and lost forever. The next generation may not value these reminders of the old days and destroy them. It would be a good plan to send all historical matter to the library, as a loan or gift, for safe keeping.

"The library needs a complete file of the Port Washington 'News,' which the editor can, no doubt, assist it in securing. We will donate a full set of "Plain Talk." Old letters, clippings, deeds, autographs, photographs, silhouettes, geneologies and similar history will be much valued by the present as well as future generations. This is a serious matter. The library needs these things, and they should be preserved."*

*It is still a serious matter. Without *Port News,* today on microfilm, and slightly tattered issues of *Plain Talk,* the early years of the Port Washington Library would have been almost impossible to reconstruct.

The Free Library

One of the most interesting annual reports the NEWS has had the honor of printing in its columns for some years past was that of the Port Washington Free Library, used in this paper on Saturday last. It contained the year's work of a most excellent institution, and betrayed one interesting fact, as well as many other good things, that the townsfolk know a good thing when they see it, and also take a wholesome advantage of opportunity, when it comes their way.

Nothing so plainly and accurately betrays the existence of culture in a town as the patronage of a library. While the NEWS is not full posted as to the class of books most in demand by the patrons of this institution, whether of the light, sometimes termed "trashey" character, or whether the higher grade, educational type of book is most in demand, something in the way of an educational result must have been attained by the dissemination by the library of the many thousands of volumes during the year which came to a close on December 31st last. In any case it may be truthfully said that no book is utterly barren of value to its readers. Some, of course, are more fruitful in this relation than others. There are books and books. Few are written without a moral, without a reason for being cast broadcast on the world. The choice lies with the reader. Discretion, though, should be used, and plentifully, as to the style of literature which should be placed in the hands of the young for the future direction of mind and life. Here the value of a library, with walls filled with carefully selected volumes, the contents of whose shelves are freely offered to the townspeople, is apparent. A wide and careful selection can be made under such conditions, and with generally the best results.

It may, then, be said that money expended on this institution was a wise expenditure. It's a valuable town asset. It should be kept up to the highest point of excellence, and in this connection it may be said that there is little fear of a backward step in its usefullness as the management is in most capable hands.

Not content to implore his readers to gather together printed matter of historical interest, Mr. Landis later added to the list such artifacts as uniforms and weapons of the wars, spinning wheels, candle molds, weaving of wool or flax homespun, quilts, homespun table linen, deeds, old books. All these contain historical matter. He ended his editorial: "Perhaps we will sometime have our own historical society."*

The final issue of *Plain Talk*, that staunch supporter of the library, its librarian, Board of Trustees, and all that a good library represents, was published on September 12, 1914. Editor Landis, in the lead editorial wrote: "Accumulating business requirements...make it necessary that less time be spent in such recreation as *Plain Talk* afforded, and as this issue makes three years, it is an appropriate time to close its career."

William Hyde, likewise a good friend of the library, continued his coverage of library matters in a most crucial time. One country after another was declaring war against its real or alleged enemies in Europe. Repercussions this side of the Atlantic were mild at first in small towns such as Port Washington. Yet readers sought out knowledge and information about the unknown—Europe. An October issue of the *News* carried in its weekly column, "Our Free Public Library," a timely list of books and periodicals about Germany which were avidly read.

BOARD OF TRUSTEES—June 1914:

Charles N. Wysong, *President*
Mrs. Mary E. McLean, *Vice President*
John S. Witmer, Jr., *Recording Sec'y*
Miss Wilhelmina Mitchell, *Treasurer*

Miss Florence McKee	Burges Johnson
Miss Mary A. Baxter	Mason Trowbridge
Mrs. Ellen B. Stannard	

The rooms on the upper-floors of the library were rented to various tenants over the years, but Mr. William H. Shields is the only one mentioned more than once. Mr. Shields had taken care of many odd jobs around the library for Miss Mitchell, and was ideal to take over the care of the grounds on a regular basis—at 50 cents per week. Later he suggested that he work full time in lieu of room rent, but the Board rejected his offer. Nevertheless, he remained as a tenant for many years and eventually rented the barn.

Miss Mitchell publicized as best she could the new books added to the library collection, usually in a *Port News* column. Not all titles were listed, of course, but as more and more non-fiction was in demand, a subject list was published:

*Only 48 years went by before Cow Neck Peninsula Historical Society opened its doors.

AGRICULTURE & GARDENING
ANGLING
ASTRONOMY
AVIATION
BOTANY
CAMPING & CAMP COOKING
CARPENTRY
CRAFTSMANSHIP
FARMING
PRACTICAL HANDBOOKS FOR BOYS
PHOTOGRAPHY
ROAD & HIGHWAY ENGINEERING
MACHINE SHOP WORK
PRACTICAL ENGINEERING
HERALDRY
TRAVEL IN CALIFORNIA
POETRY
NEW FICTION
STORY BOOKS FOR BOYS AND GIRLS
PRACTICAL HANDBOOKS FOR GIRLS

The problem of increasing the membership of the Library Association was on every agenda of Board meetings. Within their own group they could not make much headway, so in March they determined to appoint a new committee of five association members *not* on the Board—Mrs. A. F. Gray, Miss Anne McLean, Mr. A. W. Keevil, Mr. J. E. Bullard and Mr. H. K. Landis—to offer some solutions.

The effectiveness of the new committee could not be measured in one month, but President Wysong's annual report to the Association in April boasted of 43 new members making a total of 94, and 155 new book borrowers were listed on the rolls. During the fiscal year 1914–1915, 8,730 books were loaned, an increase of 414 over the previous year. Curiously enough there were 4,598 books on the library shelves and 4,434 persons attended the library during that period.

The resignation in October, 1914, of long-time Board member, Mrs. Ellen B. Stannard, to become effective in April 1915, after 22 consecutive years of service, was discussed at length by the board. The Secretary wrote to her asking her to reconsider. She wrote back insisting that they accept her decision, but it was June before they acted, and then "most reluctantly." Miss Helen Sands was elected to replace Mrs. Stannard.

The summer of 1915 brought more frequent news about the war in Europe. In the local newspaper there was coverage with photos of American and British ships sunk by German torpedoes. The *Lusitania*, sunk off the coast of Ireland, took the lives of Alfred G. Vanderbilt and Charles Frohman, the theatrical manager, both well-known in the Sands Point community.

The minutes of the November Board meeting anticipate, once again, future activity of the community:

"The Librarian, Miss Mitchell, stated that she frequently had an opportunity to speak to the *friends of the library* in favor of reducing the library mortgage and she felt that some committee should be authorized to accept for the library donations either for the mortgage fund or for general operating purposes. Upon motion Miss

At that time...

Woodrow Wilson reelected

Joseph Henry Aston, Library Board Member, 1915–1917.

The Aston Home at 26 South Maryland Avenue.

Mitchell was placed on the Finance Committee and it was made a special duty of this committee to solicit subscriptions to the mortgage or building funds."

The library year ended with election of Mr. J. E. Bullard and Mr. J. Henry Aston to the Board to replace Mr. Mason Trowbridge and Mr. Burges Johnson who both resigned.

Henry Aston built his home on South Maryland Avenue in 1906 on a 50′ by 100′ plot and later bought the same size lot to the south, both from Miss Vandeventer. The house to the north was owned by William Rose and Teresa Benet, Kathleen Norris' sister.

Mrs. Harold Aston Swanson, Henry's daughter, in an interview in May, 1991 recalled their neighbors:

"The Benets had a large trapdoor in their kitchen close to the wood stove under which a large bath tub had been installed. The top of the tub was flush with the kitchen floor, and every Saturday night for family baths it could be filled easily with hot water from the adjacent stove. *It was a marvel!*"

Mrs. Swanson remembered the library in the old Burtis house even though she admitted she did not frequent it.

Mr. J. E. Bullard, elected to the Board the previous month, became active immediately on the Administrative Committee. Within days he had the Public Service Company repiping the gas lines in the Library Room, and had *new, improved burners* throughout. Miss Mitchell's desk, always poorly lighted was treated to a *new, improved* desk lamp. And all of this was done at no cost to the library.

Mr. Bullard was also a committee of one to get better publicity for the library. In the following week's issue of the *News*, on the front page, Editor Hyde carried an article about the "gifts to the library thus indicating the (Public Service) company's interest in the good work being done by that institution."

The first mention of "reserving" books of great popularity came in March when the two-volume *Life of John Hay*, by William Roscoe Thayer, was received in the library. A timely *News* article recommended:

"This is a very interesting and instructive book and is well worth the perusal of anyone interested in the life of Hay or the diplomacy of the United States. This book promises to be very popular and it might be well to leave a post card with the librarian in order to be notified as soon as it is returned to the library."

View of the pond across the street from the Aston's.

Twenty-four years had gone by since the opening of the Library in 1892, and in May, 1916, the Board appointed a committee of five, known as the Celebration Committee whose mandate was to "make an effort to raise money to pay off the mortgage on the present property and to build a new library building"—all to be done in time for the celebration in 1917 of the library's twenty-fifth anniversary. A tall order!

Mr. Wysong's annual report continued that very line of thought. The town was growing and the use of the library was increasing. He wrote:

"There is much to be done in the future and there is a crying need for expansion. The Library room is very crowded and there is very little, if any, room for further expansion. We need a new modern library building. The land we now own is amply large and fittingly situated. Is it too wild a dream to hope for funds during the coming year to erect upon this plot such a building as we need?"

The report was published in its entirety in the *Port News* and it was followed a week later with an editorial by Mr. Hyde in which he spelled out the continuing demand on the library's resources:
"With this increased patronage, an expansion of quarters has become urgent.

"With all due modesty, the *News* refuses to agree with Mr. Wysong that 'It is too wild a dream to hope for funds...to erect such a library as we need.' Wilder dreams have become reality. If not too

Free Library Quarters

We were glad to receive the letter from "Library Enthusiast" last week, and it offered us still more pleasure to publish it.

The contention by the NEWS that the value of good literature to the reading knowledge seeking folks of the "Port," was so apparent, as shown by the large draft on the Free Library during the past year, that a general movement of residents, looking to an expansion of quarters for the use of the Institution could be counted on, appears to have been well grounded.

The NEWS still feels convinced that the Free Library will have better and more commodious quarters before the world grows many months older, or be practically assured of the possession of such quarters, at all events.

The suggestion made by "Enthusiast" that an endowment fund be created smacks of practical goodness, but the total of the fund would, of necessity, have to be placed at a larger figure than the $20,000 or $40,000 suggested. The least cost for a new building of sufficient accommodations to meet large future demands on the library would likely reach $25,000, and the additional labor to meet increased business would require a larger working force and at greater cost. Possibly the earnings of $50,000 would cover that expense.

At all events the importance of the matter to the community is such that farther and broader discussion is suggested by the NEWS. We would be glad to publish the views of townsfolk as to the best and most practical way to house our free library in a manner to make that institution more of a credit to the town, as great a visualized pleasure as is its present value as an educator.

The Celebration Committee of the Port Washington Free Library met last Tuesday and laid out a program for a year's work. It is hoped that enough of this program can be carried out to make possible a celebration next February which will be memorable in the history of the village.

The new High School building is now being started. When this is completed Port Washington will have a better educational plant than practically any other village on the Island. The building will still be beautiful and there will be ample land around it to give it a suitable setting and the pupils sufficient room for exercise and athletics.

Why can we not begin a new Library building soon? This building could either be built on the present library property or on some plot which might be purchased in a suitable location. Just as soon as the people realize how much a strictly up to date and adequate library adds to the village we shall surely build a new building. The old building has now about reached the limit of its usefulness for library purposes. A new one must, therefore, be provided before the library can do its best work.

In Louisvill, Ky., they wanted a new auditorium which would cost $250,000 and which had to be paid for by popular subscription. The money was raised in a week. There is no reason then why we cannot raise enough money for a new library and an endowment fund before next February when the 25th anniversary of the library occurs.

costly a project and given the necessary publicity through the columns of the *News,* we are of the opinion that there will be a generous and substantial response from the townsfolk."

The Celebration Committee consisting of Chairman Bullard, the Misses Helen Sands, Mary A. Baxter, Florence I. McKee, and Mr. Witmer set about their enormous task. One of the more interesting arguments put forth concerned the very valuable collection of books on Long Island history and maps of the area which urgently "need a more suitable place to house them than we have at the present time. Such books and maps are possibly of more interest to the people in such a rapidly growing community than they are to the citizens of a more conservative and easy going town."(!)

The idea of a Carnegie Library,* having been proposed and rejected in earlier years, surfaced once again, along with the suggestion that many communities had library buildings built as monuments to one or more public spirited citizens. The question was journalistically posed, "Is there any person in our village who would like to build a similar monument to himself, or would it be better to try to get a Carnegie Library?"

Thanks to Editor Hyde the town was peppered with constant reminders of the need—"…old building has reached the limit of its usefulness…a new one must be provided before the library can do its best work…a fireproof building needed…time for some of our philanthropic citizens to show their loyalty!"

The Celebration Committee came up with ideas for mailings, stronger publicity, fund-raising entertainments at the Nassau Theater, a history of the library in pamphlet form to distribute to the townspeople—all valid ideas. Yet by November, seven months after the decision to raise money, nothing really was happening.

In the December board meeting minutes, a clue to the delay was emerging. The work of the Celebration Committee in preparation for the 25th gala planned for February 1917 was discussed at length. The Board once again referred the promotion letter prepared by the Committee back to the Board. It was obvious that no one truly wished to make a commitment. There were far too many distractions for the board to get the whole-hearted attention of the townspeople for a project the size of a new library. Most citizens were well aware that the United States would soon be involved in the war in Europe.

*Carnegie Libraries were free public libraries given by philanthropist Andrew Carnegie to about 1,700 communities in the U.S. The building was donated on condition that the town would supply and maintain the library.

CHAPTER VI

The War Years and Aftermath 1917–1919

After many U.S. merchant ships had been sunk by German submarines and President Woodrow Wilson had proclaimed that "The world must be made safe for democracy," the United States declared war on Germany on April 6, 1917.

While there are no Library Board minutes of meetings for the first three months of 1917, in March the *News* carried the story of the formation of the Port Washington Home Guard with a number of distinguished citizens in leadership roles including Library Board President, Charles N. Wysong, who was Secretary and Treasurer of the new organization.

1917 *Port Washington Home Guard formed, large turnout to join— Library asks for donations of books and magazines for armed services—President Wilson kicks off campaign for fund to buy books and build portable libraries*

About 350 men crowded Liberty Hall on April 4, and another one hundred waited outside to enroll in the Home Guard. According to a telegram proudly sent to Frederick Hicks, Port's representative in Congress: "...enrollment blanks were passed around and two hundred and forty signatures, with the accompanying small fee of fifty cents for membership, were obtained. Mr. John Philip Sousa then offered to play the *Star Spangled Banner*, but there being no piano in the hall, the company sang the verses standing, without accompaniment, and (then) adjourned."

The library had many books of special interest at this time particularly books on military matters *and* on gardening. A plea was made for someone to donate a "set of the old International Encyclopedia, or any other reference books which have been displaced (in the home) by new ones, the library will be very glad to have the old ones."

In July an increase in the trolley fare from Port Washington to Mineola was announced. Effective July 15, the 9.69 mile trip would now cost $.20.

The library joined the war effort by asking everyone to donate books and magazines, Miss Mitchell suggesting that "if you write in each book your name and address, the soldier who reads it will know that someone in Port Washington or vicinity is his friend and stands ready to help him." Such authors as Kipling, Doyle, McCutcheon, O.Henry, Stockton, Tarkington and Oppenheim were sought.

By September, however, it was learned that a problem existed in the book programs for servicemen. The *News* reported:
"The numbers and kinds of books that have been donated have been entirely inadequate. There has arisen such a demand for books of a serious nature and for small portable buildings in which they may be housed and from which they can be circulated that the necessity of raising money for this purpose has for some time been apparent."

In consequence, President Wilson kicked off a campaign with a substantial subscription to a fund to be used for building portable libraries in army camps and for buying books most urgently needed. Port's share in the fund was five cents for each man, woman and child in the community, to be left off at the Library between 2 and 8 p.m., or mailed to Mr. Witmer on Bayview Avenue. Editor Hyde further dramatized the need when the first week's endeavor to raise money fell far short of the goal:
"The quota for Port Washington was 5 cents per inhabitant—the price of a beer, a car fare, a cheap cigar, a stick of chewing gum, a glass of soda or a small amount of candy...not as much money as they give to a letter mailed to New York City."

No final tally was made until the Annual Meeting on April 2, 1918 when the minutes read: "In connection with the drive for money and books for the Soldiers and Sailors libraries we raised about $120.00 and secured over 250 bound volumes which were shipped...for the soldiers and sailors."

Editor Hyde and the entire community, it is hoped, was heartened by the fact that at least 2,400 townspeople gave at least a nickel.

In the 1890's members of the Woman's Club had visited Chautauqua and the idea of holding a Tent Chautauqua* in Port Washington had been discussed. At the August 7th, 1917 meeting of the library board the Secretary was asked to determine what arrangements would be necessary if the Chautauqua was to be run as a library benefit in Port Washington.

J.E. Bullard of the Library Board worked most effectively with Editor Hyde to promote the Chautauqua, but regrettably no record exists in the minutes of board meetings or in the *Port News* of the outcome of their plan. Most of the library's fundraising celebra-

---

*Tent Chautauquas were traveling groups having no connection with the original Chautauqua Institution, a summer and correspondence school in upstate New York. Tent Chautauquas travelled from town to town during the years 1903 to 1930 giving inspirational lectures, concerts and recitals in large tents.

tions had succeeded admirably over the years. Possibly the Port Washington Chautauqua was just a casualty of wartime.

Charles N. Wysong, President of the Library Board since 1914, resigned in December, 1917, and at the following February meeting Mr. Charles R. Weeks was unanimously elected to replace him.

1918   *"Business as usual" at the library during war time—Children's room renovated—Influenza epidemic closes library ten days.*

At the annual meeting in April, the Secretary, John Witmer, cogently summarized the previous year:

"The past twelve months have seen marked changes in every form of community life and enterprise. Some lines of endeavor have almost passed from the public mind while other special forms of work and service heretofore little known have become the center of attention and effort. Changes equally great may be seen in the work of the library. During the past year there have been campaigns for Liberty Loans and for Food Conservation, for the Red Cross and for books and funds for the Soldiers and Sailors libraries. In all of these country-wide movements the libraries have been asked to help. The Port Washington Library has cooperated with the other libraries throughout the county and has been glad of the opportunity to share in the work.

"Many magazines were donated and sent to cantonments on Long Island. Thanks are due our friends for all these donations and for the use of their cars for 5 or 6 trips necessary to transport the magazines."

American Library Association
War Service Committee

This Committee acknowledges with thanks the receipt of the reading matter which you have so kindly sent for the use of the soldiers. We can assure you that this gift and further donations will be promptly cared for and will be much appreciated.

JAMES I. WYER,
Chairman.

SORTING STATION
11 West 40th Street
New York City

form m–213a [x–3–17 2m]

American Library Association "thank you" card, July, 1918.

Mr. Witmer concluded his report on an encouraging note, stating that all functions of the library continued as usual in time of war, and "that in spite of the urgency and appeal of many other activities demanding attention, our library has been able not only to maintain, but also to increase over the preceding years all of its usual lines of work."

Effects of the war were felt in many areas. Miss Mitchell reported to the Trustees:

"...during the coal shortage 10 baskets of coal had been loaned to the library by Mrs. McCreery and that this accomodation had been duly recognized. (She) reported also that kerosene lamps had been used on several evenings when the gas supply had failed.

...certain of the Library windows had been fixed and that a screen door had been removed at her request by Mr. Charles Wiggins and that Mr. Wiggins had made no charge for the work."

The library board in 1918 included:

Charles W. Weeks, *President*	Mrs. M.E. McLean
John S. Witmer, Jr., *Vice President*	Miss Helen Sands
J.E. Bullard, *Secretary*	Mrs. C.E. Tuxhill
W.H. Kellogg, *Treasurer*	Miss Wilhelmina Mitchell
Miss Mary Baxter	

During the summer major renovations were made in the children's room, eliciting from Editor Hyde the following:

"...the needs of the children received careful consideration, for the Library is meant to be a happy hunting ground for them, and their books had been so read and re-read that many were on the verge of dissolution, so a number of new books for them were ordered and will soon be placed on the shelves."

Among the titles were *Indian Heroes and Great Chieftains, Masters of Space* (Morse, Thompson, Bell, Marconi, etc.), *The Boy with the U.S. Weathermen, When I Was A Girl in Holland, A Maid of Old Manhattan, A Young Lion of Flanders* (young boy in wartime Belgium). Mr. Hyde promised to give a complete list of the new books in his column in the weeks to come.

FAVORITE BOOKS 1913–1918

Pollyanna by Eleanor Porter
Laddie by Gene Stratton Porter
Penrod by Booth Tarkington
Of Human Bondage by W. Somerset Maugham
The Calling of Dan Matthews by Harold Bell Wright
The Call of the Wild (reprint edition) by Jack London
Over the Top by Arthur Guy Empey
Dere Mable by Edward Streeter

Port Washington Free Library
December 12th 1918

The Franklin Square Agency

The enclosed list please give
your earliest attention and if any
have already been included in our
last years order for a longer time
than to January 1st 1919. make that
change on the enclosed list, I am
under the impression some may
come due in 1920.

Please send your bill to the Library
or to Mr W. H. Kellogg. Mackay Ave
Port Washington N.Y. Treasurer for
The Library,

Very Truly

Wilhelmina M. Mitchell
Librarian

Few examples of Miss Mitchell's handwriting exist. This letter to a magazine agency is the best.

Port Washington did not escape the wide spread and devastating epidemic of influenza in November, 1918. For ten days the library was closed to the staff and public alike as a precaution against the extremely contagious disease.

1919   *Post-war efforts for Memorial Library—Subscription base or tax base debated*

The citizens of Port Washington, in a burst of patriotic fervor similar to other towns across Long Island and across the nation, were eager to find a way to honor those who died in the war in Europe. On January 24, 1919 the lead editorial in the *Port News* was all about planning appropriate and lasting memorials to the town's...

"brave and noble men who so willingly laid down their lives for the sake of humanity. It is indeed pleasing to note that in nine cases out of ten the sentiment in our sister villages is in favor of Memorial Buildings—principally libraries. We say it is pleasing to the *News* for the reason that this paper has strongly advocated a Library Building as the most fitting memorial to Port Washington's boys.

"The Library has a substantial collection of books and a good site. But its old frame building is not only inadequate but unsafe for so valuable a collection of literature as housed there at the present time."

On March 1st a Nominating Committee for Board members was appointed by President Weeks with Mr. Witmer as Chairman and Mssrs. Lewis T. Knox and Edward M. Lapham, members. Mr. Lapham was father of Thomas M. Lapham, later to become President of the Library Board of Trustees.

At the same meeting William Shields petitioned the Library Board to purchase "the piece of land lying between the Main Street and the property of said Shields and north of that property occupied by the barn. The Trustees decided that this piece of property is not just now for sale." Years later the decision was corroborated when the entire property of the library came up for sale.

. Following that regular meeting, all board members attended a meeting of the "Soliders' Memorial Committee," at which time the members of the library board appeared to be convinced that if the School District *and* the members of the Library Association voted the expenditure of not less than $30,000 to establish and maintain a suitable memorial library, the board would turn over to a new free public library "the real and personal property of this library."

The Soldiers' Memorial Committee then held an open meeting at the High School, chaired by Edward J. West, to discuss whether funds should be raised by public subscription or by public contribution as a tax. The sum required had been increased to $50,000 which it was proposed to raise in two installments adding $25,000 to the school budget this year and $25,000 to that next year.

Controversy, as might be expected, immediately developed. Some wanted an ornamental shaft with an eagle atop, or a monument. Others questioned subscription or taxation. In a letter to the *News* Charles E. Hyde wrote ardently in favor of taxation and ended his letter as follows:

"I do not ask anyone to do what I myself would not be willing to do, and it is needless to say that with my vast interest in real estate, I shall be called upon to pay my share.

"Port Washington has frequently been divided in factions on important matters. Without attempting to prove or disprove the rights of such divisions, I call your attention to the fight against the incorporation of our village—the sewer tangle—the water mix-up—always factions and fighting. Such procedure is detrimental to our village interests. Why not stop such foolish quibble? We've won the war, our boys are the heroes, let us honor them properly, and do it gladly."

In spite of this and many other appeals from patriotic and civic-minded citizens, the Memorial Library proposition went down to defeat, 311 to 74, at the School District election on May 6.

The library board members themselves took a very philosophical attitude toward the outcome of the vote, perhaps even with a sigh of relief. At their meeting on May 13 they were well convinced that the proposition was rejected "more because it was felt to be an improper way to create a War Memorial than because of dissatisfaction with the present library. All present seemed a little glad, if anything, that the library is to continue under its present direction."

Handwritten notes of the October 7, 1919, board meeting once again reflect the dilemma facing the board: "A general discussion followed on the subject of the future of the library, etc. It being impossible to consider all suggestions offered, the president appointed a special committee."

At the same meeting the members of the board (perhaps eager to make up for earlier years of her *free* service to the library) voted Miss Mitchell an increase of $75.00 per month.

Final action on library matters for the year took place at the December meeting when the board passed unanimously the recommendations of the Special Committee on Library Improvement put forth by the chairman, Mr. Kellogg. These included heightened contact with the Port Washington School Board, with various civic organizations, business and professional men; a monthly bulletin; and a committee to execute a campaign to increase membership in the Association.

CHAPTER VII

The Twenties

1920   *Annual Meeting* with *dramatic reading brings crowd—Library as Cultural Center envisioned through Entertainment Course*

Library activity during much of the time in 1920, as reflected in the minutes, was limited to housekeeping problems—"the question of increasing the toilet facilities in the library building, renewing Mr. Shields lease covering the second floor, and investigating the question of electric lighting." Ads were placed in local papers offering the barn for sale, but by the end of the year, no prospects had come forward.

At the well-attended annual meeting in April, Charles R. Weeks, "our popular District Attorney and Library Association President presided, and those who attended were entertained by Reverend Walter E. Bentley, Rector of St. Stephen's Episcopal Church, with his dramatic renditions of poetry and prose. The audience was held tense by his rendition of Mark Antony's famous funeral oration from 'Julius Caesar.'"

In October the *Port News* announced a "Get Together of Free Library Members & Friends":

"Old-fashioned molasses cake and various hot drinks will be served in abundance Saturday afternoon at the home of Miss Helen Sands, Prospect Street, when members of the Free Library Association and their friends get together for an informal discussion of library plans for the year.

"The trustees of the library will attend in force to answer all questions or receive suggestions for the improvement of library service.

"As Miss Sands' 'molasses cake' is justly famous in these parts, it will be advisable for all interested to appear promptly at 3 o'clock for the beginning of festivities. Those who come late will get the best that can be served."

One of the tangible results of the previous year's Special Committee on Library Improvement was a decision to undertake a Public Library Entertainment Course starting in January, 1921.

1921 *Public Library Entertainment Courses financial success—Library improved and beautified—Gala reception for Wilhelmina Mitchell*

To make sure that the well-planned series of public programs under the sponsorship of the Public Library Entertainment Course would get the widest publicity and credibility, the trustees organized a group of distinguished Patrons from every part of town.

The list of Courses which were conducted at the High School included:

Jan. 6— Classical Program, Miss Laura Graves, mezzo-soprano and Mr. Roderick White, violin virtuoso
Feb. 10— Mr. Frank Dilnot, former Editor of *London Globe:* Topic: "Master Minds and Master Wits"
*March 10—*Stevens Institute Glee and Mandolin Club

While mention is made in the earlier minutes of five concerts between January and May, none of the board meeting minutes nor the *Port News* give details of the last two. However the Entertainment Course Committee turned over $411. to the new Board Treasurer, Winthrop K. Kellogg.

Following the success of the Reverend Bentley's performance at the 1920 Annual Meeting of the Library, the Trustees arranged with Mrs. Edwin F. Singer, first president of the Music Study Club of Port Washington, to prepare a musical program for the April 5th meeting. Editor Hyde printed the library president's annual report in full, and recognized that many unsolicited applications for membership in the Library Association had been received. He then printed the entire program of two-piano numbers, male and female singers, cello solos, dances and Russian music. The turnout was large, proving again that people come to a serious meeting when they are promised *entertainment.*

The library building during the spring of 1921 was gradually being improved both in outward attractiveness and inward efficiency. Plans included "improvement and beautifying of the ground belonging to the library building, the idea being to make that side of Main Street a fitting complement to the one opposite." (An obvious reference to the Methodist Church.) The second floor was no longer leased and the two rooms were to be used for general reading purposes and for a children's room.

Mr. Frank G. Lippert, an architect in town, generously offered to go over the building situation with the library board's Administration Committee to determine how best to utilize the second floor space. His sketches suggested that removing some partitions in the second floor would yield space for a reading room, children's room, *and* a Board of Trustees' room.

The Board of Health aided the trustees in making a momentous

*Invitation to Miss Mitchell's
Reception.*

decision: "toilets must be placed inside the building as the present outside one must be removed."

The final and major library event of the year was a gala reception for Miss Mitchell at the home of Mr. and Mrs. John Wellington Mitchell on November 21. (He was her brother Samuel's grandson.)

Not unexpectedly the *Port News* reported the event at length, excerpts from which follow:

"...the large rooms were filled with a host of Miss Mitchell's friends. Written and spoken tributes to Miss Mitchell's service to Port Washington were eloquent in their appreciation. Outwardly serene, at least, our librarian replied that she had never done anything for Port Washington which she had not wanted to do, and briefly recounted the history of the library from its start with twenty-five books, to its present prosperous state with more than eight thousand, graciously giving credit to those assistants who have worked with her throughout the years of its growth.

"Mrs. Tuxhill, the charming president of the Welfare Association then presented Miss Mitchell with a huge bouquet of chrysanthemums on behalf of her members, after which Mr. Witmer, president of the trustees, and spokesman for the library association tendered their gift, a beautiful little gold wrist watch."

Inscription on Miss Mitchell's watch reads:

*Presented to
Wilhelmina M. Mitchell
by the
Library Association
of Port Washington
As a Mark of
Affection and Gratitude
Nov. 2, 1921*

During the years 1920–1922, four new members of the Port Washington Library Board were elected or appointed to fill out terms of retirees:

Samuel J. Gutelius   H. R. Woltman
Paul D. Schreiber   Mrs. Edwin F. Singer

At the December, 1921, meeting of the board, the Administrative Committee presented an encouraging progress report on the building: "…needed repairs were progressing. The new heating plant was installed and in working order, though not quite completed. The decorating of the rooms had also been done. The weather had prevented the carpenter from putting on the new roof, but that and the work on the shelves, stoops, etc., was to begin Dec. 7. The second floor had been rented [No explanation for change in plans!] and the December rent of $30.00 had already been paid." A children's room had been decided on but it is unclear whether on the first or second floor.

The final note of the year concerned making "the Library of proper service; effort must be made to borrow books from other libraries and arrange to use the State's circulating library as well; and that prompt answer be given to all requests."

1922   *Lacking funds, Treasurer seeks short term loan—Mr. Witmer petitions School Board for $1,000 additional appropriation— Entertainment Course resumes—Card party raises $443—Miss Mitchell requests "organizer" from State Librarian's Office*

Financing of the recently completed repairs and improvements in the library was the topic of both the January and February , 1922, Library Board meetings.

The work which had been done was imperative in order to save the building from further dilapidation, and to make possible a children's room. According to the minutes, "there was no choice about contracting the debts, and to meet these a request was sent out to members of the Library Association for donations of $5.00 from each member who felt willing and able to help." About $1,800 was needed, but by mid-March the canvass had brought in only $415. The Treasurer was also authorized to make arrangements for a short term loan to cover current bills.

It was apparent to the board that additional money must be raised on an annual basis. Mr. Witmer, therefor, presented a petition to the School Board calling for an additional $1,000 annually for library maintenance. There is no record of any action on this petition until January, 1923, when Mr. Witmer reported that "the $2,000 District appropriation had been paid to the Treasurer," indicating that the increased appropriation had been passed by the voters at the April , 1922, budget vote.

Flyer advertising first 1922 Library Entertainment Course.

The Public Library Entertainment Course

PRESENTS

As the First in a Series of Five Entertainments

"NOTHING BUT THE TRUTH"

James Montgomery's world renowned

Three Act Farce-Comedy

PLAYED BY NEW YORK PROFESSIONALS

HIGH SCHOOL AUDITORIUM

Thursday Evening, Jan. 19th, at 8 O'Clock

Single Admission $1.00   Course Ticket $3.00

Either may be obtained at the door

On January 19, The Public Library Entertainment Course began its second year, presenting at the High School James Montgomery's *Nothing But The Truth,* a farce-comedy which for many years got great mileage from amateur companies and was filmed twice in Hollywood.

The success of the entertainment at the 1921 Annual Meeting of the library encouraged the board to again solicit the help of Mrs. Edwin Singer for a repeat performance on April 4, 1922. To make the occasion even more celebrated, tickets were issued to the members of the Association and their friends.

After more than twenty-one years of service to the Port Washington Library, Mary Elizabeth McLean resigned from the board as of

TENTH ANNUAL LIBRARY
ASSOCIATION MEETING

HIGH SCHOOL AUDITORIUM

TUESDAY, APRIL FOURTH, 1922
AT 8 O'CLOCK

ELECTION OF TRUSTEES — MUSICAL PROGRAM

This Card Admits Members and Their Friends

*Admission Ticket, 1922 Annual Library
Association Meeting.*

the April 4th Annual Meeting. Mrs. McLean was elected Honorary
President of the Port Washington Free Library Association and
"cordially invited to attend any, or all, of the Board of Trustees
whenever it suited her convenience and pleasure." Mrs. Edwin
Singer who had given so much time and energy to library work was
elected to succeed Mrs. McLean.

Superintendent of Schools Paul D. Schreiber, who had succeeded
Allison Wysong on the Library Board in 1920, and Mr. H. R. Woltman, who had taken Mr. S. J. Gutelius's place in 1921 were both
elected to three year terms.

THE LIBRARY BOARD IN 1922:

John S. Witmer, *President*
Mrs. Olive Singer, *Vice-President*
Miss Mary A. Baxter, *Secretary*
H. R. Woltman, *Treasurer*

Mrs. C. E. Tuxhill   Paul D. Schreiber
Miss Helen Sands   Charles W. Weeks
Winthrop K. Kellogg   (replaced by Frank G. Lippert,
                          June 1922)

In spite of urgent calls for help in improving the grounds of the
library, the Secretary lamented in the June minutes that "all at-
tempts to put the lawn in some sort of order and to secure shrub-
bery had been fruitless. On the other hand all repairs to the
building had been completed and much needed Fire Protection
apparatus was installed, including a fire escape."

During the summer Mrs. Singer organized a very successful card
party at the Knickerbocker Yacht Club which attracted nearly 300
friends of "Port's' popular institution." So successful, it seems that
Mr. Witmer wrote an open letter to Editor Hyde in which he

thanked Commodore Peter C. Gallagher for the commodious quarters and service, and Mr. Edwin Gaillard, former trustee, "for his most desirable presence and pleasing remarks pertaining to the library." The sum of $443. was cleared.

Once again the library turned to Albany for help in resolving a major problem. Miss Mitchell requested that an "organizer" from the State Librarian's office be sent to look over the book collection with a view to elimination of obsolete matter and to make suggestions on subjects requiring building up. Miss Norris from Albany spent a few days at the library in June and in the September 12th minutes Helen Sands, acting Secretary, reported her findings and suggestions:

"...to discard many books of science and many out of date...weed out all worthless fiction, then strengthen the children's section...ask the Supt. of the schools (coincidentally, Mr. Paul D. Schreiber, member of Library Board) to have school librarian(s) train children in care of books, and the teachers to cooperate...to have a workroom for the librarian, to secure her against interruptions and give her more time for real librarian work by having someone relieve her at the desk oftener."

Music to Miss Mitchell's ears!

Mrs. A. R. Haskell was Miss Norris' hostess while she was at the library, and when asked for her "bill for entertainment of the organizer" Mrs. Haskell replied that she was happy indeed to help the library, without pay.

The newly decorated and equipped children's library on the second floor became the scene of many afternoon programs called "Children's Hour" attended by elementary students and sponsored by the Village Welfare Society, Mrs. Shonts, Chairman.

1923   *Library Board meets heavy opposition to proposed $50,000 appropriation for building—Mount strong campaign to win—Lose by large margin*

The year 1923 started out as many other years had with an appeal to all the village organizations to support the appropriation by the School District of funds to be used for a new library building.

Frustration obviously plagued the Board of Trustees in their annual, even semi-annual, struggle to arouse *all* the citizens of Port Washington to recognize the urgency of building a new library. Many people paid lip service to the need, but too often they faltered at the ballot box.

Nevertheless, at the Board meeting on March 16, 1923, "a motion was made, seconded and carried that the trustees of this library sponsor a proposition to raise $50,000 by taxation from School District Number 4 for the purpose of purchasing a site and erecting a building to be used as a *public library*."

Within days of the announcement of the upcoming proposition, a lengthy letter was printed in the *News* from Mr. Charles W. Sloane arguing that the town was "going a little too fast," that school taxes were climbing, and "How much more would the tax be increased by establishment of a Library, and the expense of its upkeep?" Both legitimate questions to be answered in due course. Mr. Sloane, however, reached rather deep in the barrel for his final argument: "However handy a library nearby in which to find information on all subjects, ancient and modern, true and fabulous, the prosperity of a locality is better promoted by moderate taxation and such local advantages as, for instance, *efficient postal service*." (Insufficient funds at the national level for postal service had been predicted for May and June.) "Even though there were no other reason, this impending breakdown in the postal service might well suggest a pause before starting a Library."

Winthrop Kellogg, Treasurer of the Library Board, replied in the *News* the next week that Federal taxes were high because more than 80% go to pay for the late war and its after effects. Local taxes were not high even considering the larger budget for 1924: "And an additional $2.20 tax per $1,000 of assessed valuation is not going to fall heavily on anyone. Ask the real estate men what they think of the plan for a new library to which we can point with pride. Ask them if it is going to drive buyers of property away. Wait and see. The real estaters will be featuring the new Library shortly, and if you are one who wishes to *sell* his property here, you had better vote for the new Library."

In 1923 the population of Port Washington was between 8,000 and 9,000. Based on national and state statistics, a library for a community of this size was estimated to cost between $80,000 and $90,000.

Speaking at the School District Annual Meeting on May 1, 1923, at the High School, prior to the library vote, Arthur W. Keevil, who was in favor of the proposition to raise $50,000 by taxation, called attention to the defeat of a similar petition a few years before when it included a proposal for a memorial to the soldiers and sailors. He "allowed that the district could not afford to turn down the petition at this time."

From the opposition came W.C.W. Child who argue against the appropriation of such a large sum for library purposes. He felt that $25,000 was sufficient using the present site instead of acquiring a new one.

The tally that evening: 421 persons voted—236 votes were cast *against* the proposition and 185 *in favor*.

A front page letter in the *News* at the end of August echoed the sentiments of many in Port (and elsewhere) who felt strongly that the town needed constant improvement: "Dear Sir—I read your article regarding the establishing of a hospital at Port Washington in last Friday's *News*, and sincerely hope your idea will be carried through to its accomplishment.

It seems to me that there are four matters which should be kept constantly before the residents until they become realities. Namely:

1. A bridge over the railroad at Willow Ave. or some other advantageous point.
2. A waterfront park.
3. A hospital.
4. A suitable building for the public library.

With its superb harbor and location, its fine schools, excellent fire department, splendid train service, and the best weekly newspaper on Long Island, Port Washington is certainly one of the most desirable places to live in on the Island, and with the four improvements mentioned it would outstrip any town in the country."

Yours truly,

R.S. Van Schaick, Brooklyn, N.Y.

While the voters may have turned down the library proposition in the spring, many townspeople throughout the rest of the year continued their efforts toward building a better library—with books as well as bricks.

A headline in the *News* in August:

GARDEN PARTY NETS NEAT SUM FOR LIBRARY

**Mr. and Mrs. George Thayer's Home Grounds
the Scene of Large and Jovial Gathering**

Toward the end of the news story which followed, including a list of all who attended as well as many committees, the crucial statement appeared: "About $430 was realized in the four short hours of the afternoon and it will all go toward the fund for the Port Washington Public Library."

THE PERSONAL TOUCH

Some recollections of the Port Washington Library by long-time residents:

"We moved here in 1923. We lived on Beacon Hill, just next door to Dr. Newman. Mr. Schreiber placed me in Main Street School in the second half of the second grade that fall.

"I became aware of the library through at least one friend at school and it was open, I think, only one day a week...we could go in and take a book for a week, sometimes for two weeks. That was the Burtis store. The building was kind of a beige color. It certainly didn't reflect fresh paint. It was kind of old and musty inside and out. And the one or two days a week that it was opened, it was presided over by—I guess she was a Mitchell—I don't know that for sure. (It was, of course, Miss Wilhelmina Mitchell.)

"At long recollection I would say she was probably in her sixties. Always wore a black dress, always wore a black sort of tight hat. Stiff brim, higher than usual straw hat, and as I recall, I don't think I ever saw her smile. She took the library and her work very seriously. If anyone walked in with their hat on they were immediately admonished. The collection was certainly not modern. You saw no new books on the shelves. Certainly no dust wrappers. I never saw anyone assisting, but always Miss Mitchell and always rather prim and proper.

"We would go in after school. We got out at 3:30 and this other guy—it's a familiar name—Malcolm Anderson and I together. Now his father was a local author—Robert Gordon Anderson—and his mother was the founder of the Garden Club. He was with Putnam for a while, left them to freelance. He wrote some children's books, the '7 O'Clock Stories,' the 'Half-past 7 Stories,' the '8 O'Clock Stories'—as kids progressed in age the stories progressed a little bit, the hours referred to bedtime, of course."   *Charles W. Harper*

"The library was a little bungalow-type house where St. Stephen's property is—just as you went in the driveway, you turned to the right and that was the library. I believe the librarian's name was Miss Mitchell. I remember she was a rather heavy lady but very pleasant. I was kind of young, but I remember she was a very pleasant lady.

"There were as many books as the building would hold. A lot of children's books."   *Flora Cramer*

"My first visit to the library? Well, Miss Mitchell, of course, was the librarian and her friend, Miss McKee. They had the library in a renovated house on the Episcopal Church property. It was a nice old house and it had a front porch. You went in and there was a whole shelf of children's books. We were not allowed to take them out, but Miss Mitchell let *me* take them out!

(Interviewer: Why were you special to Miss Mitchell?)

"Because I *was* special. Evidently she knew she could trust me, I guess. *St. Nicholas* was a children's magazine. And I loved it. There were several books of St. Nicholas, too.

"The library—it was dark in there. Dark and quiet. You had to keep your voice down. It was sort of like a church.

"I'm sure my mother took me the first time and got me interested in it because there were no children for me to play with. Bayview Avenue was so far out of town.

"Miss Mitchell lived next door to us at 62 Bayview Avenue. We lived at 64 Bayview. Her house is still there. My mother didn't have to persuade me to go to the library. She and my mother read to me a great deal. The library was just part of me. That's all!"

Virginia Linder Davis

A NEW LIBRARY FOR

Next Tuesday evening, May 1, 1923, at 8 o'clock at the High School, the People of Port Washington will decide whether or not they will have a new library.

THE PROPOSAL AND COST

The proposition is to raise the money for purchasing a site and erecting a building by taxation, $25,000 in 1924 and $25,000 in 1925. The assessed valuation of the property in the District is approximately $11,500,000. If the vote is in favor of the library your tax will therefore be increased in 1924 and 1925 less than 22c for each $100 of the assessed valuation of your property.

ARE YOU SATISFIED WITH THE PRESENT LIBRARY AND ITS SERVICE?

If you are satisfied with the present library, or if you think it meets the needs of your children, or if you are opposed to improving Port Washington, or if you feel that Port Washington is too poor to spend the money, then we have no message for you.

But if you wish a better library for your children and others, if you have civic pride, if you feel that Port Washington can afford it, then go to the High School Tuesday, May 1st, at 8 o'clock, and vote for the library.

REASONS FOR A NEW LIBRARY

1. 1550 school children. The enrollments in the school are increasing at the rate of approximately 130 a year. There are hundreds of other young people, who are no longer in school, who need a good library and reading room.

2. A library is a place where a person may continue his or her education.

3. The Town is now without adequate library facilities.

4. A good library will be an economy to the reading people of the District.

OBJECTIONS OF THOSE OPPOSED TO THE NEW LIBRARY

1. Port Washington is not a library town.

ANSWER: This is sad, if true. Next Tuesday evening will prove whether it is true. The people who say this is not a library town are **opposed to any progress** — it is the best way they have of expressing themselves. Erect an attractive library building and the use of the library facilities will increase many fold.

2. Too much money is asked. $50,000 is not needed.

ANSWER: A sufficiently large site should be secured so that as Port Washington grows the building now to be erected may be added to. Say the site will cost $10,000, only $40,000 is left for the building, and a building worthy of Port Washington cannot be erected for less.

3. Too little money is asked.

ANSWER: The Trustees of the present library expect to turn over to the new library the books of the present library, together with the proceeds of sale of their property. This will give the Trustees of the new library funds to use in equipping the new library.

PORT WASHINGTON

4. Let someone give us a library or pass around a subscription paper.

ANSWER: In addition to saying that these methods have failed, we add that the raising of the funds by taxation is the fairest and most democratic way. The library is for all. It will be managed by Trustees elected in the same manner as School Trustees. A library is an extension to the school system. The library should be provided, maintained, operated and managed in the same way as the school.

LOOK AHEAD

The Town is growing rapidly. At the present rate of growth, the population will double in the next ten years. The new library cannot be ready in less than two years at the least. Do you wish to postpone it longer?

If, Mr. Taxpayer, you feel that you can afford the 22c additional tax next year and the year after, vote "YES" on the library proposition.

THE NEW TRUSTEES

At the same meeting next Tuesday evening, if the Library proposal is adopted, five Trustees will be elected for the new library. It will be their business to select the site for the new library, to prepare plans, make contracts, etc. Their task is no slight one. Vote therefore for five of Port Washington's best and most public spirited citizens.

A BROADCASTING STATION FOR PORT WASHINGTON

Speaking of the marvelous development of the last few years in the transmission of sound and of "listening in" on addresses and performances hundreds and thousands of miles away, wonderful as this is and valuable as it may prove as a factor in human advancement, it is as nothing compared with the invention of writing and printing and the creation of the modern book. It is indeed a marvel to "listen in" on a recital or an address 1000 miles away. Sitting hundreds of miles away and hearing immediately the voice or the music that is being produced in Pittsburg or Newark is a thing to stir the imagination, but what is that, either as a mere wonder or as a means of human enrichment, compared with the ability which anyone who can read possesses, of listening in to the poetry of Milton, the drama of Shakespeare, the dialogs of Plato, the songs of Homer or the parables and sermons of Jesus? The invention of printing and the creation of the modern book have made the mind of every great thinker of the last 3000 years a broadcasting station for the continuous and worldwide dissemination of the messages, ideas, thoughts and hopes that have given the world most of the things that make life worth living today. In the book we have the greatest thing that all the centuries of invention have produced. Let us not neglect the greatest of all broadcasting stations, the Library.

BY THE BOARD OF TRUSTEES OF
THE PORT WASHINGTON FREE LIBRARY.

"I recall a big house—Burtis House. You went up four steps, outside, and then a vestibule to prevent weather, I suppose. As I recall her big desk was about ten or fifteen back, and the files, the stacks, were down left and right. You went in and there she sat in her majesty behind that desk. You were greeted always with a big smile and directed to your section.

"She was sort of buxom, wore a shirt and skirt and always had a necktie, a bowtie. I can't remember if there was a belt, but usually a skirt and that was the style I suppose.

"You had to be quiet, yes, but she would take groups of us if we came in, two or three of us looking for books in the stacks, but not very long away from her desk.

"Where did we sit? Window sills. Why do I remember big window sills there?

"A friend told me that there was another librarian, Florence McKee, but I don't remember. We borrowed books, but the librarian kept the card. Somehow that book came back. I mean *we brought the books back!* We were very solicitous about that—especially if we took a new edition out.

"If you were reading a series, she would really be ready to tell you what the next book was to come along. Miss Mitchell was a wonderful person."

Gertrude Crampton Nicoll

During the spring of 1924 the School Board was persuaded to set the date of August 5th for another vote on the question of a new library. All those who had lent their names, prestige and time to further the effort worked with renewed energy. The most visible and vocal advocate was Editor William Hyde. His editorials and front page "goading" month after month brought new arguments, new ideas, and even a sense of guilt to his readers.

His headlines alone told the continuing story:

WHAT THE PORT WASHINGTON LIBRARY SHOULD MEAN TO YOU
(2/22/24)

NEW PORT LIBRARY WILL COST LESS THAN 10C PER CAP. PER WK.
TO MAINTAIN
(5/2/24)

YOUR NEW LIBRARY—WHEN? WHY NOT THIS YEAR?
(5/10/24)

WHY PORT NEEDS A NEW LIBRARY
(6/6/24)

LIVING LIBRARIES LIVE WITH US
(7/4/24)

WHAT THE FIRST TUESDAY IN AUGUST MEANS TO YOU
(8/1/24)

IT SHOULD BE APPROVED—Don't fail to do your duty, taxpayers. You won't be sorry for it! (Editorial, 8/1/24)

SCHOOL DISTRICT GIVES FREE LIBRARY $35,000 BY MORE THAN 2 TO 1 VOTE!

OPPONENTS TO RESOLUTION FAIL TO DEFEAT NEW BUILDING PROPOSITION THE SECOND TIME

In the same edition (8/8/24) Hyde could not resist adding his own "non-editorial" comment:

THE LIBRARY, THE LIBRARY
THEY CAN'T FIGHT YOU
ANYMORE

We have met the enemy and they are ours!

"The meeting at the High School last Tuesday night settled the hash of the opposition to an adequate and respectable library in Port Washington. They were beaten to a frazzle. And how! *The News* would enjoy publishing the names of the 112 who voted against the resolution. To the 243 who voted for it we say: "Here's to your good health, your family's good health, and may you live long and prosper."

On August 15th Hyde wrote a lead editorial—A LIBRARY AT LAST—which included his own strong feelings about Port Washington and the library: "...at last we are going to add another attraction to a place which is rapidly becoming one of the most delightful throughout Long Island."

1924 *Library moves from Past to Present—Views the Future with renewed energy and confidence—Now called Port Washington Public Library*

Toward the middle of October the Library Trustees petitioned the Regents of the University of the State of New York (the twelve members of the Regents having the final word on matters pertaining to education and libraries in N.Y. State) to transfer all property of the Port Washington Free Library to Union Free School District No. 4, Town of North Hempstead, County of Nassau, "for library purposes." Henceforth it would be known as the Port Washington Public Library.

Public participation in finding a suitable site was solicited by the library trustees and, of course, by the *Port News*. A list of the trustees was published on the front page along with a statement emphasizing:

"The affairs of the Library Association are open to all, and therefore the trustees will in the near future call upon the voters to en-

dorse or reject the plans that they have in view. If any reader of the
News has any suggestion to make regarding the place and erection
of such a library please communicate with any trustee."

Central location for the library was also considered by Hyde of
utmost importance, followed by size:

"One thing that will need most serious consideration is that Port
Washington is growing with astonishing rapidity and the library
should be planned and built with a view to the future use of a much
greater number of patrons."

Between 1920 and 1925 a change in the number of trustees was
voted on, reducing the Board from nine members to five. In January, 1925, when the charter came through, the Trustees included:

John S. Witmer, Jr.,   Walter S. McGrane,
Karl W. Kirchwey,   Frank G. Lippert,
              and Helen Sands.

Adding to the elation the trustees must have felt at having the
money to build a new library, and the excitement of developing
building plans based on community needs, was the major step forward of becoming a public library chartered by the State of New
York on the first of January, 1925.*

In the matter of *building* a new library, nothing had happened
due primarily to inaction on the part of the school board, a fact that
was emblazoned across the front page of *Port News* in the April 3rd
edition:

TWO BOARDS ARE SPLIT
WHILE THE PUBLIC WAIT FOR THE NEW LIBRARY

School Trustees Deny Request of Free Library
Officials for Special Meeting of District to Vote on
Proposition to Set Aside a Site on Southeast
Corner of High School Grounds

In a not untypical small town dispute the library trustees had written to the editor of their local newspaper stating:

"So much talk has been occasioned by the apparent lack of action
by the Trustees of the new public library that the said trustees now
feel that it is time for the enclosed copies of letters pertaining
thereto to be given to the public."

The letters provided rather positive evidence that school board
members had been dragging their heels for months, including the
fact that "the Library Trustees have received no part of the $35,000
voted by the taxpayers of the District last summer, which was included in the budget of the Board of Education for the current
year."

*For complete text of the Charter, January 1, 1925, see Appendix.

Inevitably the library trustees exploded when the then president of the School Board, J. Henry Decker, wrote to them after many months reporting that their petition was denied "in that the entire school grounds are needed for school and recreation purposes."

From today's perspective, sixty-seven years later, the obvious question must be asked, "Who didn't do their homework?" Just twelve years previously the idea of using school grounds as the site of a new library had been soundly trounced by a large and vocal "athletic contingent" without even a vote. In 1913 the *northeast* corner of the High School property was in question. In 1925 it was the *southeast* corner, next to Webster Avenue. Certainly delinquent in delaying their answer to the library trustees, the school board's stalling tactics, nevertheless, may have forestalled another bruising battle.

1925   *Belleview Avenue lot becomes available — Town architect selected — Great Neck contractor*

Early in August the Trustees of the Public Library announced that they had agreed to purchase a plot of land on the west side of Belleview Avenue, just south of Main Street. They invited all registered architects residing in Port Washington to meet with them "for an informal discussion" on August 17th. Following the discussion it was unanimously agreed "amongst those present that the selection of an architect should not be decided by competition but by lot. All resident architects both present at the meeting and absent were considered. The trustees announced that Mr. LeRoy Barton (who lived on Crescent Road) was selected to design the new library."

[Although there are no actual records in library files of the building of the new library on Belleview Avenue, it must be taken for granted that plans were drawn up promptly by Mr. Barton, presented to the library trustees for approval, and Mr. George A. Richardson of Great Neck was awarded the building contract. There seem to be no references to the construction project in the *News,* nor have any pertinent contracts or other official documents been found.]

FAVORITE BOOKS

1919–1925

America's Part in the World War by R. J. Beamish and F. A. March
Main Street by Sinclair Lewis
The Sheik by E. M. Hull
If Winter Comes by A. S. M. Hutchinson
The Covered Wagon by Emerson Hough
The Mysterious Rider by Zane Grey

CHAPTER VIII

A New Library,
A New Librarian—1926

Belleview Avenue

1926   *Trustees and former members of Woman's Club given preview of new library—Formal opening July 12, 1926—Original appropriation exceeded by less than $2,000*

Meanwhile during the early months of 1926 the results of the 1925 New York State Census were released; Port Washington boasted a population of 9,007.

A proposition calling for the expenditure of $695,000 for a new *high school* was voted down by just 17 taxpayers.

Former resident and now internationally famous author, Kathleen Norris, was greeted by "a host of friends and acquaintances (at Port Washington Yacht Club in May) who enjoyed the opportunity to meet and listen to a woman whose influence in modern literature is wholesome, sane and sweet," effused Editor Hyde.

Clarence Budington Kelland, Beacon Hill resident, famous author, assistant editor of the *Saturday Evening Post* and president of the School Board, brought Thomas Costain, another *Saturday Evening Post* editor and later best-selling novelist, to the High School Senior Banquet at Bradley's Restaurant. According to Editor Hyde, Mr. Costain "encouraged us to write for the Post."

By the middle of June the new Library was completed. Prior to the formal opening to the public, a special occasion was planned:

PRIVATE VIEW OF NEW LIBRARY THIS SATURDAY

"On Saturday June 26, a private view of the new library will be tendered to the founder and her fellow members of the Port Washington Woman's Club, whose labors in 1892 and many years after have given to the town a library worthy of the community.

"All of the trustees who have served so faithfully and all those who by their subscriptions supported the library when without them it could not have continued to exist, will receive as a token of appreciation the compliment of a first glimpse, even though the furniture, ordered more than a month ago, has not been received and everything but the building itself is in an uncompleted condition." (Port News, 6/25/26)

The July 23 issue of *Port News* once again gave lengthy front-page coverage to a major library event.

LIBRARY NOW OPEN TO TOWNSPEOPLE; TRUSTEES REPORT
Well Known Artist Paints Founder's Portrait Gratis

"The Port Washington Public Library is now permanently located in its new home on Belleview Avenue, having moved from its old location on Main Street to formally open on July 12, 1926. You will find the librarians ready, willing and anxious to show you through the new library and also to assist you in any way possible in regard to the reference and reading facilities offered. It remains for the people of Port Washington themselves to visit the library and satisfy themselves as to what a wonderful opportunity awaits them."

"The site and building as it stands at present represents an investment as follows:
"*Land:* The land was purchased by the Library Trustees from the Tibbetts Estate for $10,000. The Tibbetts Estate took back a mortgage for the entire purchase price of $10,000, said mortgage to run for 10 years at 6 per cent interest.
"*Building:* In the *Port Washington News* of Nov. 6, 1925, when the announcement of the awarding of the contract was presented, the Trustees stated that "the original appropriation of $35,000, together with such library funds as may be on hand applicable for use, will suffice for the erection of the library and put it into use without additional expense to the taxpayers.
To show how near this prediction came true, the actual total amount expended was $36,828.40."

Thus the new library was formally opened, all monies accounted for and special tributes publicly paid to LeRoy Barton, the architect and to G.A. Richardson, the builder; to Miss Wilhelmina Mitchell and all the trustees, headed by Miss Helen Sands, President, all of whom "put their heart and soul and most every minute of their time into the work and rested not until the beginning of the summer."

Everyone who came to the opening of the library had the opportunity to meet with Miss Mitchell and to admire her portrait over the fireplace in the Reading Room.* It was the work of the celebrated portrait painter, George H. Taggart, who had offered to paint her portrait at the conclusion of the August 1924 meeting of the Board of Education when the building of the new library was a certainty. Miss Mitchell posed for the portrait during the following summer. A resolution of thanks to Mr. Taggart for his gracious gift was adopted by the trustees at their July meeting.

*Taggart's portrait of Miss Mitchell now hangs on the east wall of the Reference Room.

The portrait of Miss Wilhelmina Mitchell, painted by George Taggart, hung in the Reading Room of the Belleview Avenue library from 1926 to 1970. It is now on the east wall of the Reference Room at the present library.

The Belleview Avenue Library as it appeared in the 1950s.

Miss Mitchell, well aware of the increased responsibility of running the new library, indicated to the board her wish to step down in favor of a professional librarian to organize the library on the latest techniques.

1926   *Miss Helen B. Curtice appointed Head Librarian—Miss Mitchell becomes Associate Librarian—Catherine Sandy appointed library assistant*

Mr. Edwin W. Gaillard who had served the library so well in 1913 and 1914 again came to the aid of the trustees by helping them find a new librarian. In November Miss Helen B. Curtice, a trained and registered librarian, took over the position. Previously she had been assistant librarian at the Jackson Square branch of the New York Public Library.

The board appointed Miss Mitchell associate librarian "so that Port Washington may keep in close touch with the one without whose devoted service through 33 years of almost unsurmountable difficulties this town would never have had a library."

The staff was further increased when Catherine Sandy, a recent Port High graduate, came to work as an assistant to both librarians. Her career at the Port Washington Public Library spanned over 48 years.

The Reading Room of the Belleview Avenue Library during the 1930s.

Christmas greens were donated by friends of the library to decorate the library during the holidays. On December 23rd a fire was
kept burning in the fireplace of the reading room. This added so
much to the attractiveness and comfort of the room that it was decided to have a fire every Saturday evening during the winter
months.

An informal note, in what is certainly Miss Mitchell's handwriting, was found in an old notebook. It is the only record of book
acquisition and discards during the '20s:

> In January, 1926   11,362 books
> January, 1927   12,068 books
> _____
> 706 books accessed in 1926
> less 1,638 discards equals total collection of 10,430

This is the last record of Miss Mitchell's activities on behalf of the library. Born in Port Washington in 1847, she took on at the age of 45 the sometimes thankless job of creating a library, nurturing it and setting the highest standards for a library its size in New York State. Just a year and a half after retiring, Miss Mitchell died in her eighty-first year and was buried in the Mitchell family cemetery on New Street in Port Washington.

1927   *Clarifying memorabilia for safekeeping at library—Bill Hyde dies—Ernie Simon buys* Port News*—$9,500 budget passed— "Absent-minded borrowing" problem*

The townspeople of Port Washington have always been conscious of their own history, every now and then asking their friends and neighbors to *please* search their attics for memorabilia about the town. Often the library was the repository for such maps, documents and other papers.

However, early in Miss Curtice's administration as librarian, she and the trustees faced a difficult decision about the type of memorabilia to accept. Mr. T. J. Turberg of Sands Point offered his collection of Indian relics, arrowheads and various stone and shell implements with the proviso that they should be exhibited in a glass case in the reading room or the children's room. Accepting the gift was discussed and debated during three different board meetings, and in spite of the fact that this new library had far more space than its predecessor, it was decided not to branch out into the field of preserving artifacts of other than local historical interest. All were agreed that documents, maps and other easily stored papers had their proper place in the library.

Editor Hyde did not hesitate to use the Board's decision as an opportunity to remind his readers that a home should be found for the furniture of Colonial times, old china and pewter, brasses, tiles, spinning wheels and other "articles of bygone days where they can be seen and appreciated by all."

In the spring an excellent collection of garden books was offered including L. H. Bailey's famous *Pruning Manual,* and other intriguing titles such as *Little Gardens for Little Money,* Kelsey's *Rural Guide*—"A Practical Handbook for the farmer, the suburbanist, and all town folk who enjoy outdoor life and hope for a rural home."

The library was not alone in its twelve-year struggle to expand. Although needed for many years, it was not until 1927 that the voters of Port Washington approved in May a bond issue of $750,000 to finance a new high school, today known as Carrie Palmer Weber Junior High. This new facility with the largest and acoustically best auditorium in town opened on April 6 and served the secondary level youth of Port Washington for twenty-four years.

Progress in a community such as Port Washington may be measured in many ways. When the library was first started in Miss Mitchell's home (1892) there were *no* telephones in Port Washington. The following year there were four: Bayles Drug store (public pay phone), and the residences, in order of installation, of Dr. W.I. Cocke, Lloyd S. Bryce (later the home of Howard Gould, then Daniel Guggenheim) and W. Burke Cockran. By contrast in 1927 Port Washington had more than 1,700 phones. The Central, as they referred to the telephone exchange, had the latest equipment and 21 operators "taking care of a very busy office."

The Long Island Rail Road, in its annual survey, reported that 128 new buildings went up in Port Washington during 1926. To this number was added in 1927 the new theatre at the corner of Main Street and Belleview Avenue "where gorgeous coloring effects, emblazoned shields and all the gaiety of medieval times combine into one of the finest gathering places on all the North Shore."

The sudden death in November of William Mackey Hyde, founder and editor of the *Port Washington News*, shocked the community. The library, the schools, and the many citizens whose civic projects and improvements he fought for mourned this outstanding town leader.

Without losing a date or a deadline for months, the *Port Washington News* finally changed hands on May 1, 1928. Ernest R. Simon and Charles D. Lewis, who had worked with William Hyde on the newspaper for many years, together purchased the paper for $75,000. They promised the readers to continue in the same paths as their predecessor. Their first editorial (May 4, 1928) concluded: "Come in and visit us anytime or call—Port Washington 35—for we shall always be glad to see you and talk with you" (an invitation that was never repudiated).

As editor, Ernie Simon continued William Hyde's firm and friendly relationship with the library. The number of news stories and especially the "new book lists" continued to receive front page notice and occasional editorial comment.

In 1926 Karl W. Kirchwey resigned from the Library Board where he had served for three years (1923–1926). Board members then elected Cedric R. Crowell to complete Kirchwey's term of five years.

Mr. Charles R. Weeks, who was President of the Library Board during 1918 and 1919 and later became Judge Weeks, was appointed Counsel to the Board of Education in 1928, bringing him indirectly in contact with the library once again.

At the August 7th Annual Meeting of Union Free School District No. 4, Frank G. Lippert gave his yearly report as Treasurer of the Library Board, Cedric Crowell was elected to a five year term, and the voters passed the proposed budget of $9,500 to maintain the library for another year.

1929   *Town growing rapidly—32 magazines subscribed to—"unrecorded borrowings"—children's library boasts over 1,200 volumes*

Over the years many gifts and bequests to the library made it possible to make purchases and improvements outside the constraints of the budget. Using such funds Miss Curtice acquired many new books for the children's room and had suitable new bookshelves built to accommodate them.

The library was growing as the population expanded. (The school census taken in August, 1928, gave a figure of *around* 10,500 total population) Continually increasing use of the library along with a book collection that was expanding each year (more than a thousand books were added in 1928) necessitated some new methods of cataloging. In addition to a system where cards were filed by title and by author, books were now to be analyzed by subject matter and a new set of "subject" cards was added to the catalog.

The days of asking readers to save and bring to the library their magazines had long since passed. The magazines to which the library subscribed were often listed at the beginning of each year in *Port News*. The list for 1929 reflects the broad interests of a growing society: *American Girl, Atlantic Monthly, Boy's Life, Century, Country Life, Current History, Etude, Every Girl's, Good Housekeeping, Harper's Monthly, House Beautiful, Ladies' Home Journal, Life, Literary Digest, Living Age, London Illustrated News, National Geographic, Nations Business, Nature Magazine, New Republic, Pictorial Review, Popular Mechanics, Radio Broadcast, Review of Reviews, Rudder, Saturday Evening Post, Saturday Review of Literature, School and Society, Scribner's, St. Nicholas, Theatre Arts Monthly, World's Work.*

Miss Curtice noted that the *London Illustrated News* was the first foreign periodical to which the library had subscribed.

Every librarian must deal with the problem of "unrecorded borrowings." In February she wrote a letter to the Editor:

"An important reference book has been missing from the Reading Room for several weeks—*Home Book of Verse*, ed. B.E. Stevenson. It is bound in bright red cloth with lettering, contains over 2,000 pages on India paper and is very little worn. It is thought that some reader must have taken it out, absent-mindedly forgetting to have the book charged. As it is needed very much at the library and is an expensive book, costing $15.00, the library authorities ask whoever has it return it immediately."

Two and a half years after the new library had opened, another progressive step forward was made in the children's room. In addition to making the room as attractive as possible, Miss Curtice, using the American Library Association catalog of recommended books for children, ordered from publishers *all* fiction and picture books listed. The children's library now boasted 1,202 volumes.

Ernie Simon, Editor of the Port News.

A summary of library activity for the first six months of 1929 shows that 18,663 books (30 percent non-fiction) were circulated to 232 borrowers. 1,000 books were added to the collection, and 100 were borrowed from the State Library in Albany. The summary went on to further explore readership:

"The librarian and assistants have been trying to find out who and how many of the people of Port Washington are *not* using the library. There are 2700 people registered as borrowers. There being no town directory, the winter telephone directory for 1928–1929 was checked. It was found that, out of the approximately 1,900 families in the directory, there were 992 who had no adult members registered at the library."

An invitation was then issued to all who had not previously used the library to visit it. The Board of Trustees and the librarians earnestly wished to make available books which fit the reading needs of all citizens.

The trend during the late twenties toward a more humanistic approach to writing history was not lost on those in charge of the library. In one *Port News* column it was noted that "new books on American history show an interest in people rather than events." Some of these so-called social histories included Claude Bowers' *Jefferson and Hamilton* and *The Tragic Era* (post Civil War), *Life and Labor in the Old South* (U. B. Phillips), and the new books by Charles and Mary Beard. These titles were among many summer acquisitions.

At the end of the year, Miss Curtice wrote a lengthy article about magazines, pointing out that five "formerly subscribed to, but little used" *(Century, Ladies' Home Journal, Radio Broadcast, Review of Reviews,* and *School and Society)* had been discontinued. In their place an English periodical, *Cornhill* and the French *L'Illustration, Progressive Education, United States Air Services, American Mercury, Bookman* and *The New Yorker* were added.

In November the many friends and associates of Mr. Edwin White Gaillard learned through the *Port News* of his death in Mount Kisco: "Mr. Gaillard had been a sincere friend of the Port Washington Free Library Association of which he was the president."

FAVORITE BOOKS 1926–1936

Outline of History (reprint edition) by H. G. Wells
The Story of Philosophy by Will Durant
All Quiet on the Western Front by E. M. Remarque
Anthony Adverse by Hervey Allen
While Rome Burns by Alexander Woollcott
North to the Orient by Anne Lindbergh
Gone With the Wind by Margaret Mitchell

CHAPTER IX

The Depression and World War II

1930–   *Literary "lights" still shine in Port—Former library on Main*
1931   *Street demolished—First branch library established in Hempstead*
         Harbor School—Sinclair Lewis awarded Nobel Prize—One-third
         of residents use library in 1931—Depression deals blow to library

In the January, 1930, issue of *Sunrise...Long Island's Own Magazine*, Editor Albert R. Beatty's lead article was titled "A Community of Celebrities—Some of the Bright Lights of Port Washington." He listed as current residents authors Clarence Budington Kelland "who has done more to bring about the deserved recognition of Port Washington than any other individual," F. W. Bronson, Eric Hatch, Clyde L. Eddy (also an explorer and lecturer), and Robert Gordon Anderson. Artists living in Port Washington at the time included John LaGatta, John E. Sheridan and Neysa McMein, who built a charming French country house on the Cornwell Estate at Barker's Point.

Albert Beatty included Christopher Morley in his list of authors even though "Morley makes his home in Roslyn, he has pushed aside the branches and become one of (this) town."

The former library building and property on Main Street were still owned by the Library Trustees when in February they decided to demolish the building which had remained empty and could become an eyesore. Ben Rogozensky, a local contractor was given the material of which the building was constructed if he would demolish it. A three-column photo of the old and revered building on the front page of the *News* gave readers "one last look."

In 1916 the school district had taken over a one-story frame building on the Goodwin-Gallagher Corporation sand bank calling it the Hempstead Harbor School to accomodate children of the employees of the sand banks. Rooms were added on the first floor and later a second story was built.

Following the policy of trying to reach as many readers in town as possible, the library opened a branch library in the Hempstead Harbor Public School, located on West Shore Road, on May 14, 1930. Each Wednesday afternoon from four until eight p.m. Miss

For twenty-seven years library borrowers found their books and magazines at this familiar old frame building across from the Methodist Church. In February, 1930, it was demolished.

Curtice or one of her assistants, in a classroom set aside for the library, issued books to both children and adults living near the sand pits, and helped readers find just what they wanted. It was altogether an interesting collection of about 300 volumes including children's books, recent and standard fiction, German and Italian books, some non-fiction such as home economics, raising children, travel history and gardening. According to a journal kept by Miss Curtice, the branch remained open through December, 1933.

The "new" library on Belleview was honored in the spring by being chosen as the site for a Library Institute, an all day meeting of North Shore librarians. At the conclusion John A. Lowe of the Brooklyn Public Library, an authority on library buildings said that "Port Washington was to be congratulated on having such a beautiful library...one of the finest on Long Island and an inspiration to the community."

Of additional interest to those close to the library was an item in
Port News in the summer:

P.W. PUBLIC LIBRARY PICTURES
EXHIBITED AT STATE FAIR BY
LEROY BARTON OF PORT

"Pictures of the exterior and interior of the Port Washington
Library with floor plans drawn by LeRoy Barton of Beacon Hill,
Port Washington, were exhibited at the State Fair in Syracuse. The
library exhibit included pictures of 'the best library buildings' of
the State and the local library was included under that heading."

Two popular and highly respected townspeople died during the
summer of 1930; both were mourned by the many who had known
them over long periods of time. In June Mrs. Mary Elizabeth
McLean died suddenly while on vacation in Vermont. From 1900
until 1921 Mrs. McLean was continuously on the Library Board,
giving freely of her time and her home to promote every forward
move toward improving the library.

In September Arthur Vance, whose 1906 home at 68 Carlton Avenue is still standing, died at age 56. For a very short period before
World War I he sat on the Library Board finishing out the term of
an unnamed member. He was, of course, most famous for the tre-
mendous and indispensable part he played in making the *Pictorial
Review* one of the great magazine properties of the world.

Miss Curtice continued writing her weekly columns about books.
Chatty at times, erudite at others, she wrote about every type of
book that would interest readers in Port Washington. On occasion

Arthur T. Vance,
1872–1930

Hempstead Harbor School, site of
branch library, 1930 to 1933.

Main Street, early Thirties, looking up toward the library, right, and Main Street School, West front.

Miss Curtice called her readers' attention to special events such as Book Week, and to special exhibitions, but always dear to her heart were children and children's books about which she wrote frequently.

Former Port Washington author, Sinclair Lewis, was awarded the Nobel Prize for Literature in November, 1930. He was the first American to be so honored. The prize was for his satirical novels. Miss Curtice did not miss the opportunity of stating in her column: "Those of his novels which will be found at the library are *Main Street, Arrowsmith, Mantrap, Elmer Gantry, Dodsworth,* and *Babbit,* the book which decided the judges in favor of Mr. Lewis."

Although by all customary measurements library statistics for 1930 far exceeded those for 1929, Miss Curtice never slackened her efforts to attract more readers to the library and to broaden the collection. Her report to the Library Trustees which was given a double-column spread in the February 6, 1931, *Port News* was headlined:

ONE-THIRD OF PORT RESIDENTS
USED LOCAL LIBRARY
DURING THE PAST YEAR

Public Librarian Helen Curtice Makes A
Very Interesting Year's Report—
1,927 New Volumes Added—50,419 Books
Taken From Library During 1930

Miss Curtice rejoiced in the fact that almost 2,000 new books were added at a cost of $2,000, "resulting in a collection of books much more adequate to meet the needs of this community," she wrote, "*though still below the state standard*." 10,000 more books were circulated in 1930 than in 1929; 24 per cent of the whole were children's books. Foreign language books were added, and the facilities of the New York State Library and the New York Public Library were called on frequently for special requests.

The remainder of the article was true to form—if a third of the population uses the library, how do we reach the other two-thirds? The question was answered partially by listing the hours and days open, eligibility (just live in town!), and the fact that an unlimited number of books could be borrowed.

In April another feature article appeared demonstrating once again the newspaper's interest in promoting the library. The headline:

GREATER USE SHOULD BE MADE
OF PORT WASHINGTON PUBLIC LIBRARY

"Provides Store House of Valuable Information for
Youth—Should Serve Parents as Excellent Help in
Development of Children—Are Movies Taking Place of
Good Reading?"

Each point in the sub-heading was dealt with at length. Sixty years have seen vast physical changes in the library since Ernie Simon wrote that headline. He would not be far from the mark, however, if he were writing about our society today, even though movies are no longer the primary target.

The country-wide Depression had its effect on Port Washington not unlike that of many towns in Long Island. The library was not exempt from problems. At the end of December the Bank of North Hempstead where library funds were deposited was forced to close. At the time those funds amounted to $5,537.00: $1,000. Endowment Fund, checking account of $537., and Savings Account of $4,000 from taxes. (Eventually a portion—amount unknown—was restored.) The Board of Education kindly gave the Library Trustees an advance of $2,000. based on anticipated tax revenues of $9,500. due in April.

Ironically, Miss Curtice had a column in the December 11 *Port News* headed:

BOOKS ON THE DEPRESSION

"These difficult times of unemployment and financial depression have caused a satisfactory increase in the use of the Public Library, both in the borrowing of books for home reading and in the use of the Reading Room. In spite of this increase, the trustees and librarian believe that many residents do not realize that the library offers everyone in the village free books, either to take home or to read in the attractive Reading Room, and these opportunities are given entirely without cost to the individual.

"To those with more free time this winter the library gives the chance of education for a possible better job or of getting more fun out of leisure hours."

1932   *Port Library receives high rating—Miss Curtice and Miss Sandy maintain high standards doing the work of three*

The Library Extension Division of the University of New York issued a rating of 101.55% on the Port Washington Library in 1932. The report showed the present condition and standing of the Port Washington Library in comparison with other libraries in the state serving approximately the same population. There were four parts to the rating: book stock, circulation, finance, and staff and service.

Shortly after this favorable report was announced from Albany another report, this time from the Board of Trustees, was published in the *News* to the effect that circulation of books at the Port Washington Library had increased from 16,445 in 1926 to 60,473 in 1931—an increase of 268% in *six years.*

In spite of this good news, a new and acute problem faced the Trustees. Early indications were that circulation would jump to 72,000 in 1932. The staff of the library consisting then of the librarian, Miss Helen Curtice and her assistant, Miss Catherine Sandy, had remained the same since the new library opened.

Ernie Simon's April 23rd article stated:
"One full time trained worker for every 20,000 books circulated is the standard set by the Library Extension Division.
"It was therefore, necessary last year for the librarian and her assistant to do the work for which the State standard demands three workers holding State Certificates, and it is greatly to their credit that in spite of the pressure of extra work, they have maintained the high standard of the library so that the rating last year was 101.65%."

The library budget for 1932–33 was up from $9,500 to $10,500, and for the first time was not included with the School District budget, as the school trustees felt that the Library budget, not connected with the school affairs, should appear separately. A major step forward for the library!

Both budgets passed on May 3, 1932. The school and library budgets combined called for a tax rate of $1.07 per $100 assessed valuation.

1933   *Children's librarian added to staff—Miss Curtice's book reviews*
        and news about books, authors and publishers popular—New
        names on Library Board

One of the rewards of the budget increase was that in January, 1933, a new member of the library staff was added. Miss Elinor Baker, a graduate of Ohio Wesleyan University and the School of Library Services of Pratt Institute, was hired as children's librarian. Her previous experience included a year at the New York Public Library and a year in the Cleveland Public Library where she took graduate courses at Western Reserve in child psychology and children's literature. Miss Baker filled a much needed position in helping children choose books and parents in selecting reading for their children.

Miss Curtice continued her weekly column, *P.W. Public Library News,* in the local paper, offering forty-four informative and sprightly articles throughout the year. Subjects were diverse covering wide areas of interest such as "technocracy," technology, war debts, international involvement, Bermuda, old New York, Westerns, the Classics, children's books, travel, politics, poetry, theatre, fiction, in short, the entire spectrum of literature—all described with the purpose of luring the reader to the library.

Each year the library was able to boast of increases in circulation, use of Reading Room and reference area, number of books borrowed (actual circulation in 1932 was 76,868) and, of course, the new children's librarian was heartily welcomed not only by children but by parents as well.

Miss Curtice was an exemplary librarian, and she was also a student of books and of publishing. Her services as a speaker on the

Overdue book reminder card,
November 1933.

The Literary Mountains

It was not so very long ago that London was the literary center of the universe. The great publishing houses were there; the greatest accolade an American writer could receive was acclaim from the English critics. As a result, American literature took to aping its foreign cousin, and for a while the "fashionable" American authors were more English than the English.

All that has changed. England still has her great literature—but the highest literary mountains are to be found in this country. The American book publisher leads the world—not merely in the promotion of sales, but in bringing before an audience new talents, new ideas, new and vital experiments. Much of this he does without hope of gain, knowing from experience that deficits are almost inevitably the result of adventuring of this kind.

We need not, however, feel sorry for the American publisher because of that. He has earned a very definite reward. It is to the presses of America that much of the world now looks for pungent volumes of criticism and political philosophy; for the greatest biographies, for the most important fiction. America has produced a native literature and in it are names which are almost as familiar in Paris and Vienna and Leningrad and Cracow, as in San Francisco and New Orleans and Sauk Center. It is a literature which, because it is fundamentally native to a land, is really international in spirit.

And the better American publishers who have given so much of time, effort and hard-earned money to aiding that development, when more profitable, if less commendable, enterprises beckoned, deserve more of the credit than they generally receive.

Port News, *January 6, 1933.*

topic of books, both new and antiquarian, were often in demand and her observations about the role of publishers and publishing were on occasion printed in the Port News (see sidebar).

Editor Hyde of the *Port News* occasionally printed the entire Annual Report of the Port Washington Public Library. Such was the case on January 26, 1934. The following news item includes the Treasurer's report followed by Miss Curtice's report on 1933 statistics:

PORT LIBRARY SPENT $11,217 IN 1933, BUT RECEIPTS ARE $11,836

Spent More Money for Books in 1933
Than in Other Years, Report Trustees

"The annual meeting of the Board of Trustees of the Port Washington Public Library was held Wednesday, Jan. 17. At this time reports for 1933 were received from the Librarian and Treasurer, and officers were elected.

"The treasurer reported that for the last two years the item for repairs had been small as the labor was contributed through the local Unemployment Committee (a group of concerned citizens who made it their business to help victims of the Depression find paying jobs) This has made possible a larger expenditure for books. The item for salaries includes janitor service, three full-time librarians and one part-time librarian.

Members of the Library Board included Cedric Crowell, President; William Haskell, Secretary; Miss E. Jane Brown: and Mrs. Alan Gould, Treasurer. (The fifth member's name is not known.)

LIBRARY REPORTS BOOK CIRCULATION OF 90,736 IN 1933, A GAIN OF 18 PER CENT

The Port Washington Public Library had a total circulation of 90,736 during the year, 1933, it was disclosed in the annual report of the librarian, Miss Helen Curtice. The average daily circulation was 299.1.

In comparison with 1932, the year just ending showed a gain of 13,868 in book circulation, or 18 per cent. The annual report as given by Miss Curtice:

Circulation   Adult: Fiction, 47,823
                        Non-fiction, 19,691
                        Periodicals, 2,460—total, 69,984
                Juvenile: Fiction, 13,871
                        Non-fiction, 6,591
                        Periodicals, 290—total, 20,752
                        Total circulation, 90,736
Days open, 303.

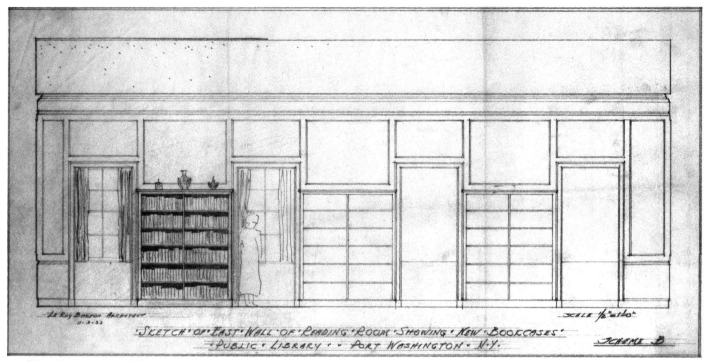

Architect LeRoy Baron's "Sketch of East Wall of Reading Room Showing New Bookcases" installed in 1934.

Foreign book circulation and interloans from Albany and New York Public Library increased. The total number of borrowers was 4,316, almost 40 per cent of the population, and the library added 1,706 new books.

1934– *Local artists share studio and display works—Model airplane*
1935   *exhibit creates interest in books—32 High School students dis-*
        play Indian crafts—Library Garden Project formed to beautify
        grounds—Trustees urged by N.Y. State to apply for WPA funds

The place of the library in the community was enhanced significantly during 1934 with a series of exhibits in both the Reading Room and Children's Room. In February the Port Washington Sketch Club which had started three years previously held an exhibition in the Reading Room of water colors, pastels and oils. Both professionals and amateurs were members, sharing a studio in the old Plaza Building, Main Street and Haven Avenue. Each week, weather permitting, they gathered together for outdoor sketching "about the sand banks or along our picturesque harbors."

The following month an exhibit in the Children's Room gathered together forty-six model planes crafted by boys in town. Fourteen flying models and five solid scale models were suspended from the ceiling and twenty-seven smaller models displayed in cases, all of which showed an excellent amount of skill, patience, exactness and knowledge of aviation.

In her library column in the *News* two weeks later, Miss Curtice wrote:

"The interest shown in the exhibit of model airplanes by the boys who loaned their models and by those who have been looking at them indicates that aviation holds an important place in their lives. Adults, too, want aviation books and new titles are constantly being purchased."

Then followed a list of new books such as *Complete Model Aircraft Manual, Prize Winners Book of Model Airplanes,* books for all ages, interests and skills.

Another exhibit of young peoples' work went on display in May in cooperation with the Art Department of the Senior High School. Thirty-two students demonstrated their skills in design, representation, costume design and sketching. It was felt that an exhibition in the library would reach far more people than the annual display at the High School during Education Week. Miss Curtis wrote:

"Indians have fascinated so many young readers at the Port Washington Public Library that this month (July) some books have been purchased which tell stories and legends of the Indians and describe their customs and handicraft work...some easy stories and picture books for the younger readers, all of which, added to the books already in the library, make an interesting collection on the subject."

Ever since the library opened in 1926 when a minimal foundation planting was made, much had been discussed, but little done, about

The new Port Washington Post Office a few weeks before dedication, November 16, 1935

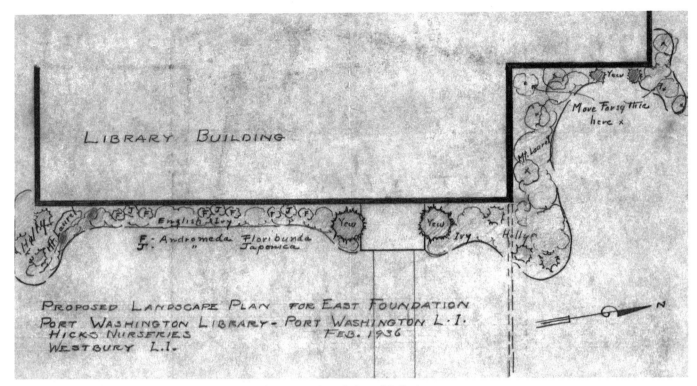

*Landscape Plan by Hicks Nurseries for plantings along East Foundation of Belleview
Avenue Library. Port Washington Garden Club's Library Garden Committee completed
plantings in Spring, 1936.*

improving the grounds around the library. Consequently a group of
garden club members organized the Library Garden Project, en-
rolling members at $1.00 per year for two years.

In October Hicks Nurseries in Westbury submitted an estimate
of $153.34 (!) for 22 evergreens, 35 flowering trees and shrubs, 105
ground covers and 136 bulbs to be planted in the back yard of the
library. The estimate was accepted and materials planted the next
spring.

Over the following two years money was raised to complete the
Library Garden Project, and according to a notebook kept by the
committee, a total of $315. was expended between April, 1935, and
June, 1937 for landscaping the entire grounds of the library, all out
of donated funds. As one $1 donor commented, "Grass, flower bor-
ders and shade trees have created this beautiful garden, a lovely
place for the children's hour in the summer."

The year 1935 started not unexpectedly with the re-election of
Cedric Crowell as president, William T. Haskell, vice-president,
Mrs. Alan Gould, treasurer, and Miss Jane Brown, secretary. (Still
no clue as to who was the fifth member of the board.) One other
lapse in detailed information: although only two years had passed
since Miss Elinor Baker had been appointed children's librarian, it

was noted in the *News* that "Miss Josephine Smith will continue to act as librarian of the children's books. Miss Helen Curtice, librarian, will be assisted by Miss Catherine Sandy and Miss Cleo Thompson." Miss Baker's departure is unrecorded.

The trustees and the librarian, while not publicly taking bows, could well have been pleased that the library statistics continued improving and that "among the 23 libraries in New York State serving communities with a population of 10,000 to 15,000, The Port Washington Public Library received the highest rating for service rendered during 1933, according to reports from the Library Extension Division."

The Depression and its aftermath brought a variety of Federal and State public works programs, or offers of programs, to communities as small as Port Washington. Frank L. Tolman, Director of the Library Extension Division in Albany, wrote to the Port Washington Library, urging the trustees to submit a list of "present or future needs for library buildings and extensions." His letter went on to tell of new library projects around the state all of which were paid for, partially or totally, from Federal Public Works funds, WPA in particular.

The trustees and Miss Curtice evidently agreed to follow up on what appeared to be a rather enticing offer of help in making some improvements and building a small addition. Letters went back and forth between the library and Albany, architects were consulted, local governmental officials met with the Board, and the correspondence became onerous. Mr. Crowell was writing two-page letters attempting to get answers. The architects were concerned about getting paid for their plans. The last letter on file from Albany lists a number of libraries in the New York City vicinity that had received Federal funds, and a slightly longer list of those libraries which had applied.

Whether out of concern for raising additional funds to supplement government money, overall cost of the project, or just plain frustration, no further steps were taken by the Board.

An entirely government-funded project that did reach completion at the end of the year was the new Federal Building at Port Washington, N.Y. otherwise known as the Post Office. Some striking murals, painted by WPA artists, still adorn the walls.

1936–   *Elizabeth Smedley replaces Josephine Smith as Children's*
1937   *Librarian—Port Washington authors published in Fall season—*
         Library again receives top State rating—Miss Curtice's reviews
         popular

The latter half of the 1930s was marked by normal year to year progress in library activities and rewarding recognition from the State of New York for the outstanding accomplishments of the Port Washington Public Library.

In all four rating categories, Book Stock, Circulation, Finance, and Staff and Service, the library achieved a rating of 121.9 percent of the state standard of 100 percent which led Editor Simon to write in the February 7, 1936 *News:*

"This would certainly indicate that the residents of Port Washington are obtaining from the library a measure of service not only in excess of the standard, but far in excess of the normal expectancy from the funds available."

On June 15, 1936, Miss Elizabeth Smedley commenced her career as children's librarian at the Port Washington Library just two weeks after receiving her degree in library science from Columbia.

REMINISCENCES

From an interview with Betty (Smedley) Wood (with occasional help from Moyer Wood):

"My interview with Miss Curtice was in April or early May (1936). The interview, I think, went fairly well. I wanted the job very much. I was a little worried because Miss Curtice said after my interview that she was going into the city and would ride back with me. I was so afraid that I would say something wrong and completely ruin my chance!

"I was very happy when I finally got the job and began work June 15, 1936. And so began my love affair with library work with children which has lasted all my life.

"Miss Curtice was then head librarian. She had been a children's librarian, you would know it to look at her—small and lively, very friendly. A wonderful person to work for.

"Shortly after I started work, a young man came up to the desk where I was on duty and asked, 'Have you seen my sister?' And I, of

Local Work Pictured In Book Written By Tangerman, of Port

"Whittling and Woodcarving" is the title of the new book just written by Elmer J. Tangerman of Port Washington. The book was published by Whittlesey House in New York and went out for sale the week before Christmas. Included in the book are a number of beautiful pictures taken of different examples of woodcarving.

Mr. Tangerman, who has been a resident of Port Washington for many years, is well known in the field of whittling and has been written about in one of this newspaper's columns.

Pictures of work done by Albert Wood and Five Sons and of several pieces done by young Bob Bartlett of Reid Avenue are included in Mr. Tangerman's book which is being prominently displayed at all New York book shops and may be secured at Miss Cramer's Gift Shop in Port Washington.

A special display of some of Mr. Tangerman's work was shown at Macy's in the Arts & Crafts Department during Christmas week.

Tangerman Whittling book

course, said 'What does she look like?' He said, 'Well, she looks just like me only she doesn't have a moustache.' So I had to look at him very carefully. Let Moyer tell you.

Moyer: "Well, I cut Betty's picture out of the paper when it was announced that she would be the new librarian and I had carried it in my wallet for about a week."

Betty: "We were introduced formally a couple of days later through a mutual friend. Soon after that we fell in love, but neither of us was in a position to get married. So we had the brilliant idea that while we were waiting we would design and build a house that we would move into when we did get married.

"The children's room at the library at that time, before the later addition, opened off the main lobby opposite the front door—a lovely, light, airy room with windows on three sides and a small patio outside for summer story hours. In those days the fireplace in the big reading room worked, so we had winter story hours occasionally in front of the fire.

"I was fortunate to inherit from my predecessor, Josephine Smith, a carefully chosen, well-balanced collection of children's books and a tradition of story hours and book clubs.

"Miss Curtice had warned me that the Library Board had a policy of not employing *married women* (customary in many schools and libraries in pre-World War II days), so in 1938 when Moyer and I decided to get married and have a family, that temporarily terminated my library career."

Miss Smedley, Miss Sandy and Miss Curtice comprised the entire professional staff, sharing all the work of the library—circulation desk, shelving books, reference work, opening boxes of new books from Baker & Taylor, opening the door before 9 A.M., changing the dating stamps on pencils, counting circulation—in short, "a good introduction to hands-on library work."

Miss Curtice's columns in the *Port News,* announcing new acquisitions, giving information about children's and young people's programs, and generally promoting the library, were published faithfully, if not weekly, certainly twice a month, throughout the '30s. She was particularly concerned that readers know about Port Washington authors.

It was unusually fortunate that during one publishing season books by four Port Washington authors were published, giving Miss Curtice the opportunity of reviewing them simultaneously. Highlights of those reviews follow:

"Honors this month should go to Port Washington's own authors, for three of the new and popular books at the library are by local men:

Voyaging Down the Thames, by Clyde Eddy, well-known lecturer and author, is a delightful intimate account of a trip down the Thames

from its source, Cricklade to Nore Light where the river meets the
sea.

John J. Floherty's book, *Your Daily Newspaper,* answers all the questions which the average young person might ask about how a newspaper is produced, and the jobs and careers associated with newspaper work.

In *Stars to Windward,* Bruce and Sheridan Fahnestock of Plandome tell of their adventures on a three-year voyage on their schooner, 'Director,' through the Panama Canal, to the South Sea Islands and on to Manila."

Dr. Everett N. Whitcomb,
Vice President, Library Board,
1937–1946.

The State Education Department periodically inspected all libraries to assure that State standards were maintained. The 1937 inspection of the Port Washington Public Library received the following rating:

Book Collection	Good
Income	Sufficient for Current Expenses
Librarians	Competent
Library Hours	12 hours daily
Financial Report	Annually submitted
Library record	Accurate and complete
Classification	Dewey Decimal
Loan & Registration Record	Adequate loan system; Up-to-date Registration
Librarian Certification	3 certificates held
Building and Grounds	Attractive but rapidly outgrowing. Plans for expansion being discussed.

Recommended for further registration. Attractive building,
well-managed. Meets all state requirements.

Nurturing and sustaining children's and young people's interest in and love of reading continued to be a high priority with Miss Curtice. The ambiance of the children's room, displays and posters emphasizing timely subjects, story hours, and continuing acquisition of new books attracted large numbers of young readers throughout the late thirties.

In July, 1937, a Travel Club was organized for boys and girls who were nine years or older and registered borrowers at the library.

All interested were asked to talk with Miss Smedley to get their passports and decide which European countries they would like to visit in their reading. England, France, Holland, Norway, Germany, Russia, Hungary and Sicily were all visited via specially selected books.

John P. Marquand's *The Late George Apley;* R.C. Hutchinson's *Shining Scabbard;* the winner of the All-Nations Prize Novel Competition, *The Street of the Fishing Cat* by John Foldes, the Hungarian entry; Josephine Lawrence's *The Sound of Running Feet; Rich Man, Poor Man* by Janet Ayer Fairbanks; Vera Brittain's *Honourable Estate; Naked to Laughter* by Dorothy McCleary and finally William Saroyan's collection of stories, *Three Times Three* were the subjects of Miss Curtice's reviews in January 1938.

Special events and exhibits, primarily in the Children's Room, were featured throughout each year: A pottery exhibit by children in Flower Hill School in March; a Book Circus in May for the Children's Book Festival—a three-ring circus of favorite books; a Girl's (11 to 14) Library Club to plan "worthwhile programs and some good times" including a ghost party, reading aloud and dramatizing stories. At Christmas in 1938 the Girls' Club built a creche which was displayed in the Children's Room, along with an exhibit of Christmas celebrations in other lands—wooden shoes and St. Nicholas from Holland, Christmas tree of Germany, Yule log of France, Three Kings of Spain, and many others.

1939   *Popular novels in great demand—Books on little theatre and Broadway find eager readers—War in Europe creates demand for background books on Europe*

During 1939 over 100,000 books, pamphlets and pictures were borrowed from the library. Of these Christopher Morley's best seller, *Kitty Foyle* was by far the most popular. According to Miss Curtice, "There are more people, as a matter of fact, waiting for this novel than any other book in the library. Fifty-two people have put their names down for it."

Grapes of Wrath had a waiting list of 36, Oscar Levant's *A Smattering of Ignorance* the same, and as a result of the much publicized movie of the same name, *Gone With The Wind* came in for a second round of popularity. Even *Anthony Adverse,* published a few years earlier, was still in demand.

"Drama and the 'Little Theatre' has always had an important place in Port Washington," wrote Miss Curtice in the spring of 1939. "With the coming of Kenneth Macgowan, one of the leaders in the art of the theatre in America, to speak to the Play Troupe, this interest should be greatly stimulated." Her column continued:

"The Public Library at all times tries to make available to residents of Port Washington books which are related to matters of current appeal. Consequently, at this time, the attention of readers is called to books about the theatre and books of plays which will be found in the library."

Mr. Macgowan's *Continental Stagecraft* and *Footlights Across America* were two books of special interest along with the plays, *Berkeley*

Square and *The Cradle Song,* both at the time on Broadway, and *Trelawney of the Wells*—all on the library's shelves. Miss Curtice concluded:
"Since *Outward Bound* by Sutton Vane has been chosen for the spring production of the Play Troupe, many people will wish to read it. The novel, as well as the play itself, has been ordered."

The storm over Europe was on every front page and in everyone's conversation. A partial list of the books Port Washington was reading in an effort to both understand and keep abreast of the war included: *Europe on the Eve,* Frederick L. Schumann, *Europe in Retreat,* Vera Dean, *Handbook of the War,* John C. deWilde, *The Voice of Destruction,* Hermann Rauschning.

There were also many titles in the library reflecting the point of view of neutrality which was stimulated by a lecture, "Keep America Out of the European Brawl," delivered at the High School in February, 1940, by retired major general, Smedley Butler. In the following week's *Library Listings* column in the *Port News* (Miss Curtice varied the names of her column every year or so), appeared the following statement:

"In order to get an idea of both sides of the question and of all the problems involved, a few books available at the Port Washington Public Library are suggested here as helpful reading:

"Stuart Chase, in *New Western Front,* quotes Thomas Jefferson thus, 'I have ever deemed it fundamental for the United States never to take an active part in the quarrels of Europe.'

Can America Stay Neutral? by Allen W. Dulles and Hamilton Fish Armstrong—the pros and cons of the possibility of the U.S. remaining at peace by means of legislation while the rest of the world is at war."

Other titles in this column (among the best of many fine book reviews by Miss Curtice) were *Neutrality for the United States, America Faces the Next War* and *Union Now.*

Lists of Defense Program Books available at the library offered such titles as *The Fifth Column is Here, Mobilizing Civilian America, A Navy Second to None, Zero Hour, Complete Flying Manual, Aircraft Blueprint Reading,* and *The Army Way* by Philip Wylie.

Aware of the problems created by the great demand for best sellers, more than the usual number of copies were ordered and a duplicate pay collection was established. Books in this collection could be borrowed at a charge of 5 cents per day. This additional service for patrons, started as an experiment, was a big success and was continued over many years.

In 1940 a long-time wish of the Trustees and staff of the library for better cooperation between the public schools and the library was fulfilled. An agreement was reached with the principals of the

At that time...

FDR defeats Wendell Wilkie for presidency

grade schools to include in the regular school curriculum each year (at the third grade level) a class visit to the library.

Another reminiscence about Belleview Avenue Library:

"I was seven or eight years old. You had to be very quiet or those two ladies (Miss Curtice and Miss Sandy) stared at you. I think we were afraid to walk past the desk. Once you got to the children's room, there was a friendly atmosphere.

"Later, in high school, I remember going to the library at night and using the Reading Room because you had a crush on a boy who was there maybe doing homework or something like that. You probably never spoke to each other, but you could look at each other and that was it."

— *Peggy Seaman Aitken*

CURRENT LIBRARY FAVORITES

(According to reports from the public libraries of twenty-six cities *)

FICTION

Author	Title	Points
1. A. J. Cronin,	*The Keys of the Kingdom*	249
2. Marguerite Steen,	*The Sun is My Undoing*	211
3. Mary Ellen Chase,	*Windswept*	175
4. Edna Ferber,	*Saratoga Trunk*	155
5. Louis Bromfield,	*Wild is the River*	102
6. Richard Llewellyn,	*How Green Was My Valley*	87
7. Eric Knight,	*This Above All*	56
8. Frances P. Keyes,	*All That Glitters*	48
9. Ernest Hemingway,	*For Whom the Bell Tolls*	46
10. Henry Bellamann,	*King's Row*	39

NON-FICTION

Author	Title	Points
1. William L. Shirer,	*Berlin Diary*	217
2. John Gunther,	*Inside Latin America*	175
3. Pierre Van Paassen,	*That Day Alone*	134
4. Joseph Edward Davies,	*Mission to Moscow*	115
5. Louis Adamic,	*Two Way Passage*	103
6. Clifton Fadiman,	*Reading I've Liked*	88
7. Jan Valtin,	*Out of the Night*	62
8. Margaret Leech,	*Reveille in Washington*	47
9. Adolph Hitler,	*Mein Kampf*	37
10. Rebecca West,	*Black Lamb and Grey Falcon*	33

COMMENT: The two leading titles on the fiction list remain the same as last month, with the two following, *Windswept* and *Saratoga Trunk* swapping places. *All That Glitters* is new to the fiction list. The three non-fiction leaders also retain top places. First appearances are *Mission to Moscow* and *Black Lamb and Grey Falcon*.

CHILDREN'S BOOKS: First in popularity are: *An American A.B.C.*, Maud and Miska Petersham; *Paddle-to-the-Sea*, Holling C. Holling, *Little Town on the Prairie*, Laura I. Wilder; *Loopy*, Hardie Gramatky; *Defending America*, Creighton Peet.

* Atlanta, Baltimore, Birmingham, Boston, Brooklyn, Buffalo, Cleveland, Dallas, Denver, Des Moines, Detroit, Indianapolis, Kansas City (Mo.), Los Angeles, Louisville, Memphis, Minneapolis, New Orleans, New York City, Newark, Pittsburgh, Portland, Salt Lake City, San Francisco, Seattle, Springfield (Mass), and Toronto.

Wilson Library Bulletin, *March, 1942, current titles most requested at libraries across the country.*

CHAPTER X

Fiftieth Anniversary 1942

Pearl Harbor brought drastic changes to Port Washington similar to the disruptions of every day life in every other community. Air raid wardens were appointed, blackouts were mandated, and all townspeople joined in the nationwide dedication to Civilian Defense.

"If Miss 'Mina' Mitchell, prime mover and first librarian, were here today, she would be surprised but, one feels sure, not at all dismayed to see the 1942 staff of the library learning to put out incendiary bombs."

Thus began a January 9, 1942, *Port News* article by Ruth Bornn, a Port Washington writer whose help in publicizing the Fiftieth Anniversary of the library was truly appreciated. Two weeks later just prior to the week-long celebration at the library, Miss Bornn's next article, one full page including photos of the three libraries which preceded the Belleview Avenue site, carried a banner headline plus two-column subheads:

PORT WASHINGTON LIBRARY
CELEBRATES 50TH ANNIVERSARY ON JANUARY 27

Program, Exhibits Continue All Week; Reception Jan. 31

Founders, Still Living, Will be Honored; Organization
Created in 1892 When Population Here Was 800; Historic
Displays In Building A Feature

Line cut from The Library Journal, *April 1, 1942.*

The Reading Room was handsomely decorated for the anniversary. The then president of the library Board of Trustees, Cedric R. Crowell, wrote in a Fiftieth Anniversary article which appeared in the April, 1942, issue of *The Library Journal:*

"Again 'Friends of the Library' (!) lent a hand. Sigurd Hartell, a New York decorator and Port Washington resident, and Charles Gulbrandson, local artist, converted flat-topped tables into distinctive display spaces. Display steps were placed on table tops, and beaverboard background uprights were painted a soft terra cotta with design and lettering in a light gray to match the walls."

One exhibit captioned, "Do You Remember?," consisted of pictures, clippings, minutes of early meetings, names of the founders, a watercolor of Miss Mitchell's family home on Shore Road at Pleas-

Half-Century Scoreboard

The most popular and the "most influential" books of the past 50 years were collected and displayed by an enterprising Long Island library last week. To celebrate its 50th anniversary, the Public Library of Port Washington chose the popular books from the best available sales figures; and asked a group of "informed people" to say what books "have most profoundly affected the thoughts and actions of mankind" since 1892. On the jury were Charles A. Beard, Henry Seidel Canby, John Dewey, Jerome Frank, Henry Hazlitt, John Kieran, Walter Lippmann, Somerset Maugham, Christopher Morley, William Lyon Phelps, Norman Thomas, Carl Van Doren. Their first ten choices, in order of recommendations received:

1) & 2) Hitler's *Mein Kampf* and Freud's *Interpretation of Dreams* (tied). 3) William James's *Varieties of Religious Experience*. 4) A. T. Mahan's *Influence of Sea Power upon History*. 5) Einstein's *Relativity; the Special and the General Theory*. 6) Shaw's *Man and Superman*. 7) Spengler's *The Decline of the West*. 8) William Graham Sumner's *Folkways*. 9) & 10) Veblen's *Theory of Business Enterprise* and *Theory of the Leisure Class*.

Next came *The Education of Henry Adams* and John Dewey's *Democracy and Education*. Henry James's *Golden Bowl* edged out his brother's *Principles of Psychology* for 13th place, and Lenin's *Imperialism; the State and Revolution* nosed out his master Marx's *Das Kapital*. Also rans: Charles Beard's *Economic Interpretation of the Constitution of the U.S.*; Bergson's *Creative Evolution*; Frazer's *Golden Bough*; W. H. Hudson's *Far Away and Long Ago*; William James's *Moral Equivalent of War*; Lewis' *Babbitt*; Parrington's *Main Currents in American Thought*; Tolstoy's *What Is Art?*

Henry Hazlitt was the only juryman to name Joyce's *Ulysses*. John Kieran, who appeared to miss the point, named as "books that I prize most" the works of Masefield, W. H. Hudson, Rostand.

(continued opposite)

ant Avenue, and other (historical material). The "Best Sellers" of the last fifty years were assembled on another display table in groups of six or eight with corresponding cards on which the titles were listed in the chronological order of publication.*

Through the generosity of the Grolier Club of New York the Library was able to exhibit examples of beautiful typography and book design of the period.

Another exhibit which attracted much attention in the Reading Room was a collection of books assembled as the result of replies from twenty distinguished people to a letter written by the trustees, asking their opinion as to what books published in the last fifty years have most profoundly affected the thoughts and actions of mankind.

In the children's room a display headed "Fifty Years of Children's Books" included "Early Books of Information Which Have Survived"; "Fifty Years of Children's Book Illustration"; "Manners Then and Now"; and "Newberry Medal Books." More than 100 children attended the Saturday morning, January 31, children's story hour when the then famous Marjorie Flack, popular author and illustrator, delighted her audience with stories and sketches.

That same afternoon a tea and reception was held in the Reading Room in honor of the founders and former trustees, and in spite of the cold and snowy weather, two of the four living founders arrived as well as past and present trustees.

During the year of the Fiftieth Anniversary the members of the Board of Trustees included:

Cedric R. Crowell, *President*
Dr. Everett N. Whitcomb, *Vice President*
John C. Crawley, *Secretary*
Mrs. Sigurd N. Hartell, *Treasurer*
Mrs. A. Valentine Fraser (who had served as a *Trustee* also in 1903!)

At the end of January Miss Marion Lathrop Simmons, who replaced Betty Wood as children's librarian in 1938, resigned to take a position in Rochester, N.Y. The railroad was still a potent factor in transportation because the *Port News* noted:

"The Empire State Express will carry the librarian to her new destination Sunday morning and all her friends join in wishing her farewell and good luck."

Townspeople brought to the library 4,000 books for servicemen and women in the Victory Book Campaign, although the quota set by the county for Port Washington was just 1,400 volumes. Miss

*There were seven lists, each of which appears in the appropriate years of this book.

Curtice augmented the Civilian Defense efforts which were of vital importance to everyone. One notice in the newspaper exhorted everyone: "Be Informed! Read these books and pamphlets which may be borrowed from the Port Washington Public Library":

CIVILIAN DEFENSE BOOKS

This Is Your War, M. W. Child
Civilians Must Fight, F.R. Daniell
Bomber's Moon, Negley Farson
Bombs and Bombing, Willy Ley
Air Raid Safety Manual, Burr Leyson
Aircraft Spotter, Lester Ott
Civil Air Defense, A.M. Prentiss
Ernie Pyle in England, E.T. Pyle
Digging For Mrs. Miller, John Strachey
Air Raid Defense (Civilian), Curt Wachtel

PAMPHLETS

Blackouts, War Dept. Office of Civilian Defense
Handbook for Air Raid Wardens, (same)
Handling Animals in War Emergencies, American Red Star Animal Relief

The most popular books of the half-century, by estimated U.S. trade sales:
▶ In a class by itself at 8,000,000 copies: C. M. Sheldon's *In His Steps.**
▶ Around 2,000,000: *Gone With the Wind, Anthony Adverse* and Gene Stratton Porter's *Freckles.*
▶Around 1,500,000: Mrs. Porter's *Girl of the Limberlost* and *Laddie*; John Fox Jr.'s *Trail of the Lonesome Pine*; Owen Wister's *The Virginian*; Harold Bell Wright's *The Winning of Barbara Worth*; Jack London's *Call of the Wild*; J. L. Hurlbut's *Story of the Bible*; Wells's *Outline of History.*
▶ Around 1,000,000: Stevenson's *Treasure Island*; Du Maurier's *Trilby*; E. N. Westcott's *David Harum*; John Fox Jr.'s *The Little Shepherd of Kingdom Come*; Florence Barclay's *The Rosary*; *Rebecca of Sunnybrook Farm*; *Pollyanna*; *The Calling of Dan Matthews*; E. M. Hull's *The Sheik*; *America's Part in the World War,* by R. J. Beamish and F. A. March, which was published in 1919.
* A religious novel of the '90s.

Time Magazine, February 9, 1942, picked up the story of the "most influential" book list at Port Washington Public Library.

In November, 1942, the library and the schools cooperated in celebrating America's first wartime Book Week. The theme, appropriately, was *Forward With Books.*

The following month the trustees and librarians welcomed the good news, spread across the *Port News* front page, that the library once again had been honored by the University of the State of New York for outstanding performance in 1941. A rating of 115.6 percent was achieved, "appreciably higher than the standard set by the state for libraries in communities of comparable size."

YOUR LIBRARY GROWS
1892 TO 1942

1892:		*1942:*
800	Population	13,823
430	Books	19,504
37	Borrowers	5,939
855	Circulation	94,143
$25.20	Budget	$12,900

CHAPTER XI

The Forties

1943– *Books for servicemen urgently needed—Record low budget—*
1944 *Memorial fund for garden books established—Cedric Crowell resigns as Board President, writes first library policy statement*

Responding to an urgent request from the Army and Navy, the American Library Association, along with the American Red Cross and the U.S.O., together sponsored a Victory Book Campaign for men in the Armed Services. Miss Curtice sent out an appeal to the town for books in *good condition* published since 1930. (Textbooks since 1935)

The previous year Port Washington contributed 8,000 volumes, of which 4,800 were suitable for the Armed Services. "Let's do as well this year," Miss Curtice requested, "and make sure the men are supplied with books they will find enjoyable and useful."

One of the first memorial funds to be established at the library came in the spring, the gift of Dr. S.A. Brown of Harbor Acres. The Charlotte Cowdrey Brown Memorial Fund honored a real "hands-in-the-dirt gardener" who was a moving force in the Port Washington Garden Club and a former president of the State Federation. Garden books of all types were to be purchased from the Fund proceeds.

For three months the library had opened at noon due to oil rationing, but by some fortunate circumstance in May, regular hours (9 AM to 9 PM) went back into effect. That same month Vice President John Crawley presented an $11,000 library budget which set some kind of record—it was $500 less than the previous year's budget and understandably passed with ease.

The "budget honeymoon" did not last long, however. In April, 1944, Crawley was back before the voters to explain an increase of $1,400 for 1944–45—mostly for periodicals and books, but payroll also accounted for much of the total.

Children's librarians moved in and out of that position during the early 1940s. Miss Helen S. Canfield took over the position in the spring of 1944. By September she had resigned and Miss Mimi Trippe was hired. In March of 1945, Miss Trippe reported that she had been offered another job at a better salary, but the Board being reluctant to lose her upped her salary and in May paid her a bonus. During the summer while she took courses in library science at

Columbia, Mrs. Alan Wile, a teacher at Manhasset Bay School, took over the summer Saturday morning Story Hour for six weeks. Thereafter Miss Trippe remained as a very popular librarian with young people until she departed in September 1948.

The letter of resignation in November, 1944, of Cedric R. Crowell, who had served on the Library Board since 1926 when he was appointed to fill out the term of Karl Kirchwey, initially brought great consternation. Crowell proposed at the same time that a statement of current policy of the Trustees of the Port Washington Public Library should be prepared. As most frequently happens in such proposals, the *proposer* ended up, with Miss Curtice's collaboration, writing the document which was unanimously adopted by the Board and has become the foundation on which all later policy statements have been based.

In essence, the principles embraced the belief that the library must be "an open forum where free speech is nurtured"...where "no censorship by any political, religious, or racial minority" is tolerated, and "where services must be free without favoritism or discrimination."

The *Port News* reported at length the contributions Cedric Crowell had made:
"In 1926 the present library had just been opened. The expansion of library activity in Port Washington was beginning and Mr. Crowell brought to that work his wide experience as publisher, bookseller and business executive, together with his intense interest in the successful operation of a community free library...the outstanding quality of the Port Washington Public Library is largely attributable to the loyal guidance that Mr. Crowell has given to its policies during the 18 years of his active trusteeship."

His fellow Trustees accorded Crowell Honorary Membership on the Board which would turn out to have been a particularly astute decision.

Linus E. Kittredge was appointed to replace Cedric Crowell, and Mrs. Hartell's tenure was extended by the voters for another five years.

1945   *Expansion of library contemplated—consultant hired—report favors new site for new library—analysis of consultant's report by local resident and "friend"*

Although far from over, World War II was winding down: V.E. Day ended war in Europe, United Nations Charter signed in June, Japan surrendered on August 14.

Already Miss Curtice was anticipating the need for expansion of the Belleview Avenue Library. The Reading Room was crowded, the Children's Room had long since run out of available space for

The book stacks in the basement of the Belleview Avenue Library had reached capacity by 1945—just one of the reasons expansion was needed.

books *and* children, and the stacks in the basement were reaching capacity.

In June, 1945, she was authorized to contact the Director of Library Services in Albany for help in finding a library consultant. She was put in touch with Mr. Joseph L. Wheeler who came to Port Washington with Albany's highest praise, "if you can get him, you could do no better." His assignment was to examine the blueprints submitted in 1935 for expansion and make recommendations for 1945 and the future.

Wheeler lived up to his advance billing, submitting a 13-page report after just two days of concentrated study of the library's annual reports, assessment of the population ("it is clear that Port Washington is a community of far above average reading habits"), anticipated post-war population growth (in 1945, the population was 12,729), and detailed recommendations for enlarging the building.

Unfortunately Wheeler was unimpressed by the location of the library on Belleview Avenue and so indicated to the Trustees by writing almost four pages at the outset of his report—a few excerpts below:

"...the location of this library building is exceedingly poor... 300 feet from Main Street, on a side street, on a sloping lot...one has to climb fourteen steps to the front door...the amount and vitality of the reference work of the library would be greatly increased and improved in a suitable location, on the main pedestrian traffic stream. A library is not something remote, books are not something to be approached with a "Sunday clothes" attitude: they are agents for bringing highly valuable information, new viewpoints, new purposes and ambitions, into the life of the community."

In the balance of Wheeler's report he outlined a modest program of improvements "if nothing can be done now about a new site, and if a new building is to be secured within eight or ten years." His recommendations included doubling the book stack wing on the main floor and basement using *wood* to cut costs by 1/3 to 1/2, creating additional space for adults, additional shelving, recessed space for catalog and vertical files, and more work room space.

Initial reaction to Wheeler's Report is not recorded in the minutes of Board meetings. However, the Trustees asked Mr. Ray Finlay to analyze the Report from the standpoint of "a local resident and friend of the library" and a public relations expert. His comments:

"I for one like the present library location. Even if there were funds available for constructing a new streamlined library on Main Street, I would question the wisdom of sacrificing the qualitative advantages of a quiet, peaceful side street environment in favor of the quantitative advantage of those few people who were not sufficiently interested to walk a half block out of their way and climb fourteen steps."

Ray Finlay then suggested that Wheeler's recommendations be implemented by getting building estimates and "if it is found either impossible to obtain building material (because of continuing postwar shortages), or that the expense is prohibitive...first consideration be given to a stack room on the first floor."

Further discussion about library alterations took place mid-summer when Mr. Wheeler addressed the Board. The September minutes make clear that "Mr. Wheeler emphasized (again) his view that the library should be housed in a new building in a more nearly central location."

1946   *Old library lot on Main Street up for sale—logical purchaser St. Stephen's Church—21 month project*

At the September, 1945, meeting consideration was given to the sale of the library lot on Main Street, and Mrs. Hartell offered to inquire of Mr. Hollenback, one of the wardens of St. Stephen's Church, whether the church would be interested in buying the lot (next to church property). Subsequent Board meeting minutes make brief references to the possible sale, but nothing of consequence transpired until the following spring.

In June 1946 at the Board meeting members again brought up the land sale, making the suggestion that "the property should be disposed of by sale to the town if possible and that the attractiveness of the street would be lessened if the property were used for a gas station, but the library should not continue to maintain the property for park purposes."

Cedric Crowell (who had not left town "indefinitely" as he had anticipated) returned to the Board replacing the recently retired Dr. Whitcomb. Crowell initiated further discussions with Dr. Woon, Rector of St. Stephen's, "on the possibility of selling to the Episcopal Church."

From the minutes of September 10, 1946:
"Board members agreed on the inadvisability of selling the property to anyone whose use of it would substantially change the appearance or be detrimental to that section of Main Street. With that in mind, Mr. Crowell was asked to contact the Vestry of the church and notify them that the Library will have to offer the property for sale unless the Church will make an offer which can be brought before a town meeting for approval."

In December Mr. Crowell "read letters from Mr. Enscoe and Mr. West indicating that members of St. Stephen's Church are not interested in acquiring our Main Street property." The Board agreed to put it into the hands of an agent and to ask permission from the taxpayers to sell at the next School District meeting.

A public notice appeared in local papers during February, 1947, offering the Main Street property for sale ($750), subject to the approval of taxpayers at the Annual School District Meeting. Within a few weeks Mr. Crowell reported that St. Stephen's Church had offered $500 for the property. The April 15th meeting notes reveal another wrinkle in the Board's efforts to make the property pay:
"Although the Trustees would be glad to see the Library free from the expense of maintaining this property, it was felt that this was an extremely low price and Mr. Crowell was authorized to find out if they would be willing to lease the property for $30 per year, the lease terminable on ninety days' notice."

Not without some glee, one can surmise, Cedric Crowell announced to his fellow Board members on May 13 that St. Stephen's had offered $750 for the lot. Everything thereafter fell into place with ease: Library Board members agreed, the proposition as placed before the voters passed without dissent, and on December 9 Mr. Crawley turned over to Miss Curtice a check for $750 to deposit in the Port Washington Bank and Trust Company.

At the annual budget meeting, Mrs. Robert Kelley was elected to take the place of Mrs. Fraser and in June the Trustees elected John C. Crawley President.

1948   *Budgets increase, voters undismayed—Special joint meeting of
       Library Board and School Board*

At that time...

**Harry Truman elected 33rd
President**

During the 1940s library budgets increased yearly as did the
school budget and most other civic operations: 1945 ($15,790),
1946 ($18,065), 1947 ($22,830), 1948 ($24,750), 1949 ($25,900). It
is clear that Port Washington voters strongly supported the library
over the years; rarely was the "no" vote more than 30% of the total
votes cast.

The Library Board voted $300 to renovate the Staff Room in the
basement "to provide a more pleasant place for staff to retire to and
that some accommodations to make lunch and tea be provided."

At their invitation the entire Library Board met with members of
the School Board in December:
"The purpose of the meeting was to discuss the proposed new
school buildings and the possibility of the Library occupying a
building on the site of the school property.
"*School Board's position:* Library would have better chance of getting
new building if included in community plan...Building would be
heated by school plant and serviced by school custodians...School
would eliminate High School Library...Special rooms for student
use...School would cooperate in supervising students.

*John C. Crawley, Library Board Member for
15 years, with his wife, Ellen, and
daughters, Janet and Adelaid.*

"*Library's position:* Might lose identity as Public Library…Parking already difficult would be worse at community center…perhaps building on nearby site, e.g. at Port Washington Boulevard and a new street, but School Board insisted building must be on school grounds, attached or connected to High School buildings."

One week later at their regular Library Board meeting, Miss Curtice reported that Miss Vetter from the State Library would be in Port to look over property and discuss advantages and disadvantages of the proposal. This led to a general discussion of library problems and the possibility of enlarging the present building.

Miss Vetter met with Miss Curtice as planned and early in January, 1949, she wrote that she was against such a plan. In summary: "People did not generally like to go to the school to get books—
Staff found administrative problems increased—
It is doubtful that the school would be allowed to eliminate the High School Library—
Establishing a Friends of the Library Association to stimulate interest in a new library should be considered. (!)"

1949   *Music appreciation for children—Forum on children's reading—*
        Budget held to $1,000 increase—Crawley re-elected

With the idea of guiding young music lovers in the right direction, Miss Curtice announced that the library's record collection "now ranges from the lighter works of Handel and Haydn to nursery rhymes, sea songs and marches." Saturday morning programs were scheduled for children 6 to 12 who were also invited to bring their own favorite records to be played.

Also in February a forum on children's reading tastes and how to shape them attracted a large audience which heard from teachers in elementary, junior and senior high school, and from Miss Curtice and Mr. Barlow of the Education Association.

A controversial proposition on the school budget for a reserve fund for recreational facilities was voted down and the budget itself was passed by a mere 46 votes in May, 1949, while the library budget sailed through by 255 to 125 votes. Longtime Board member, John Crawley, was re-elected.

At the May Board meeting the familiar topic of "Where do we find a children's librarian?" came up once again. Miss Trippe had resigned in August of the previous year and no qualified candidates had appeared. The frustrations of the librarians are obvious in these notes from the May, 1949, minutes:
"Miss Curtice reported that, as a result of her inquiries at Adelphi and Hofstra, she had received several applications for the position of Children's Librarian, and felt that two of the applicants would be acceptable. Neither one has had library training but intends to study Library Science while working. Miss Curtice thought that if

one of these girls is selected a schedule could be worked out to enable her to do this and suggested that the Library give her time for at least part of the studies. Inasmuch as we have been unable for a year to secure a Children's Librarian and as none of the library schools holds out any hope from this year's graduates the Trustees agreed that this might be the Library's solution to its present difficulties."

Acting on this agreement with the Board, Miss Curtice hired Miss Hymes to start work on July 1, giving her half of Friday morning and her free day to attend Columbia. By October 11, to everyone's regret, Miss Hymes had taken off for greener pastures and was replaced on a part time basis by Mrs. Barlow who lived in town.

Once again "to find a children's librarian": Miss Jean Stooksberry arrived on the scene in December and "made a very favorable impression (on Miss Curtice and Mr. Kittredge), which together with her past records and references influenced the Board to offer her the position," to commence work as soon as possible. Miss Stooksberry made an equally great impression on the users of the library, and remained in Port Washington for many years.

Cow Neck/Port Washington has occasionally been thought of as isolated—a peninsula thrust out into Long Island Sound away from the mainstream. Geographically isolated, perhaps, but never provincial. It has been said that a more cosmopolitan community does not exist on the North Shore.

When World War II ended and a better world was in everyone's thoughts, interest in the United Nations reached a peak here. The library in cooperation with the League of Women Voters organized a display of UN pamphlets, clippings, books, and copies of the UN Charter which appear to have been eagerly consumed and replaced often. When the United Nations Association came into being Port Washington's North Shore Chapter was one of the first.

In a community where sailing has always been the leading sport, experienced sailors and novices alike found the collection of sailing books extensive and useful. Along with nautical books were the equally sought-after sports fans' "armchair books." One of the most popular authors was "Doc" Ehre, Port Washington high school English teacher, who collaborated with Irving T. Marsh of the Herald Tribune on *The Best Sports Stories of 1949*.

Another former resident of this town, Stanley Woodward, wrote *Adventures in Marine Painting* which was equally in demand by artists and sailors.

CHAPTER XII

The Fifties

1950 *Special book plates distinguish books of Memorial Collections— Miss Stooksberry continues children's story hours—Nassau Library Association begins long trek toward becoming service organization (NLS)—Special Collections featured—Censorship*

By 1950 three active memorial collections attracted readers who were interested in the fields of cybernetics (Graham L. Montgomery), sailing (William T. Haskell, former Library Trustee), and gardening (Charlotte Cowdrey Brown) whose collection grew steadily from interest earned on the original grant. Each collection was shelved according to its classification and designated by a unique book plate.

Booklists from library users were encouraged and published in the *Port News*. One in particular came from Robert H. Ball, whose home was across Locust Avenue from the present library and who left his vast personal book collection to the Public Library. He included in his recommendations such divergent titles as Tom Lea's *The Brave Bulls*, Jane Austen's *Emma*, *The Warden* by Anthony Trollop, Samuel Pepys' *Diary* and *Hamlet, Revenge,* by Michael Innes.

Mrs. Malcolm Vendig, Mrs. Arthur Utz and Mrs. Gayle Talbot also responded with their own lists with titles which Miss Curtice put on the shelves whenever possible.

On the same ballot with the Library Budget of $25,000 (up only $200. from 1949) was a referendum for the Port Washington Board of Education to construct neighborhood schools in Manhasset Bay Estates, Manorhaven, and New Salem for a total cost of $325,000. In addition new administrative offices and a bus garage for $100,000 were on the ballot. Voters gave the nod to all school projects and the library budget. Work commenced the same summer on the new high school (to be named after Paul D. Schreiber, former Principal and Superintendent, as well as Library Board Member) which the voters had approved the previous February.

Plans were under discussion to expand the Nassau County Library Association (NCLA) into a service organization. From January, 1950, until December, 1960, every year or so the pros and cons of organizing and joining came in for further debate. In 1952 two members of the NCLA Committee on State Aid to Libraries delivered to the Board a contract for discussion which appears to have gotten nowhere. The Port Washington Board voted against adoption of the plan and continued their opposition for the next eight years. On November 9, 1960, two years after Edward de Sciora became Director of the library, the Port Washington Library Board finally joined Nassau Library System.

The *Port Washington News* almost weekly kept the town up-to-date on events at the library as well as news about new books and collections, due in large part to publicity writer Dorothy Hagenbuch's constant flow of library news releases. Miss Stooksberry's children's story hours continued their great success quite possibly as a result of her frequent visits to Main Street, Sands Point and Flower Hill Schools.

Two new memorial collections were donated during 1951:

The Martha Mott (Mrs. A. Valentine) Fraser Memorial Collection, established in May, 1951, included travel, gardening, Long Island history and American history volumes. (At the time of her death Mrs. Fraser lived in the Old House, Mott's Point; she also had served as a Library Board member in earlier years.)

The Leonard C. Ball Memorial Collection, new children's books received through donations from friends and members of the Washington Bureau of the New York Herald Tribune.

The League of Women Voters, in their widely distributed pamphlet, *This Is Port Washington,* also publicized the library with a full page article on its history.

Library policy has always required that complaints from library users concerning allegedly offensive books must be handled promptly, with tact and firmness. Minutes of the October, 1951 Board meeting and subsequent communication provide a good example:

"Miss Curtice reported that a member of the Library had indicated that a book entitled *The Big Sea,* by Langston Hughes, published by Alfred A. Knopf, 1940, is highly objectionable and should be removed from the Library shelves. Miss Curtice was asked to advise her that it would facilitate the Boards' consideration if she would put her objections into writing."

On November 26 Mr. Crawley, President of the Board, replied to Miss Curtice (following page).

There followed just a short time later Cedric Crowell's second letter of resignation (following page). He was leaving town for his retirement home in Roxbury, Connecticut, and took the opportunity to reinforce the convictions expressed in John Crawley's letter the previous month.

Dear Miss Curtice:

Having just finished reading Langstron Hughes'
The Great Sea (Knopf, 1940), I sympathize with any other reader
who has found it immoral and vulgar.

Comparisons are unavoidable, however, and I am
obliged to say that on the whole there is no more immorality and
somewhat less shocking vulgarity in this book than may be found
in most of the best selling novels put out during the decade since
this book was published. It is possible, of course, that I missed
something in this book that a more alert reader has found particularly objectionable, but unless I have done so it seems to me that
we have no substantial reason for knocking out this book so long
as public taste requires us to keep many other books that seem to
me much more offensive.

In short I simply do not know how a rule can be
formulated under which we can fairly exclude this particular book
without excluding also scores of books that have much greater
popularity and which the ordinary canons of public library practice
require us to put in stock.

Sincerely yours,

Letter from John Crawley, Board member to Miss Helen Curtice, Librarian.

Dear Kit,

Due to my imminent departure from Port Washington, I herewith submit my resignation from the Board of
Trustees of the Port Washington Public Library. When I
was a candidate for Board membership last spring, we had
not sold our home here, and there seemed reasonable prospect that we should continue residence in Port Washington
for several years.

It has been a great pleasure to serve on the
Board for about twenty-five years and to have had this
long association in its growth under the very able administration of Miss Helen Curtice as librarian.

Naturally I hope that the Board and the community
will see to it that the Library continues to be "free",
not only in respect to the circulation of books to the
residents of the community without charge - except for
taxes - but of equal importance, in respect to free
speech and free press within the limits of the federal
and state laws.

I have a firm conviction that the most effective
antidote for any alien ideology is a free press in which
a wide variety of ideas is expressed and given a public
hearing in communication media, including those available
in the Port Washington Public Library. I have a sure faith
in our form of government, subject as it is to adaptation
to changing conditions as they develop - a faith sufficiently sure so that there is no necessity to abandon freedom,
without which "security" is a hollow drum.

So long as the Library does remain free in the
large sense, there is more likely to be tolerance of others
and their opinions, even when they are at variance with our
own. If the Port Washington Public Library can stand in the
van of tolerance of every honest point of view - except
intolerance - the Library will serve the community well.

Sincerely yours,

Cedric R. Crowell

Letter from Cedric R. Crowell to Linus Kittredge, President of the Library Board.

1952   *Classical recordings for home use—Gardening and other hobbies—*
        Marie Dunnells replaces Mrs. Kelley on Board—Library expansion
        once again

At that time...

**Dwight D. Eisenhower resigns
Supreme Command in Europe;
elected 34th President**

An announcement in "Found This Week at Your Library," the
name of the *Port News* weekly column, brought many music lovers
to the library seeking some of the new Long Playing classical recordings recently acquired: operas, symphonies, piano music, light
classics and vocal music.

The Port Washington Garden Club and the Port Washington
Public Library have maintained a long friendship from two points
of view: the library's shelves have been stocked with the best and
newest of garden books, and the garden club at Christmas time and
throughout the year has supplied bouquets and arrangements to
decorate the library, a welcome tradition that has brought pleasure
to the staff and patrons throughout the years.

"Hobbyists—from birdwatchers to photographers and from bee-
keepers to potters—can find the book or other materials to advance
them in their chosen interest" at the library was the oft-repeated
enticement in the newspaper, not to forget square dancing, water-
coloring, and breeding tropical fish.

In addition to appointing Mrs. Clifford (Marie) Dunnells to the
Library Board to replace Mrs. Robert Kelley, a search was on to find
a clearly qualified candidate to fill out Cedric Crowell's unexpired
term. After John Crawley (always a busy trustee) interviewed candidates, a special meeting was held in the spring at which a unanimous vote brought to the board a new member who would serve
with distinction for the following nineteen years: Mr. Thomas W.
Lapham.

A new study of library expansion was entered upon which included visits by members of the board to libraries in Hempstead,
Scarsdale and White Plains. By November the search for an architectural firm was completed with the appointment of Lorimer and
Rose who were retained to present a plan for expanding the present
building *and* a tentative plan for a new library.

1953   *Population growth exceeding predictions—Construction Program*
        for Library pondered by Board—Budget increase held to $300—
        Growth in use of library

The postwar boom in housing in Port Washington, starting with
the first garden apartment, Dolphin Green in 1949, continued una-
bated for many years: areas south of Revere Road with names such
as North Salem and South Salem grew rapidly as did Morewood
Oaks and Manhasset Bay Estates, attracting young families most of
whose breadwinners commuted to New York.

In the four year period from 1948 to 1952, the population grew from 15,831 to 19,851, and many of the new residents would help swell the ranks in the schools and the library.

At the library the younger generation accounted for the largest increase in circulation in 1952, 28% more books were borrowed from the children's room than the year before. Miss Curtice reported that only lack of space kept the total collection at 27,530 volumes. An increase in discarding books for which there were few demands was the only solution.

The Annual State Grant, fines, invested funds and a $2,000 surplus from 1952–53 placed the Library Board in the happy position of increasing the budget by only $300.

Although Mr. Kittredge met with the architects to facilitate plans for expansion, it was decided to delay until the fall any district-wide meeting. Thoughtful consideration was needed to plan well for the future especially since the proposal presented by Lorimer and Rose for construction of an addition recognized the consequences of the rapid growth of the town: from 1940 to 1952, over 47%.

A welcome innovation in library-sponsored programs was the Great Books Course suggested by Mr. and Mrs. Leo Forman. Not only did the Board react favorably, a motion was passed to purchase two sets of the books required by the course.

The cooperation between the library and the *Port News,* established in the early part of the century, must be credited with much of the success of attracting readers month after month. In well over 60% of the newspapers studied there were articles about the library—reviews and lists of new books, programs for children, art exhibits, building projects and news *about* the librarians who made it all happen.

Within the library itself the staff worked hard to make it a pleasant place to be and easy to use. An article in the *Port News* announced a new public relations endeavor:

"POSTERS TO TELL OF SERVICES AT PORT'S LIBRARY
HOW WELL ARE YOU ACQUAINTED WITH YOUR LIBRARY?"

"To answer this and, at the same time, give a clear picture of the many services offered, the Port Washington Public Library is presenting a series of posters designed by Mrs. Roland L. Loiseaux and Mrs. Edwin Bostick, the first of which may be seen on the bulletin board just inside the main entrance.

"Here is shown a floor plan of the library to aid visitors in locating reference books, and in using the card catalog, with their indexing by authors, titles and subjects, in both the adult and children' sections. Included in the "heart" of the library is the circulation desk where staff members are always on duty to help readers. This first poster also shows how books that are not readily available may be reserved."

Then followed month by month a series of posters which guided readers to specialized subjects such as theatre, humor, essays, history, the picture file in the Reading Room with over 30,000 items—all designed to help visitors get better acquainted with the library's many facilities.

1954   *School Board gets first view of Library expansion plans—Open House for residents to stress needs—Voters approve expansion*

President Kittredge and other members of the Library Board met with the School Board in March to show plans and discuss the proposed expansion. He explained that the library board had considered the possibility of an entirely new building, "but decided that, in view of heavy costs involved, it would be more feasible to enlarge the present building to meet the immediate need for more space."

Public announcement of the proposition along with a detailed floor plan was made in early April and later that month residents of the community were invited to an open house at the library. Miss Curtice, Trustees and the architects hosted the event "so that voters may become better acquainted with their library, and also see the need for larger quarters than the present building offers."

Following approval by the voters in May, Lorimer and Rose were authorized to go ahead with final plans. Pollock and Wysong were appointed general contractors and commenced work in September. Disruption of regular activity in the library was kept to a minimum: some children's books found a temporary home in the Reading Room, and Miss Stooksberry, in a small basement room with no chairs or tables, "made do" with books for older readers.

The books of Port Washington authors—then and now—have always received special attention at the library. In 1954 there were three:

Know Your State, Mrs. Ruth Bornn, Editor, and Mrs. Robert Fulton, Illustrator, published by the League of Women Voters of New York.

The Long Road of Father Serra, by Theodore Maynard, "the inspiring story of the founding father of modern California and its missions."

Faith in Fusion, by Charles Belous, about the formation of the political fusion movement in New York City in the 1930s.

1955   *Library reopens after closing for building construction—Mrs. Harold (LuEsther) Mertz elected to Board—Wysong and Merriman collections praised*

After six months of activity on both levels of the library and a month's closing, the library reopened on March 28, 1955, to an enthusiastic readership. On March 5th, closing day, over 1,000 books had been checked out and about the same number returned four weeks later.

On June 18th the Trustees and Miss Curtice hosted an official Open House for all residents of the area. Tours of the new, roomier building were conducted by the staff and Trustees, one of whom, LuEsther Mertz, had been elected to the Board in May.

The Library Board, the Play Troupe and a multitude of friends in Port Washington learned with great sadness of Cedric Crowell's death in Roxbury, Connecticut, late in June. He had demanded the best from those he worked with in business, in the library and in the Play Troupe, at the same time setting and reaching the highest goals for himself.

The new Adult Study Room was of particular interest because of the Long Island Historical Collection, housed in a special cabinet designed and built for the library by Albert Wood and Five Sons of Port Washington. Charles N. Wysong's collection of books, documents, deeds and other papers handed down through his family from the days when Cow Neck was part of Queens County, was the first major gift to the new room and is still referred to by researchers and historians today.

Trustees of the Port Washington Public Library, June 18, 1955, at the Open House for the recently completed expansion: front row, l. to r., Marie Dunnells, Helen Curtis, Head Librarian, LuEsther Mertz (elected in May); back row, l. to r., Thomas Lapham, Linus Kittredge, Grace Hartell, John Crawley, Herbert Rose, District Treasurer.

Open House, June 18, 1956, Linus Kittredge, President of Library Board showing visitors, Mrs. Hungerford and Miss E. Louise Hungerford, relatives of Wilhelmina Mitchell, the treasures in the Long Island Collection.

In writing her famous book, "Tales of Sint Sink," Miss Charlotte E. Merriman, former principal of the Main Street School, compiled six notebooks covering the Indian days, the Revolutionary Period, the nineteenth century and up to 1918, which were made part of the new collection.*

1956–   *Cedric R. Crowell Memorial Fund established—Port authors*
1957   *continue flow of new books—Censorship—Increasing use of library—Chamber music scores added—Betty Wood rehired after 19 years—Marie Dunnells reelected—Major reference books acquired*

The *Port News* carried the story of a new book fund in memory of Cedric Crowell:

"A memorial to the late Cedric R. Crowell, one of the founders of the Play Troupe of Port Washington and for many years President of the Board of Trustees of the Library, has been established through the gifts of Play Troupe members and friends of Mr. Crowell, it was announced at the March meeting of the Play Troupe by Richard D. Whittemore, President.

"Mr. and Mrs. Homer Bartlett and Paul Nicholson were the committee in charge of the Cedric R. Crowell Memorial Fund. In presenting a check for $385 to be used in setting up a drama bookshelf

---

*"Tales of Sint Sink" remains today one of the most delightful accounts of the early history of this town. Copies are available at the library.

at the Library, Mr. Nicholson reviewed Cedric Crowell's many contributions in time, talent and guidance toward developing the Play Troupe, now an integral part of this community.

"Linus Kittredge, who accepted the gift on behalf of the Library Trustees and Head Librarian, Helen Curtice, recalled the wonderful spirit of friendliness and leadership that Cedric Crowell brought to his duties as Library Board President. 'Through Mr. Crowell's efforts the Port Washington Library has attained its position as one of the finest libraries on Long Island,' Kittredge said.

"In the Cedric R. Crowell Memorial Collection at the Library two of Mr. Crowell's greatest interests will be commemorated—his love for the theatre and a lifelong devotion to books."

Books purchased by the Fund were marked by a special book plate and a plaque was mounted marking the section where books were kept.

That Port Washington continued to attract authors to its hospitable ambiance was demonstrated by the publication in August of books by five residents, copies of which were placed on display at the library:

Elbert Robberson, *The New Book of Small Boats*

Edward Hunter, *Brainwashing: The Story of Men Who Defied It*

John K. Winkler, *William Randolph Hearst: A New Appraisal*

Theodore Maynard, *The Life of Thomas Cranmer*

Father Francis B. Thornton, *Cross Upon Cross: The Life of Pope Pius IX*

A major publishing event in 1956 was the University of Chicago/Brittanica, *Great Books of the Western World*, in 54 volumes encompassing 443 works by 74 authors from Homer to the Bible to the 20th Century. The Port Washington Library was selected to receive one of the 1,600 sets distributed by the American Library Association under a grant from the Old Dominion Foundation.

Once again Miss Curtice reported to the Board that a reader had insisted on her removing an "unsuitable" book ("The Untidy Pilgrim") from the shelves. The Board promptly determined that "censorship is not part of a library's services to the community," and the book was returned to circulation.

At the October meeting, the Board passed a motion to authorize the expenditure of $100 to establish a collection of chamber music scores as the result of Mrs. Paul (Lucretia) Harrison's efforts on behalf of fellow musicians. Just two months later this innovative addition to the library's collection was on file and it has grown yearly since that time.

In January, 1957, the Board "approved the *re*-employment of Mrs. Betty Wood as a children's librarian." She was to substitute for Mrs. Loiseaux. In her reminiscences Betty recalls:
"In the years that followed (my resignation when I married) I kept in close touch with the library, often called to fill in when needed. More than once Miss Curtice baby-sat my toddlers while I took over the story hour. I kept up with the latest children's books while reading to my growing family. When our youngest was about ten, I asked Miss Curtice for a part-time job, and for the next several years worked with Miss Stooksberry in the children's room."

The circulation of books jumped 20 percent in 1956: 151,802 books borrowed; 2,400 new volumes were added bringing the collection to over 33,000; and 8,231 borrowers were registered in early 1957. Keeping up with the need for up-to-date reference books, Miss Curtice added the latest editions of World Book, Encyclopedia Brittanica, Collier's Encyclopedia and the two-volume London Times Atlas.

The budget of $57,910 passed handily and Marie Dunnells was nominated from the floor and reelected for a second term.

1958   *Unique slogan for Library Week — Budget passes, Kittredge reelected — Barbara Hackler Memorial Fund — Miss Curtice announces resignation — New Director search commenced*

"Every week is Library Week and every day is Library Day" was the slogan selected for the 1958 celebration in Port Washington. Greater circulation of books and encouragement of reading was stressed on bulletin board notices and in the eagerness of the staff to help the inquiring mind."

Library Card used in 1958.

The occasionally stormy waters of school and library budgets and of elections had remained relatively calm throughout the Fifties. In 1958 both passed by comfortable margins and the voters seemed

Edward de Sciora

well satisfied with their schools and their library. Linus Kittredge was reelected for another term.

Kenneth A. Hackler presented a check for $413.50 to the library. The money was contributed by Mrs. Hackler's friends after her death in August to establish a memorial fund for the Children's Room in recognition of her love for children and of her interest in children's books during the years when she served as a children's librarian.

Although rumors were about that Miss Curtice was contemplating retirement after 32 years as Head Librarian and Director, the September Board Meeting minutes reveal the first formal announcement, after which:

"...a discussion (took place) with respect to her possible successor, the Trustees concluding that in view of the increasing administrative duties falling upon the Director of the Library, it seemed desirable to obtain the services of a qualified Director, preferably someone with substantial administrative experience."

After the announcement it became obvious that much activity had taken place on the part of the Trustees in seeking a new Director well before the public announcement.

Board members at that time included Linus Kittredge, Marie Dunnells, LuEsther Mertz, John Crawley and Thomas Lapham.

From the Board Meeting minutes, November 18, 1958:

"The Trustees reviewed their activities which have extended over a period of several months in interviewing possible candidates for the Directorship of the Library. Mr. Kittredge was (then) authorized to offer Mr. Edward de Sciora, of 242 11th Street, Brooklyn, N.Y., a provisional appointment as Director, and to so inform Mr. de Sciora. Upon communicating the offer to Mr. de Sciora by telephone, Mr. Kittredge reported that Mr. de Sciora had accepted the offer and would endeavor to arrange for his early release from the New Lots Branch of the Brooklyn Public Library where he is now engaged.

"Mr. Crawley was authorized to write Mr. de Sciora confirming the Board's action and expressing the hope that his appointment may be made permanent after the publication of the prospective Civil Service List of eligible candidates."

Edward de Sciora started working at the Port Washington Public Library the first of December, 1958.

In the 66 years since Wilhelmina Mitchell took on, voluntarily, the daunting task of creating, nurturing, and directing a library in Port Washington, there had been only one other head librarian, Helen B. Curtice. Many in this community still remember her charm and her businesslike approach to librarianship.

Thus ended the second era of the library. A new director was about to point the way to entirely new directions.

CHAPTER XIII

New Director—New Directions 1959–1969

Just under 28,000 people resided in Port Washington in 1959. Each workday morning one third of the wives sent their husbands off to the Long Island Rail Road station, or drove them in the family car (two-car families were just beginning to emerge). The trip to New York was close to half an hour, one of the great attractions of the town. Most of the children walked to school, another great attraction since neighborhood schools were scattered about the peninsula convenient to most families.

The Port Washington Public Library Board of Trustees and staff at this time included:

Trustees—Linus E. Kittredge   John C. Crawley
         Marie P. Dunnells   Thomas W. Lapham
         LuEsther T. Mertz

Staff—Edward de Sciora   Everett Landwehr
      Catherine Sandy   Dorothy Hagenbuch
      Jean Stooksberry   Dorothea Loiseaux
      Cynthia Randall   Alice Ritter
      Edith Goodwin   Betty Wood

Historical exhibits always popular in an historic town: February, 1959, display of photos and books about the Tibbits Homestead on Old Sands Point Road.

OLD TIDEWATER MILL, NEAR PORT WASHINGTON, L.I. BUILT 1693

A woodcut of the Old Tidewater Mill by Bill Galloway.

As Port Washington has fostered literary and journalism celebrities, so has the community welcomed artists—painters in oils and watercolors, sculptors, etchers, wood carvers and lithographers.

At the April, 1959, Board Meeting the desirability of exhibiting the works of art of local artists was discussed enthusiastically, and on motion, approved unanimously. Within weeks a full schedule of one-man or one-woman exhibitions was announced, aiming to help the public become better acquainted with the talent in this community:

Fleurette R. Withers	*May*	William K. (Bill) Galloway	*September*
Mario Cooper	*June*	Frank Kleinholz	*October*
Carl Buck	*July*	Barse Miller	*November*

The exhibits were attended by many in town who expressed their surprise at seeing for the first time oil paintings, watercolors (especially those of "old-timers," Carl Buck and Bill Galloway, who painted familiar landmarks of Port Washington), and portraits—all painted by neighbors and friends.

The first time the idea of opening on Sundays came up at a later Board meeting as the exhibits were being planned. It was agreed that the library should not be open on Sunday afternoon *for this purpose alone,* the meeting minutes reported and continued: "the suggestion may be brought up for discussion at a later time if there seems to be any public pressure for such a special opening."

Frank Kleinholz, one of the artists whose work was seen in the library during October, proposed to the board that a committee be formed to advise and assist financially the library art exhibits. During the spring of 1960 the Art Advisory Council was formed not only to assist in art programming, but also to expand the scope to include shows in various art forms and media such as prints, sculpture and photography. Included on the Council were four well-known artists who had already exhibited at the library along with seven members of the community who had an active interest in art *and* the library:

Norman Blankman   Mrs. Roland Loiseaux
Mario Cooper   Mrs. P.A. Marcussen
Theodore Davis   Barse Miller
Frank Kleinholz   Mrs. Louis Rappaport
Edward Lawrence   Mrs. Ben Slater
              Paul Wood

The first decision of the Art Advisory Council (AAC), after electing Edward Lawrence their Chairman, was to announce an Open Art Exhibition in June of artists within the Peninsula, Port Washington, Sands Point, Plandome and Manhasset. The four artists on the AAC comprised the jury and local business enthusiastically participated by offering prizes. Thirty-four of the ninety-four paintings submitted to the competition were placed on exhibit and the *Port News* happily announced that the winners were "a high school student, a housewife, an ex-Navy man and a college student."

The Art Advisory Council has remained over the years one of the committees that contributes unceasingly to the vitality of the library. Members are approved by the Board of Trustees and, to avoid conflicts, a separate bank account is maintained for funds raised by annual mailings to the community.

Romance touched the lives of the Trustees in May, 1959, requiring a special meeting of the Board: Miss Helen Curtice, since her resignation six months earlier, had become Mrs. Clyde Eddy. She was now requesting an appointment as a senior librarian. Three members of the Board present and two by proxy voted unanimously to approve the appointment.

After serving 17 years as a Trustee, John Crawley resigned that month and Benjamin E. Haller was elected.

With continuing community use of the library, inevitably space again was at a premium: just one example, insufficient room for reference books. Action was postponed then, but Mr. de Sciora and the Trustees knew that the crisis would have to be faced early on.

Although the exact date is not recorded, Linus Kittredge died in November, 1959. A Memorial Collection in his name, with appropriate commemorative bookplate, was approved by the board in December, the proceeds were used to purchase art books.

At the first Board meeting in 1960, Hedley W. Donovan, then Editorial Director of Time, Inc., was appointed to complete the unexpired term of the late Linus Kittredge, and Thomas Lapham was elected president.

Hedley W. Donovan, elected Trustee February, 1960.

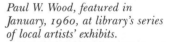

Paul W. Wood, featured in January, 1960, at library's series of local artists' exhibits.

Peninsula Artists' Show Winners in 1962 competition at library: l. to r., Joan Piel,
Ginnie Haussler, ??, Ed Lawrence (Chairman, Art Advisory Council), Catchi (Childs),
Ann Pellaton, Jo Poulson.

In 1960 the previous year's very successful series of exhibits was repeated, this time with local artists Grace Cooper, Ora Brian Edwards, Dorothea Loiseaux and Paul W. Wood.

A new and more efficient system of charging out books to borrowers was installed and by autumn de Sciora reported that overdue books were reduced to less than 1% from the previous 5%.

The year ended on an optimistic note for the library when the trustees happily accepted the offer by the Girl Scout Brownies to plant spring bulbs in front of the library.

Old and exotic auto license plates were
displayed in the lobby of the library in
celebration of National Library Week in
April, 1961 which also included a
vintage car motorcade through town.

1961–   *Participation in Nassau Library Service (NLS) explained—Art*
1962   *exhibits still newsworthy—Outreach from library—Censorship—*
         Library expansion discussed—Idea of Friends of Library *moti-*
         vates workshop

With the library now a member of the Nassau Library System, borrowers started taking advantage of the Central Reference Collection which represented materials above and beyond the average needs of the local library. This collection was available to patrons on InterLibrary Loan facilitated by System trucks maintaining daily schedules. NLS also provided a newly developed 16mm Film Library System of more than 100 films: documentaries, health, Child Study, everything from Art to United Nations. A further advantage to the Port Washington Library was low-cost book purchasing through the mass buying power of NLS.

The library art exhibits kept pace with the community interest in local artists throughout the year. Some of the exhibits included: works by Leonard Goldblatt, Mario Cooper, Virginia and Ted Davis, Barse Miller and Ruth Eckstein.

Of particular interest to the trustees and the director were the role the library should play in the community, how Port Washington Library measures up to neighboring institutions, and where the public library and the school libraries overlap or complement each other.

In his search for ways in which the library could better serve the public Mr. de Sciora met with officials of St. Francis Hospital, the results of which are told first-hand by Betty Wood who had returned as Children's Librarian:

"We discovered that in the pediatric units of St. Francis there were boys and girls with congenital heart problems who were mostly ambulatory and in need of quiet activities. For several years, accompanied by Jean Stooksberry, Margaret Ripton or a volunteer, I carried large canvas bags of books every week to St. Francis, gave book talks, told stories and took requests for books."

Barse Miller

Betty Wood also investigated how more productively public and school libraries might work together:

"There had never been much communication between school and public libraries in Port Washington. The popular concept that the two were vying for the children's patronage seemed ridiculous; on the contrary, (they) have a common goal: to stimulate and encourage children's reading, and it seemed logical that they should work together."

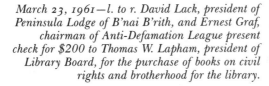

March 23, 1961—l. to r. David Lack, president of Peninsula Lodge of B'nai B'rith, and Ernest Graf, chairman of Anti-Defamation League present check for $200 to Thomas W. Lapham, president of Library Board, for the purchase of books on civil rights and brotherhood for the library.

130 parents and children attended a Family Story Hour at the library conducted by Spencer Shaw for children in third through sixth grade *and* their parents—presented not just for entertainment, but to encourage Family Reading Aloud and Storytelling as a means of building family tradition, encouraging reading and developing vocabulary. Shaw, who had conducted similar programs for children *only* in the past, was a consultant and advisor to the Nassau Library System.

Cooperation with the schools continued as the Trustees voted to co-sponsor at the library a lecture/workshop for parents on children's books over a period of five weeks in October and November.

In 1962 the question of censorship was raised concerning *The Tropic of Cancer* by Henry Miller. The U.S. Justice Department had just lifted its twenty-seven year ban on importation of the book from France. More than fifty adults from Port Washington had reserved the book when publication was announced. Replying to one reader's letter suggesting limited circulation (not "complete censorship"), President Thomas Lapham agreed that to him the book was "repulsive," yet conceded that many critics had affirmed the novel's literary merit.

He wrote:

"The Library does not know how it can formulate a rule which can fairly restrict this particular book without restricting also scores of other books. We do attempt to exclude purchase of weak, incompetent or cheap sentimental writing, as well as the solely sensational, morbid or erotic novels.

"The Board feels strongly that in a free society each individual is free to determine for himself what he wishes to read. Freedom is no freedom if it is accorded only to the accepted and inoffensive."

This issue of book censorship in the library will probably never be settled to every person's satisfaction in Port Washington or in any other community where books are freely available to the public.

The tradition of Family Evening Story Hours was continued early in 1962 when Port Washington resident, Jean Ritchie one of the nation's most famous folk singers, literally had a red carpet rolled out for her (courtesy of D. Kalfaian and Sons, rug merchants in Manhasset) "to warm up the polished vinyl in the Reading Room and create a friendly home atmosphere." This was a singing story hour with Jean Ritchie and her family and all the other families who joined in an evening of songs and singing games. What made the evening uniquely pleasurable was her famous Kentucky Mountain dulcimer which she used for accompaniment.

Other successful Family Evenings included a Halloween story hour spree in October and another featuring old favorites with Ben and Margaret Haller along with their six children in December.

Mrs. Lena Ruppert was elected to the seat on the library Board

Jean Ritchie

vacated by Marie Dunnells, but served for only three months. Theodore W. Davis was appointed to replace Mrs. Ruppert until the next school/library election.

In 1962, Trustees were once again tackling the problem of space—there was never enough space in the Port Washington Library from the day seventy years earlier when Miss Mitchell opened her front hall to neighbors who wished to borrow books. Mr. de Sciora and the Board set up a two-point plan for moving ahead. One was to prepare a written formulation of community needs, and at the same time to advance the idea of forming a "Library Council" or "Friends of the Library" through workshops and community discussion groups.

During the fall the Board had reached the stage of agreeing on needs and assessing available sites for a new library and had arrived at a consensus of services essential to a new building.

1963   *Science Wing for H.S. on ballot—Library Budget passes by 46 votes—Library Bill of Rights—Three important library posts filled*

The space problem at the library was brought home compellingly to some members of the public when films on Rembrandt and on Toulouse-Lautrec were offered; only 70 seats were available for more than twice as many ticket applicants.

A proposition to build a Science Wing on the High School ($1,094,000) and the regular school budget were voted down in one of the largest voter turnouts in years, 3,070 out of 3,626 registrants. The 1963–64 library budget of $145,632 squeaked by: a vote of just 1,494 to 1,448. Robert Fried replaced Hedley Donovan who had retired and Ted Davis was reelected.

Nassau Library System, quite possibly because Edward de Sciora had been elected president, put its many problems behind and was rapidly becoming a vital force in the management of libraries in the county. He was reelected for a second term in April 1963.

Harrison Salisbury, author and N.Y. Times correspondent, center, congratulating Edward de Sciora on his reelection as president of the Nassau Library Association, April 4, 1963, at the NLS annual meeting. Roger Jones, left, director of Lynbrook Library, looks on.

Margaret Neville, appointed Young Adult Librarian, took her Master's Degree in Library Service at Rutgers.

Problem-solving was not just a challenge for NLS. In Port Washington, librarians continued to find pages torn from books, particularly reference volumes. By installing and publicizing widely a self-service, coin-operated copy machine, de Sciora said "it is hoped that this machine will eliminate damage from torn-out pages of books." A further aggravation, overdue books, was tackled with a strong series of letters signed by the Director, from a polite reminder to a listing of fines due, a copy of Education Law concerning books kept over thirty days, and finally a threat to discontinue borrowing privileges.

The Trustees in 1963 formally and unanimously adopted a Statement of Policy, excerpts from which follow:

We believe that man's greatest invention is the written word, the ability to communicate his observations, experiences, hopes, meditations, fears, joys and sorrows across all barriers of time and space.

We believe the role of a public library in a free society is to hold open a window through which free men and women may freely view the whole panorama of human thought and experience in literature, science, art, philosophy, religion, history and politics, and in every field in which man's thoughts have been recorded.

We believe this is the role which we, as trustees of such a library, have a duty to fulfill, limited only by the physical and financial resources made available to us.

We oppose any attempt to shape our collection of library materials by any standards of literary, political, religious, artistic or social orthodoxy which we believe would impair the fulfillment of this duty.

Two major staff appointments and one major promotion took place in the fall of 1963:

Mrs. Virginia Parker—appointed Assistant Director
Mrs. Pat Lubar—appointed Clerk, responsible for library
    publicity
Mrs. Elizabeth (Betty) Wood—promoted to Senior Librarian,
    Head of Children's Work

Mrs. Virginia Parker, assistant library director, appointed December, 1963, she served the library in many capacities in her twenty-eight years in Port Washington.

1964 *Director, Brooklyn Public Library, consultant to Port Library—*
Microfilm introduced—Young Adult Librarian appointed—
National Library Week theme: Reading Is The Key—*Special*
programs planned—Budget passes—Haller reelected—Muriel
Neville elected to balance of LuEsther Mertz's term—Preliminary
contracts signed with architects for new building

At that time…

Lyndon B. Johnson elected 36th President

On January 31, 1964, Francis R. St. John, Chief Librarian, Brooklyn Public Library, commenced his work as consultant to the Trustees to advise them "on the adequacy of the library's facilities and whether the library needs to be expanded, if so the most economical and advantageous way in which to do it."

The staff was further implemented by the arrival of Margaret Neville, a Young Adults Librarian, who felt her new job was a "creative challenge" perhaps because she found over 600 volumes of the Young Adult collection piled on the floor of the workroom.

While Schreiber High School students (foreground) do research in the traditional manner, fellow classmates (rear) use (l. to r.) the microfilm cabinet, the reader-printer, and the microfilm reader in the reference department.

Plans were afoot early for celebrating National Library Week, April 12–18. The theme in Port Washington, "Fifty Years Ago—1914," sparked many ideas including a booklet prepared by Reference Librarian Catherine Sandy, *Unlocking The Past,* a charming look back at the Port Washington of 1914.

On April 16, Margaret Haller presented a nostalgic talk on famous authors residing in the town in 1914 which she later expanded into an excellent eighteen-page article in *The Journal of Long Island History* titled "Main Street, Port Washington—1914."

In a message to the electorate, Tom Lapham emphasized that there would be no increase in the present tax rate of 17 cents per hundred assessed valuation, and that "we expect during the year to present for your consideration definite plans for a bigger and better library which will meet the needs of this community." The budget was passed and Mrs. Muriel Neville, no relation to the recently appointed Young Adult Librarian, was appointed to fill the unexpired term of LuEsther Mertz who had retired.

Curtis and Davis, nationally famous library architects selected to recommend a site for a new library building, met with the Library Board in November, contracts were signed, and in December specifications charts were submitted.

1965 *Expansion program gaining momentum—Business as usual first half of year—Friends of New Library formed—*Port News *heavy supporter of plans—Few opposed—Bond issue vote October 21*

More than 60 townspeople crowded the Reading Room at the library on January 21 to hear architect Walter Rooney of Curtis and Davis outline how a library must be tailor-made to meet the needs and budget of a community. One resident, Mrs. Paul Harrison, pointed out that at the Belleview Avenue site the flight of steps below the entrance prevented handicapped and elderly persons from using the library. This was only one of the many suggestions leading to a final consensus. The most pressing needs were a meeting room, parking facilities and a much enlarged book collection.

Possible sites for a new library included property at the corner of Vandeventer and Port Washington Boulevard, the five-acre Monfort property adjacent to Campus Drive and a lot at the end of Belleview Avenue at Main Street. By far the most popular site among Board members and the architects was the Methodist Church property, but it also seemed to be the most unattainable because of the probable high cost. Nonetheless Mr. Lapham commenced discussions with members of the Methodist Church.

During the winter and spring, programming blossomed with an art exhibit sponsored by AAC of stage and costume designer, Lucinda Ballard, and her husband, Howard Dietz, librettist and song writer, residents of Sands Point; storytellers Edsel Ford McCoy and Rolf Myller, architect and children's book author; another Open Competition by AAC and a display of original lithographs by Honore Daumier, famed cartoonist and political satirist of the 19th century.

In June Pat Lubar sent out releases to the local papers announcing the formation of the "Friends of the New Library" Committee which included Mrs. Stanley Bernstein, Mrs. Robert Fieldsteel, Mrs. Hayden Johnson, Mrs. Benjamin Haller, Mrs. Sydney Margolius and Mrs. F.T. Ward. She wrote: "The Friends will solicit support from residents of the community interested in good library services, and will urge construction of a new facility. Specific pro-

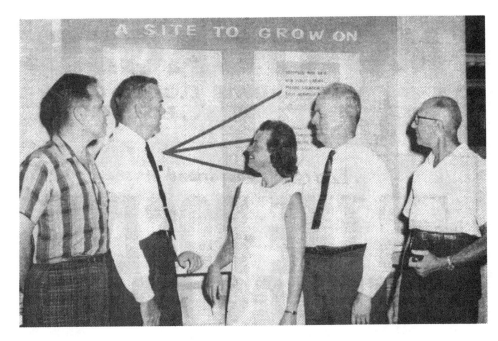

*Proposed site of the new library viewed
by trustees, l. to r., Benjamin Haller,
Thomas W. Lapham, president, Muriel
Neville, Theodore Davis, Robert Fried.*

posals will be presented as soon after Labor Day as possible, followed by a referendum."

By the first of August, the *Port News* reported:

"Plans for a new Port Washington public library moved ahead this
week with the announcement by Thomas W. Lapham that a contract had been signed with the First Methodist Church for purchase of its 1.9 acre site at Main Street and North Washington.

"The church has announced plans to relocate in Sands Point.
Construction of the new library, if approved by the voters, could not
begin until early in 1967, after the church has obtained new
quarters."

As should be expected differing points of view were expressed
following the announcement: *one,* Ernie Simon's editorial in the
News pointed out that "A town with the excellent cultural and educational reputation of Port Washington should not have to put up
with library facilities as inadequate as these (Belleview Avenue library)"; *two,* in the same issue of the *News,* a skeptical tax-payer
wrote:

"How much is the land going to cost? Did the Board or its publicity experts figure this information should be spoon fed to the taxpayers? Will the figure be hidden in an overall one later? A little
more candor on the part of the Board would indicate higher respect
for public opinion and voter intelligence."

Editor Simon's Note following the letter stated: "The cost of the
land is in this issue of the News. It was not announced earlier because library and church officials had not yet agreed on the final
price."

Young Friends of the New Library, Elizabeth Roger, Howard Russman, and Claudia Hartley, all vacationing college students, helping library committee ready the program for presentation of plans and model at Methodist Church.

The cost of the property was $150,000. The Friends of the New Library immediately organized an informal meeting for residents at which the architect, W.J. Rooney, described criteria used to judge each of eight sites for a new library. The Monfort property, long considered by many as a desirable location, was taken out of the running when, according to Lapham, "it became apparent that a building there would be tucked out of sight behind the post office truck parking lot, next to a cemetery, and convenient only to the neighboring school complex." The only other proposal seriously discussed was to expand the Belleview Avenue building, an alternative that would not have been easy since "longtime residents of that neighborhood, understandably, were not inclined to sell and condemnation would have been costly and unpleasant," said Lapham. "The resultant library would still have been unsatisfactory in size, design and accessibility."

Curtis and Davis were given the go-ahead in mid-August to start work on plans. Final cost figures and detailed drawings were completed by the end of the month, and on September 8, the Friends of the New Library, with 126 resident sponsors, held their first public meeting at the Methodist Church.

More than 100 people were present at the Methodist Church meeting hall to view the dramatic unveiling of a three-dimensional model of the proposed new Port Washington library. The meeting was chaired by Benjamin Haller, who introduced Board President Lapham Library Director, de Sciora and architect Walter Rooney.

A breakdown of the costs of the new library was given along with a pledge that the Library Board would maintain total communication and total honesty with the public regarding the proposal for a new building:

> Total cost estimate: $1,581,000 with a Federal grant of $200,000 bringing the cost down to $1,381,000.

> Based on the average house assessment of $10,000, a homeowner would pay $13 additionally per year on his taxes.

> Parking facility for 72 cars would be provided.

No one living in Port Washington, no matter how remotely connected with the library, can fail to remember the exuberance of the weeks from September 16 to October 19, 1965 when the referendum on the bond issue was scheduled. Every group or association who would listen had an advocate from the Friends at their meetings, explaining the need for a new library, answering questions (occasionally fielding some tough ones such as, "Do we really need a building of such ostentatious magnificence?") and exhorting their listeners to support the bond issue.

It was estimated that 5,000 people examined the model for the

Unveiling of scale model of proposed new library was greeted with pleasure by (l. to r.) Edward de Sciora, director; Robert Fried, member, library board; Thomas Lapham, president, library board; and Benjamin Haller, member of board.

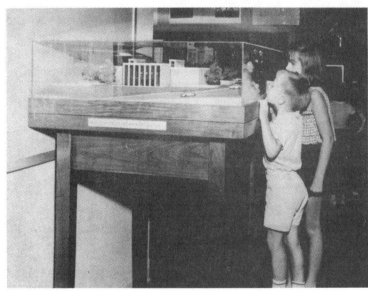

Town Supervisor Sol Wachtler presents National Library Week Proclamation to Muriel Neville, Library trustee, and Margaret Haller of the Friends of the New Library.

Even the youngest were eager to learn about the New Library.

new library, not just in the foyer of the library itself, but in banks, shopping areas, movie houses and on the sidewalk. Volunteers transported the 95-pound model by station wagon to set it up any place where there was heavy pedestrian traffic.

Letters to the Editor proliferated, mostly in favor of the new library. The greater Port Washington Civic Council (Harbor Hills, Southport, Monfort Hills and New Salem) unanimously approved the building.

The League of Women Voters, following a summer workshop headed by Mrs. Ruth Bogen, urged a "yes" vote on the bond issue slated for October 19. They also reminded voters to register unless they had voted in previous school district elections. The League leaflet about the new library contained the questions—and an-

To the Editor:

Last Tuesday, Oct. 19, Port Washington voted in favor of the proposals and plans for a new public library.

This approval is most gratifying to the Board of Trustees of the library and to all who understood the importance of the improvements and expansion of library facilities for our town.

Now it becomes the responsibility of the board to transform plans and proposals into actualities. Many good and helpful suggestions have been made at the meetings we have attended. These suggestions will be given careful consideration as we move forward to final working plans and construction.

Meanwhile, we wish to express our appreciation to that dedicated group of hard working people, the Friends of the New Library. The time and effort, the money and enthusiasm they contributed to the library cause have been an outstanding example of active good citizenship in our community.

Therefore, to the Friends of the New Library as well as to the many organizations who gave us their support and to all of the individuals who worked and voted for our new library this most sincere ''thank you.''

Board of Trustees
Port Washington Public Library

Port Washington News, October 22, 1965

Helping to chalk up the record vote in the library referendum, October 19, 1965, was Mr. U.F. Sacco, signing the register for Betty Linacre and Gertrude Stearns.

swers—most frequently asked of the library trustees and was distributed at meetings in town and at the library.

Not just the *Port News* but the *Port Mail* and *The Port Reporter* gave enthusiastic support to the proposed new library.

The vote on the budget came up on Tuesday, October 19 and on Thursday morning, October 21, the *Port News* was out with a banner headline:

BOND ISSUE FOR LIBRARY APPROVED THREE-TO-ONE

At the Board meeting the evening after the unprecedented vote on the bond issue (2,047 votes cast, 1,621 in favor, 476 opposed), it was business as usual with finances a priority agenda item: interim financing, bond anticipation notes and the sale of bonds. Kendrick Smith, Library Attorney, and Bertram Daiker, School Board Attorney, were immediately called on to clarify the many outstanding issues resulting from this major undertaking of library and school board.

The Board of Trustees expressed eloquently their thanks to the town and all who helped get approval for the new library. (See sidebar.)

The question of Sunday openings, long an issue of conflicting opinions, surfaced again, but no decision could be reached until the November board meeting when results of a county-wide study would be announced, i.e. the feasibility of Sunday service on a regional basis or by individual libraries.

Miss Stooksberry retired in September and the search was on for a replacement.

1966 *Interlibrary access introduced—Large type-size books available—Friends elect officers—Board member Davis acts to speed up church property take-over*

"If you have your library card specially stamped, you can borrow books from any of 30 other libraries in Nassau County" was the message made public by Director de Sciora, "and you can return them here or to the library where you borrowed them."

This Direct Access program caught on with patrons and was used extensively even though the library interloan system was in place.

Another innovation in library services, acquistion of large print books, brought many readers with limited vision to the library. "Lay your magnifying glass aside" was the tempting slogan used by Virginia Parker, Assistant Director in charge of Adult Services, in the hope that "many persons with vision problems who have been unable to read would now be able to enjoy books again."

In response to publicity for New York State grants up to $3,000 to assist college graduates to receive training as professional librarians, 21 candidates from Port Washington applied for Librarian Training grant applications.

Mrs. Miriam Gierasch, library staff member, and Bruce Cornell look at one of the many new large type books, a collection which has expanded many-fold from its start in 1966.

Howard Haycraft, right, president of H.W. Wilson Company, presented the John Cotton Dana publicity Award in 1966 to Director de Sciora and Patricia Lubar, library public relations consultant.

The organization which had worked so vigorously to help get out the vote for the bond issue decided to continue its efforts on behalf of the library, dropping "New" from its name. A first slate of officers for the Friends of the Port Washington Public Library was elected: Thomas C. Linacre, President, Mrs. F.S. Brewster, Mrs. Benjamin Haller and Richard D. Whittemore, as vice presidents for Program, Membership and Publicity. Mrs. S. Horsky was elected as Secretary and Norman Freed, Treasurer. A few months later Mr. Linacre moved out of Port Washington and Mr. Whittemore was elected president of the Friends of the Port Washington Public Library.

In June the library received the distinguished John Cotton Dana Award for "outstanding publicity" created by Pat Lubar during the 1965 bond issue campaign. The award, sponsored jointly by the American Library Association and the H.W. Wilson Company, cited the publicity for its quality and sophistication and for imaginative use of visual media.

Funds were obtained from the Nassau Library System to open a satellite library in the Littig House, a community center serving Harbor Homes and Bay Green Lane residents. There were 300 books in a tutoring and reference collection placed in Littig House, along with 600 paperback titles.

In June, 1966, when the Federal and New York State authorities approved the Library Services and Construction Act Grant of $200,000 for building the new library, a stipulation was made that

Peter Spier, a Port resident and prominent children's author, illustrator and ship model builder, born in Amsterdam, Holland, often regaled seven-year olds (and up) with stories and on-the-spot drawings of his native land.

Spencer Shaw, popular story-teller and children's consultant for Nassau County Library System, visited the Port library frequently.

construction must commence before March, 1967. Since early spring Ted Davis had been in contact with the Methodist Church about releasing the property to the library, and notification of the construction grant brought greater urgency. After many meetings and exchanges of correspondence, Mssrs. Lapham and Haller met with the Methodist Church Board and Building Committee in December. Their report to the library board was that "a new contract has been negotiated and the church has agreed to vacating the premises on June 30, 1967, so that construction will start on July 1." An extension of the Federal and State Grant was then negotiated.

The other major hurdle was the closing of that part of North Washington Street bordering the west side of the church property. Baxter Estates officials, the Police and Fire Chiefs and utility companies all had to be consulted, and approvals received.

1967   *New building principal topic of board meetings—Behind the scenes action speeds approvals from State, County and Village— Budget passes—Belleview Avenue library stretched to capacity, but AAC continues exhibits—Children's programs ever popular*

Board members Lapham, Neville, Fried, Haller and Davis met frequently in special sessions, in addition to regular monthly meetings, to resolve the many problems arising from the imminent start of construction.

Director de Sciora and architects from the firm of Curtis and Davis secured approval for construction from the Educational Facilities Division of the State Education Department by traveling to Albany and presenting the library plans in person. They reported that the examiner was very pleased with the plans and that he felt them to be of outstanding quality.

The annual budget, up $32,000 to $232,000, was passed and Ted Davis was elected to a five-year term.

Library attendance kept climbing, children's programming widened, and during the year the Art Advisory Council sponsored seven exhibits including drawings by Janet Compere Harwood whose former teachers included Larry Goldblatt, and Aida and Dan Whedon. The eighth annual all-County competition and the fourth annual Sculpture and Graphics Exhibit, also open to all Nassau County residents, attracted artists from the entire area.

Early in the week of September 15th, after a fence had been erected around the entire property, wrecking crews arrived at the Methodist Church accompanied by a contingent of local "sidewalk superintendents." The demolishing of this 1883 Port Washington landmark in just a few hours was watched with mixed feelings by townspeople, especially as the original church bell was removed, later to be mounted in the new church building on Middle Neck Road in Sands Point.

The fence around the property, instead of becoming an eyesore to the community, was transformed on Saturday, September 30, into an imaginative storyland of paintings surrounding the soon-to-be new library. Under the direction of Lucy Fitzgerald, many junior and senior high school students, armed with specially mixed paints she had prepared, joined a "paint-in," decorating hundreds of five by eight foot plywood panels. Favorite characters, favorite books, nursery rhymes and fairytales were the subjects the students

Lucy Fitzgerald, Guggenheim School art teacher, gives help and encouragement to junior and senior high schoolers painting the fence around the site of the new library, below left.

Friends of the Library donated funds to support the "Paint-In" on September 30, 1967.

picked themselves. They also painted ads supporting the Community Chest of Port Washington for which the Chest was most grateful.

The following day at 2:30 p.m. ground-breaking ceremonies were held on the new site followed by a reception at the Belleview Avenue Library hosted by the Friends and the AAC. Former Board members, LuEsther Mertz and Marie Dunnells, accompanied by Ellen Crawley, wife of long-time Board member, John Crawley, purposefully shoveled the dirt for the cornerstone.

Contracts with M. Stark Construction Company (general), Island Air Conditioning (heating, ventilation and air conditioning), G.T. Geelan & Sons (plumbing) and Aldoro Electric (electrical) had been signed in September. John A. Rossworn of Port Washington was appointed Clerk of the Works setting the stage for start of construction.

Opening the library on holidays was deemed successful at the November Board meeting when it was revealed that "so far the use of the library during the hours 1 to 5 P.M. on holidays had been extensive, making the additional expense and planning incurred worthwhile."

Reaching out to the younger generation and to the community had become standard procedure on a larger scale than ever before. In December Betty Wood, Children's Librarian, reported that 175 pre-schoolers were attending five story hours weekly. In spite of adding a fifth session in the fall, there was a long waiting list for these "popular programs." Nursery school and second year pupils visited the library on "field trips" while Betty Wood and Margaret Neville, Young Adult Librarian, also included in their busy schedules weekly trips to Littig House and St. Francis Hospital.

By November 20, excavation was completed and concrete forms in place. However Mr. Rossworn reported to the Board in December that "it may be necessary to bring construction to a halt in order to secure proper materials and *be sure the weather is suitable for pouring concrete!*" Also he felt that Stark Construction Co. had been slow.

This was just the beginning.

Groundbreaking for cornerstone of new library, October 1, 1967; (l. to r.) Marie Dunnells, Board of Trustees member, Ellen Crawley, wife of long-time member, John Crawley, and LuEsther Mertz, also Board member.

1968   *Private book collections donated—Space dwindles in library— Contest for seat on Board—Construction delays push back opening date—Priscilla Ciccariello appointed to staff—Friends donate funds for circulating art collection—*

The excitement generated by the activity going on at the construction site a few blocks away was reflected in the increased hustle and bustle at the "old" library, primarily because space was at a premium.

*Construction workers hoist "birdcage," form for concrete. New library to be
concrete and solar gray glass.*

From a news release in *Port News*, February 1, 1968:
"In the past few years, despite shortages of space, the library has
budgeted for increased book purchasing in anticipation of the
larger collection the new library will be able to offer.

(The total collection at that time was 64,777 books, with between
16,000 and 18,000 in circulation at one time).

"By curtailment of reading and staff rooms it has been possible
to cram nearly 10,000 more books into the library. Shelves have
been put in the former Long Island Reading Room and the down-
stairs floor has been converted to a back periodical and microfilm
reader room. All story hours, except for pre-schoolers, have been
eliminated...book storage in the basement has almost taken
over...almost all duplicate copies have been removed."

By coincidence three prominent citizens of Port Washington donated at the same time their personal book collections to the library
(which were, of course, carefully packed away awaiting the opening
of the new library):
Theodore M. Black, former reserve colonel, First U.S. Army—
books collected as military counter-intelligence officer during
World War II.
Robert H. Wessman, sailor, world traveler, photography buff who
combined libraries and book-collecting as chairman of the N.Y.
Yacht Club—well-made, finely bound books on sailing and
photography.

A Legacy for the Future

A scant two years ago, a group of Port Washington residents, concerned over the obvious lack of adequate library facilities for a community of more than 30,000 persons, formed what is now familiarly known as The Friends.

Dedicated to the principles of promoting continuing usage of the library for study, research and recreation, of stimulating financial support and gifts, and of sponsoring cultural programs of importance to the community, The Friends are now seeking to enlarge their membership rolls.

We urge you to become a member. By adding your support, you can help achieve the objectives of The Friends and will be taking an active part in the development of a new library determined to become one of the finest on Long Island.

As a matter of fact, Port's new library on Main St. will be so wonderful that librarians across the nation are already studying the plans and talking about its potential as the community's greatest asset. When finished in 1968, the library will be the result of a 20-year-long dream by those Port Washington residents with the foresight to realize that better-than-adequate library facilities are our legacy for the future.

A Legacy for the Future—Editorial, Port News, *October 14, 1965*

Howard C. Parsons, descendant of early Long Island family—Encyclopedia Britannica, complete works of George Eliot, out-of-print titles including the 1885 "Cyclopedia of Painters."

Another sign of the times was chairman of the Art Advisory Council Henry Solomon's announcement that because of diminishing wall space in the library, the AAC would accept for the Nassau County open competition only miniatures in oil and watercolor, no larger than 16 inches in any dimension.

Robert Fried, elected to the Library Board in 1963, was challenged by Donald C. Christ in a particularly heated campaign in the spring of 1968. Voluminous Letters to the Editor appeared, lauding the qualifications of the incumbent and the virtues of a more youthful candidate. In years past contested elections for library board trustee had been few, and the *Port News* announced the week before election:

"(This newspaper) will not favor one of the library candidates over

*In May, 1968, candidates for both school and library seats presented their
five-minute resumes to the public, sponsored jointly by Parent's Council and
League of Women Voters. From l. to r.: Mrs. L.R. Cieciuch, moderator;
Mrs. Imogene Brewster, Council president; Donald Christ, Library Board
candidate; Robert Fried, incumbent Library trustee; George Conklin, School
Board candidate; and Winfield Firman, incumbent School Board member.*

the other. They are both well qualified for the job. One offers the
wisdom of age and the other the vigor of youth: it is impossible to
decide which quality is more desirable."

   Donald Christ won seventy percent of the vote. The school and
library budgets passed as did a proposition affecting the library:
1486 out of 1900 voters approved the closing of North Washington
Street from Main Street to Locust Street and opening of a new road
at the east end of the property.

   By the end of June a shortage of carpenters and electricians set
back the construction schedule two weeks, yet Stark Construction
continued promising completion of the new library by fall, 1969.

   During 1968 two appointments to the library staff had far reaching effects on the library. Priscilla Ciccariello was hired for the
clerk-typist staff. Later she would receive her degree in library science at Queens College, hold many positions of responsibility in the
library, and finally become Head of the Information Services Department. Pat Lubar, the other appointee, became full-time Community Relations Consultant. Pat's determined efforts in getting
the bond issue passed as well as in keeping Port Washington well
informed about the often erratic building construction program
earned her the thanks of all her associates.

Donald C. Christ

*Magic Carpet: Betty Wood spinning a tale
for five to eight year olds in the garden
outside the Belleview Avenue Library
children's room.*

1969   *Sheldon Turtletaub appointed Legal Counsel—New York Times
        lauds new library as "Place for People"—*Friends *launch new
        member drive—Final art shows in "old" library—International
        Children's Book Awards and Exhibit—Budgets squeak through—
        First Book and Author Luncheon in May—Summer Library cadet
        and volunteers conduct survey—Building* almost *on schedule—
        Fines on overdue children's books abolished*

On January 21, 1969, Mr. Sheldon Turtletaub, Port Washington
attorney, was introduced to the Board of Trustees upon taking up
his duties as Legal Counsel to the Board. At the same meeting a
report was made concerning the January 5th New York Times article by architectural critic, Harry V. Forgeron. Although still under
construction, the new Port Washington Public Library was cited as
"a library for people, not just books."

Critic Forgeron went on to name the new Port structure one of
nine new libraries designed by architects who have taken library
structures "out of the dark ages." Curtis and Davis were designers
of three of these buildings: Port Washington, Worcester, Mass. and
New Orleans. "In designing the new Port Washington library," the
article continued, "the architects developed a vertical plan to accomodate severe grade changes on a site that offers a commanding
view of Manhasset Bay. The exterior will be of poured-in-place concrete, left exposed inside and out...a structure of mass and form,
light and shadow."

Littig House librarian, David Horton (center), shows off the community house library (sponsored by the Public Library) to Community Chest area chairmen.

The final open painting competition to be held in Belleview Avenue building on March 30 was announced by Henry Salomon, chairman of the Art Advisory Council. Other exhibits scheduled during the year included favorite children's author and illustrator Peter Spier's collected illustrations; and an exhibit in May of Alexander Calder's famous mobile, "Red Ghost," with Pedro Guerrero photographs of Calder at work.

The New Library: John Rossworn, supervisor of construction, showing Thomas Lapham, Board president, the last section of the roof to be covered over; the story hour rotunda (temporarily flooded), and finally, sharing the famous view of lower Main Street and the Bay from one of the 17 foot high window openings. Spring 1969.

Richard D. Whittemore

National Library Week, April 20 to 26, was marked by a very special occasion, the completion of the roof on the new library which was celebrated by the work force of 35 men in the traditional manner by hoisting a tree to the finished roof.

Another special event, destined to become an annual tradition in Port Washington, took place at the Plandome Country Club on May 16: the first Book and Author Luncheon sponsored by the Friends of the Port Washington Library. Four author-experts on four aspects of contemporary life—the home, theatre arts, family economics, and religion—were invited. Melanie Kahane, *There's A Decorator in Your Doll House;* Gerald Weales, drama critic for *Commonweal* magazine; Sidney Margolius, a Port resident who was a well-known, outspoken advocate on behalf of consumers. Moderator for the first luncheon, Rabbi Eugene B. Borowitz, also a Port resident, authored "How Can A Jew Speak of Faith Today?" Sandwich, dessert and coffee were $5.00.

Both school and library budgets were passed by narrow margins and Richard Whittemore was elected to replace Benjamin Haller who retired from his seat on the Board.

Friends of the Library now numbered 243 members (up from just 61 a year before). While Board member Christ was heading up the Special Gifts Committee, Esther Margolius, president of the Friends of the Library (which now numbered 243 members), organized a campaign to solicit gifts for furnishings and other appurtenances for the new building not covered under contracts.

As spring moved into summer it became apparent to all con-

Friends of the Library book sales were a primary source of fund-raising. Here Mrs. Benjamin Dewey, in charge of the booth, sold $160 worth of books before the rains came down. These young people departed with a few pounds of books each.

Normand Dumont joined the staff of the library in December, 1969, as assistant director for operations: technical and clerical services, building and general office management.

New Public Library (taken from Goodyear Blimp by Leo Stoecker) dominates lower Main Street as it awaits completion

cerned with the building program that it was slowing down at an unacceptable rate. The completion date had been postponed month by month by such dilemmas as elevator installation mechanics going on strike, and the unforeseen problem of the sewer connection on North Washington having to be switched to Main Street. In September an opening date of March, 1970, was scheduled.

Residents for a More Beautiful Port Washington, headed by Myron Blumenfeld, generously offered to review the library site for landscaping, and Mrs. Catherine Morrison, landscape architect and member of "Residents" submitted ideas in a written report on landscaping the steep slope to the west of the property.

A major innovation proposed by Betty Wood to eliminate fines on late children's books was approved by the board and has remained in effect since 1970.

CHAPTER XIV

A Library of Distinction

The twenty-one year history of the Port Washington Library—from dedication in 1970, through Decade, *the 10th Anniversary celebration in 1980, to the Centennial Year of 1992—literally explodes like a huge kaleidoscope when viewed from the middle of 1992.*

Each year has brought new technology to Information Services giving patrons young and old the opportunity to use computers…to conduct research from data banks near and far. When the reference shelves or the stacks are found wanting, invariably the needed volume is obtainable overnight from one of the libraries in the Nassau Library System or elsewhere.

The shelves of the book stacks overflow with modern, recent and centuries-old literature…a reader can borrow any regular circulating book without charge (adults only must watch out for overdue fines!).

A modern children's library with three librarians occupies a large, colorful, recently redecorated room looking out on a patio where story hours are held in good weather. In addition to overflowing book shelves, computers are available.

The three major volunteer organizations within the library—The Friends of the Library, The Art and Music Advisory Councils—plan programs year-round.

With their seasoned awareness of the community's tastes, interests and needs, the staff has excelled in choosing programs which appeal to the wide and diversified interests of Port Washington.

The welcoming ambiance of the library building itself and the dedicated staff sustain this pleasant and well-ordered environment for children, teenagers, and adults who frequent the library.

Later in this chapter the accomplishments of those twenty-one years are reviewed, accomplishments which have brought plaudits from many quarters and, through the efforts of the University of Illinois Graduate School of Library and Information Science, the designation of the Port Washington Public Library as one of the 50 outstanding public libraries in the United States.

Librarian Catherine E. Sandy locks doors of the Belleview Avenue Library for the last time. Miss Sandy had the distinction of being the only staff member who worked in the library from the time of its opening in 1926 to its closing in 1970.

After 44 years of service to the community the familiar red brick Belleview Avenue library building was closed on Saturday, May 16, 1970. Regular service to library patrons was suspended while over 75,000 books plus office supplies, records, filing cabinets and furniture were moved 'down the street' to their new home where 2,000 feet of sectional book shelving was in place.

Opening of the new building, scheduled so many times and delayed many months by heating and carpeting delinquencies, took place on June 8, 1970. On hand to guide patrons were volunteers from the Friends of the Library and 24 junior library aides. Whether it was the excitement of the new building or pent-up demand for borrowing books, more than 2,000 were checked out and an equal number returned, and 400 people signed up for new library cards that day.

Formal dedication of the new library was postponed until Sunday, September 18 because, in President Lapham's words, "The important thing is to get the building open and serving the public." During the summer news stories and editorials in the three local newspapers, *Port News, Port Mail,* and *Port Reporter,* along with attractive mailings to the entire community, proclaimed the dedication one of the major events in the history of Port Washington.

In his moving dedication speech, former Library Trustee and Editor-in-Chief of Time, Inc., Hedley Donovan congratulated the library trustees, director, staff and taxpayers "on this magnificent new library" and continued:

"This town, this northern part of the Cow Neck peninsula, is in many respects not a community but simply a place. For a community to take shape there must be at least a few institutions that have the whole town, all ages and interests, as their constituency. Not everybody will use the institution but anybody might. It must seem to express the best aspirations of the community; the people who run it must command respect; ideally it must be housed in a building memorable enough to serve as a community symbol. And it should work. That is, not break down, keep running the way it is supposed to; no simple matter for any institution today. In all these ways it seems to me this great new library is just such an institution, perhaps the first Port Washington has ever had, and a tangible beginning toward what we want Port Washington to mean."

In October, Pat Lubar, Public Relations Consultant, reported that the new building was its own most effective public relations agent, "attracting a wider variety of individuals of all ages and more diverse interests than ever before."

When asked his philosophy of the ideal library, Director de Sciora replied that "it was a coming together of people who are concerned about other people and want to improve their lives." He continued:

"A library must provide the means for people to gather the information that they need to perform adequately in today's very rapidly changing world. The Port library has books, thousands and thousands of books, and it has records and microfilms and lectures and videotapes and magazines, utilizing all forms of communication.

"Today's library reaches out into the community to encourage the use of the library and to encourage and stimulate discussion about

Graphics for all library printed matter were designed by Dennis Wheeler.

They heard speeches and saw a ceremony; they ate 40 pounds of pastry and drank almost 40 gallons of punch; they filled the meeting room and had to move to upper rooms; they heard a horn and wind quintet in the reading room and three guitarists in the children's room. And they said, formally, that a grand new building was now the home of the Port Washington Library.

The five or six hundred Port residents who came to the library's formal dedication last Sunday were welcomed at the door by library director Edward de Sciora and Thomas Lapham, president of the library board of trustees.

The meeting room wasn't large enough to hold all the guests for the dedication ceremony, so others listened in the upper rooms through the public address system.

The ceremony was begun and ended with a fanfare by Paul Dukas played by Margie King, Bill Levitan, Mark Hoffman, John Gaeta, Gary Finger, David Feingold, David Spann, Paul Deyo, and Dan Bartlett in a brass choir.

Library board president Lapham welcomed the guests, called for a moment of silent prayer, and then introduced dedication speaker Hedley Donovan, a Port resident, editor-in-chief of Time Inc., and a former library trustee.

Refreshments were provided and served by Friends of the Port Washington Library.

A horn and wind quintet played in the reading room. Its members were Raymond Alonge, Ruth Feingold, Don Ashworth, Wally Kane, and Walter Wegner. Guitarists Christie Pines, Peter Ptckow and Richard Lanik played in the children's room.

It was a good, well-run party; everyone seemed to have fun. The library reports that the first punch was not spilled in the children's room until at least 4 p.m. and guests were still at the library at a quarter to five.

Port News, *September 17, 1970.*

The new library, just prior to opening day.

the terrible and good things that happen in our society, helping people understand what's around them."

The promise inherent in de Sciora's blueprint for an ideal library was just beginning to take shape.

One of the first major steps forward in reaching out to the community and making it truly part of the library experience came about in 1971 when the first grant request and approval from the New York State Council on the Arts funded a VTR (video transcription recording) project at the library. (see page 184) From that time on the library received hundreds of thousands of dollars in grants that enabled it to offer services and programs that normally were not provided for in the library's operating budget. Funds came principally from the New York State Council on the Arts, the New York State Council on the Humanities, and the National Council on the Arts. In addition to video and film programs the state and national councils funded photography, art and music presentations.

View of the gallery at time of dedication.

Lapham's death mourned...Meeting Room named in his honor...
Budget vote split from joint school/library election...Esther Margolius
elected Trustee...Library Drive and Main Street major traffic problem

"One of my major goals," Trustee Lapham said when announcing his retirement in January, 1971, "was to see that Port Washington got the library it deserved. That is now accomplished." Although he felt that 19 years was too long, his fellow trustees and the library community could only reflect on his fine leadership and wish him well in his retirement from the board.

It was with great sadness, therefore, that the news of his sudden death in 1974 was announced. The following spring in a formal ceremony Hedley Donovan once again stepped forward to address a full house at the library, this time to dedicate the Thomas Willetts Lapham Meeting Room and memorial plaque designed by local artist, David Stone.

The *Port News* announced to the public that the library would hold its budget vote and trustee election on March 28, 1971, five weeks before the school district meeting, a departure from the traditional school/library procedure by virtue of a change in the State Education Law. The School Board's consent was necessary and confirmed by a 5-2 vote. Several years later the then president of the School Board, Fred Read, confided that the board was grateful "not to have to sit up half the night struggling with a second budget."

Esther Margolius was elected to the Library Board, but since an item in the budget for Sunday openings caused concern among more than half the voters, the budget was voted down. Weeks later the budget was presented again with Sunday openings as a separate proposition. The budget was passed, but Sunday openings were not.

Donald Christ succeeded Tom Lapham as president of the board.

Esther Margolius

Henry Salomon

Children's room showing the popular "womb chairs."

The meeting room of the library will be dedicated to the memory of the late Thomas Willets Lapham this Sunday, Sept. 21, at 3 p.m. Mr. Lapham, who died last year after a boating mishap, served on the library Board of Trustees as a member from 1952 to 1959 and as its president from 1959 until June, 1971. A major achievement of the Library Board during Mr. Lapham's years in office was completion of plans for the new building on Main Street which now houses the library.

The meeting room, which opened on June 8, 1970, has served more than 150 of the community's organizations. It seats 240, and artists who have performed there in concert say it has excellent acoustics.

The brief dedication ceremony on Sunday will begin with the poem, "Summons," written by Patricia Benton. It has been set to music by composer Jeanne Singer, who will accompany baritone Richard Anderson as he sings the selection.

Current Library Board President Richard D. Whittemore will introduce Hedley Donovan, longtime board associate and friend of Mr. Lapham. Donovan's message will be followed by the unveiling of a memorial plaque to be installed on the Lapham Meeting Room wall. The plaque was designed by David K. Stone.

Following presentation of the plaque, Friends of the Library will provide refreshments. Hostesses for the event will be Elizaneth Teitler, Carolyn Fellows, Ruth Yanowitz, Fran Stein, Lauren Richerick, Nadine Heyman, and Natalie Shipley.

The Garden Club of Port Washington is providing special floral decorations for the Lapham Room dedication. The members in charge are Mrs. Frederick Donner, Mrs. Edward Lapham, Mrs. Charles Richards, and Lillian McCormick.

Library dedicates Lapham Room
Port News, *September 18, 1975.*

During the first full year in the new library a serious problem in traffic control developed at Main Street and Library Drive. Crossing Main Street from the library was hazardous to both children and adults. The local police, the Accident Prevention Bureau, the *Port News,* Main Street School and Home Association, the School Board, Friends of the Library, Residents for a more Beautiful Port Washington and Donald Christ together offered, counteroffered, studied and restudied solutions to a perfectly obvious traffic peril. It took many years before the Nassau County Director of Traffic Engineering finally put his stamp of approval on a standard, timed traffic light at the intersection.

The book collection had reached 90,220 volumes, and 15,352 adults had borrowed books in the first eight months of 1971. Margaret Lucha was appointed Community Relations Director and promptly redesigned and edited the monthly calendar/newsletter and received approval to mail it four times per year.

Aside from a leaky roof that defied all efforts of roofers and other contractors to repair permanently, a spate of broken windows in the reading room and children's room (rocks and .22 pellet guns suspected) costing $21,000 to replace in 1974, and elevators that occasionally refused to go up or down, the new building was a huge success and remained so.

The Art Gallery was the scene of monthly exhibits which attracted to the library many art lovers who were later seen browsing in the Reading Room and in the stacks.

One of the pleasures in entering the lobby of the library was always the joy of seeing beautiful floral arrangements throughout the year, climaxed at Christmas time with spectacular wreaths and evergreens—all courtesy of the Port Washington Garden Club.

During the '70's the Board of Trustees changed markedly. Ted Davis who had served for 10 years retired in 1973 and Henry Salomon was elected to his seat on the board.

Donald Christ stepped down as president of the board, Richard Whittemore replacing him as president in 1975.

That same year Joan Kent was elected to the board and Farrell Jones was appointed to fill out Christ's term. In 1977 both Jones and Salomon were elected to five year terms.

By 1978 a new Young Adult Librarian, Suzanne Ponzini, had joined the staff, also assuming responsibility for the Littig House program. Corinne Camarata and Carrie Ayres were the Children's librarians at the time.

Farrell Jones (left) and Henry Salomon (second from left) at L.I.R.R. station offer paperbacks during newspaper strike.

Joan Kent

When the newspapers went on strike during the summer of 1978, the library did its part in helping hapless commuters cope with the ride to Penn Station. A portable lending library (card table) was set up (see photo) stacked with paperbacks. "Help yourself and please return the books to the library when you're through!" was the message. The response was overwhelmingly enthusiastic to the point that several commuters who were already carrying books brought more books to donate the following day.

Few major changes took place, structurally, in the library building during the 1980's other than finding ways to alleviate the crowded conditions when departments such as Media Port needed to expand. Special Collections which robbed the trustees of their board room actually had doubled as a conference room for years.

Farrell Jones

The library's 10th anniversary celebration continues at the library this week with daily showings of "A Multi-Image Experience." Depicting 10 years of happenings at the library, the wide-screen slide show delves back into the history of the building's construction when bulldozers dug deep, and local school children decorated a temporary fence around the construction site.

With the doors of the new building opening in June, 1970, a decade of community service followed, and the "multi-image" show documents of that..

The preparation of the multi-screen showing took more than four months, supervised by George Pickow with the assistance of Patricia Platzman, Martin Vogel, Bob Johnson, and Frank Daniel.

The 20-minute show will be screened with narration four times each day, at 10 a.m. and 1, 7:30, and 8:30 p.m. on Monday, June 16, through Friday, June 20. On Saturday, June 21, there will be two showings, at 11:30 a.m. and 3 p.m.

"A Multi-Image Experience" will have its premiere showing at the library's 10th birthday open house on Sunday, June 15. The open house will begin with remarks at 2:30 p.m. by anniversary committee head Richard Whittemore. He will introduce Timothy Costello, president of Adelphi University, whose talk will be followed by a concert by soprano Carol Dougherty-Heierman and bass Raymond Buckingham.

The concert will be followed by the narrated screening and an open house reception sponsored by Friends of the Library. The celebration is open to the entire community.

Multi-Image Experience *shown daily at library* Port News, *June 12, 1980*

Acquiring neighboring property for possible expansion (and to protect the library from encroaching commercial development) came under discussion after twelve years in the new building. In 1985 fortune smiled on the trustees when Mr. de Sciora discovered that half of the Baker Funeral Home property, adjacent to the library on the east side, was for sale. After considerable negotiating the library and the Baker family agreed, and the land and building were purchased.

Six years later the other half of the Baker property was acquired, giving the library two full lots next to the parking area running from Main Street to Locust Avenue.

The voters elected Janet Reinhardt to the library board in 1979 on Richard Whittemore's retirement. In 1983 when Mrs. Reinhardt resigned to move to Pennsylvania, Daniel Kurshan was appointed then elected to a full five year term in 1984.

Henry Salomon had served for ten years when he retired in 1984. Elected to Salomon's seat on the board was Eileen Hickson who had previously worked at the library for many years prior to becoming principal clerk.

No vacancies existed on the board for seven years. In 1991 the voters elected Fred Kramer to a five year position.

A major renovation was undertaken in 1991 to completely redesign and reconstruct the Children's Library into an even more colorful and adaptable area. Of great interest to adults (especially those who no longer had small ones at home) were the three computers (donated by the Friends) in constant use by first or second graders, and even more startling, by pre-schoolers who needed to be lifted to the seat, but needed no help using the computer.

DECADE — A CELEBRATION FOR THE 80'S

On April 13, 1980, a full house in the Lapham Meeting Room, including television reporters from Channel 12 and their equipment, greeted the opening program of the 10th Anniversary of the *new* Port Washington Library. Chairman of Decade, former trustee Whittemore, welcomed the guests:

"Today Decade celebrates the people of Port Washington who have made this library a major influence on our lives...the trustees who have had the good sense to set sound policy and allow the staff to implement that policy...the director who for more than twenty years has been one of the trendsetters in American libraries and whose foresight has brought valued innovations and prestige...the staff of dedicated professionals whose commitment and loyalty is unprecedented in this field...and finally to the many library support groups who have volunteered their energies to exploit the time and talents of so many people in the community."

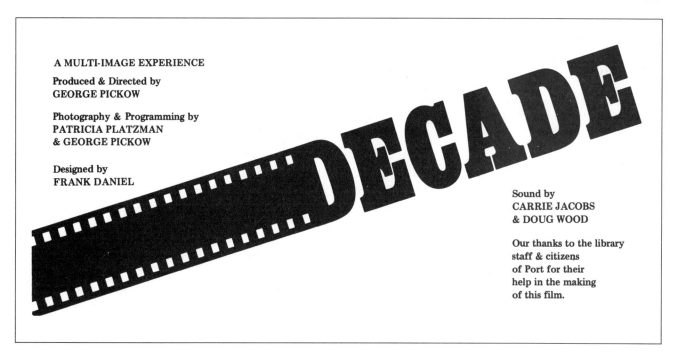

A MULTI-IMAGE EXPERIENCE

Produced & Directed by
GEORGE PICKOW

Photography & Programming by
PATRICIA PLATZMAN
& GEORGE PICKOW

Designed by
FRANK DANIEL

Sound by
CARRIE JACOBS
& DOUG WOOD

Our thanks to the library
staff & citizens
of Port for their
help in the making
of this film.

Joseph Papp, founder and producer of the New York Shakespeare Festival, and Elizabeth Swados, writer and folksinger, were the first of a long line of distinguished guest speakers/entertainers.

Two weeks later the momentum of Decade continued with "This Is My Song," a musical accolade to life based on the writings, poems and letters of the elderly.

Jean Ritchie opened the festivities in June with a concert of her own compositions, followed a week later by the multi-gravitational aerial dance troupe, *Aerodance,* performing on scaffolding set up on the west lawn.

Probably best remembered of all the events was *Decade: A Multi-Image Experience,* produced and directed by George Pickow. Truly the pièce de résistance of the season-long celebration, Pickow and his crew constructed a huge projection screen on which multiple images from eight slide projectors were blended into one 20-minute documentary saluting the library's anniversary.

In September Maggie Kuhn, founder of the Gray Panthers, the country's most noted advocate of the rights of all ages, brought the message: "Be your own person in this age of self-determination. Age is the one thing we all share."

A four-hour International Festival in the parking area of the library celebrated Port Washington in all its ethnic variety.

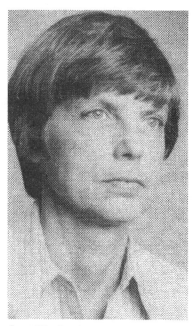

Janet Rinehardt

At that time...

**President Nixon reelected in near
record landslide**

TWENTY-ONE YEARS OF CULTURAL EVENTS

During a period of 10 days in August, 1979, a Library User Survey was conducted which revealed to no one's great surprise that over 98% of the people (200) who responded came to the library to borrow or return books or other material. In descending order, reasons for visiting library were "just browsing," the exhibits, copy machines, children's room, meetings, programs, or studying.

A survey conducted in 1991 produced 2,000 responses, 1,200 of which included written comments. The greatest concerns of patrons at that time were parking, more books, quiet places to study, more children's programs and more comfortable meeting room seats.

The library is first and foremost a repository of *books*, some 130,000 books in today's collection; available also are audio and video tapes, compact discs, books on tape, and LP records. In addition thousands of people flock to the library each year to look, to listen, to learn and just to enjoy themselves at a wide variety of events.

Here are some of the programs and events sponsored by the staff over the past 20 years, followed by highlights of programming by the volunteer organizations.

Programming by the Library Staff

For many years in charge of general programming, assistant director, Virginia Parker, exercised skill and insight in finding the programs which had wide appeal without neglecting those which might have a smaller audience but brought pleasure to the few and prestige to the library.

On occasion Mrs. Parker set her sights on prospective speakers who would attract a large audience but were elusive. Luck and a bit of audacity worked in her favor at least once. She confided:

"One summer [1971] I was at LaGuardia Airport, just coming back from a library convention, and I saw this tall, distinguished-looking gentleman and I knew it was Averill Harriman. As it happens, he had a summer home here in Port Washington. He'd just written a new book and I had written to him, but we hadn't been able to work out a time for him to come as a speaker. But when I saw him there, I introduced myself and said I hoped that at some point we could arrange it. He said, "Well, I'm on my way out there now and will be there for the next month," and so, within two weeks, we worked it out so that Averill Harriman came here as a speaker and I think that was our first big program at the new library. It was a lot of fun."

Isaac Asimov, known primarily as a science fiction writer, but equally prolific in writing children's books, popular fiction, mysteries and atomic and nuclear energy books, was a "catch" at the height of his career in the 70's.

Martin Luther King

Programs honoring the memory of Dr. King were held in the library annually from 1972, some celebrations lasting two days. Music, particularly spiritual, jubilee and gospel, Pablo Casals award winning cellist Alvin McCall, films, plays by Littig House Players, group singing all contributed to the mid-winter celebration of this man who changed the country.

The "Books Sandwiched In" series, started in the early 70's, was probably the most consistently popular program. These Friday lunchtime get-togethers in the Meeting Room with knowledgeable book reviewers derived their name from the fact that patrons brought their own sandwich with coffee served by the Friends. According to programming specialist, Pleasance Coggeshall, "we try also to get artists and musicians who will come and talk about their work and their development."

Education

Adelphi University's President Timothy Costello, admired for creating an MBA program for commuters on the Long Island Rail Road, brought the idea of an experimental MBA program to be given at the Port Washington and Manhasset libraries. A two-year course leading to a graduate degree attracted over a dozen enrollees and in 1975 eight of the original candidates received their degrees at a full cap and gown ceremony in the Lapham Meeting Room.

The library and Adelphi also cooperated in a series of ABLE (Adult Baccalaureate Life Experience) courses offering undergraduate degrees. Hofstra University and SUNY at Stony Brook both offered graduate courses at the library, some taught by videotape.

On a different level training courses were given by Literacy Volunteers of America to adults interested in teaching reading to other adults.

Ethnic Outreach

The ethnicity of Port Washington enriched the library's outreach, giving the staff opportunities to attract many who might never enter the doors.

Latin American Week at the library introduced young people to piñata parties, Mexican movies, Latin American foods and music.

During Afro-American History Month in 1979 folk tales from Long Island's first Black and Indian Historical District were presented in costumed dramas.

A Molly Picon film, traditional Jewish dances, Jewish art, and the film "Lies My Father Told Me" were presented over the five days of Jewish Heritage Week in May, 1984.

Lectures, operas, and a wide variety of other entertainments were featured during the annual Italian-American Week celebrations at the library co-sponsored by Marino Lodge of the Sons of Italy.

On three occasions during the 80's Japanese ladies and their children shared their many traditions with the community in costumed dance ceremonies, traditional Japanese food, and music at the library.

Over 400 people attended the August, 1971, meeting to hear Averill Harriman discuss Russian–U.S. relations. Former County Executive Eugene Nickerson was moderator.

Italian Heritage and Culture Month Program, 1991

Daniel L. Kurshan

Senior Citizens

A variety of services for "over 60's," were provided, from hypertension screening to consultation on aging problems to employment assistance. Gray Panthers held their meetings, and *Senior Connections* for information and referral were in the lobby twice a week.

Nautical Center

Established to maintain a collection of books, photographs, artifacts, cruising guides and selected nautical charts relating to the history, people and boats of Manhasset Bay, the Center sponsored lectures and exhibits for sailors and lovers of the sea who visited the library from throughout the metropolitan area.

Workshops, Clubs and Courses

As community interests emerged in almost any field the library responded by encouraging patrons to join clubs and workshops for chess, photography, genealogy, archaeology and travel.

THE ORAL HISTORY PROGRAM

Founded in 1980 in order to document and preserve the voices of residents whose lives have collectively spanned the past century, the Oral History Program, directed by Elly Shodell, completed projects about African-American Families, sandmining, maritime traditions, workers on Great Estates. All were exhibited at the library, three publications were developed from the extensive research and were published by the library: *Particles of the Past: Sandmining on Long Island, 1870's to 1940's; It Looks Like Yesterday to Me: Port Washington's Afro-American Heritage; In the Service: Workers on the Grand Estates of Long Island, 1890's to 1940's.*

Teen Age Programming

Under the direction of Suzanne Ponzini, the Young Adult program featured wide-reaching attractions: workshops on ten-speed bicycles, juggling, handwriting analysis, organizing, researching and writing term papers, interviewing skills.

The most popular and long-lasting program for teen science fiction buffs was the weekend SCI-Fi and Fantasy Festival started by a small group of fans. Films, art contests, trivia contests, and an occasional costume contest kept things moving.

The Youth Advisory Council (Y.A.C.), is a group of volunteers, grades 7 through 12, working to improve and enhance library collections, programs and services for teen-agers.

Eileen Hickson

Children's librarians, Corinne Camarata, Carey Ayres, and Rachel Fox in one of the colorful "castles" in the redesigned Children's Library.

For Children Only

Winter Vacation Festivals: Original animated science films by Port students…"Port Children on Videotape"…Puppet shows for over fives…Marine scientists program for eight and up.

"Summer Specials": animal films, puppets…kite making and flying contests…"Monster Hunt" reading contests.

For the Whole Family

Annual summer "Happenings": music, mime, performances, fortune telling, graffiti (under control)…Parents as Reading Partners…folksinging.

Especially for Women—since 1971

"Woman as Artist"—exhibit by members of the National Association of Women Artists…Elizabeth Janeway, *Man's World, Woman's Place,* speaks to large audience…"Sexism in children's literature"…"In Celebration of Women"—films by women filmmakers "Project turning point" for *women in need of direction about their future.*

An exhibit of 200 photographs by ten women photographers—sponsored by New York Council on the Arts, National Endowment for the Arts, and the Levi Strauss Foundation—drew crowds of viewers during the full month it was in the Gallery.

Two plays about women were presented in the Meeting Room, one, a musical celebrating the Bicentennial, *Sisters of Liberty,* the other about the life of Margaret Fuller.

Frederic S. Kramer

Officers & Directors, 1992

Amy Bass, *President*
Julie Geller, *Vice President*
Nancy Wright, *Treasurer*
Stan Spielman, *Secretary*

Ruth Bogen, Joyce Fieldsteel, Beverly
Halm, Doris Hunter, Robert Lewis,
Kaethe Ohiso, Don Parker, Anne
Sayers, Bette Sue, Andrea Watson

A Few of the Distinguished Authors
Who Spoke at the Book and Author
Luncheons

Meyer Levin
Roger Kahn
Vincent Canby
William Safire
Felicia Roosevelt
Ken McCormick
Margaret Mead
Budd Schulberg and
Geraldine Brooks
Gail Sheehy
Sally Olds
Jay Anson
Lynn Caine
Norman Garbo*
Isabell Holland
W.S. Kuniczak
Peter Wyden
Wilfred Sheed
Susan Isaacs*
Carole Klein
Quentin Crisp
George Vecsey
Kate Simon
E.R. Braithwaite
Marian McPartland**
Sandra Blakeslee
Donald Axinn

*Susan Isaacs spoke at three luncheons
and was moderator at a fourth.*

**Marian McPartland also played the
piano.*

# indicates resident of Port Washington.

FRIENDS OF THE PORT WASHINGTON LIBRARY

It is impossible to imagine the library without the Friends of the Library. Their efforts, year after year from 1965 on, first in spearheading the six-month campaign to promote the Library Bond issue, then raising money through memberships in the Friends, book sales and the Book and Author Luncheons all of which provided the funds for special programs which the regular library budget could not support.

Among their "gifts" to the library, the Friends sponsored a Winter series of live programs on the Bible, drama, ballet, a songfest, band concert and made a $500 donation to the Music Advisory Council piano fund.

–Paid for library budget and trustee vote, set up a speakers' bureau and purchased a lectern for the Meeting Room.

–Sponsored a foreign film series, the Port Black Teen Theatre, Guitar Workshop holiday songfest, and co-sponsored the Library's Third Anniversary Party.

–Funded programs by storytellers, local authors, a film trilogy of a Bengali family, and each year set aside $2,500 or more for future programming.

–*Friends* volunteers covered voting machines at annual elections...sponsored Story Theater Company...Science Film Festival...Nicolo Marionette Theatre...Barbara Merjan's Percussion Workshop for Youth...Two reviewers for Books Sandwiched In (3 series).

As recently as 1991 *Friends* donated $14,000, $10,000 to the Oral History Project and the balance for computers for the Children's Library.

ART ADVISORY COUNCIL

Founded in 1960 the Art Advisory Council earned a reputation for outstanding exhibits throughout the ten years prior to the opening of the new library, even though the facilities at the Belleview Avenue address were far from favorable.

With the opening of a new library with its handsome gallery offering natural light from skylights and artificial light designed for the gallery, the Art Advisory Council accepted the challenge for the Dedication. Their exhibit was "Two Hundred Years of American Art," twenty-six privately owned works by Port Washington collectors, loaned for the special occasion. On display for a month the exhibit attracted hundreds of visitors who could also enjoy viewing for the first time the architectural triumph of their new library.

From the beginning the Council achieved variety and quality by offering the works of renowned artists, carefully screened local artists, and by encouraging Long Island artists through annual competitions.

Over the years the library has hosted such artists as Balcomb Greene; modern great, Max Weber, whose gouaches and pastels were loaned by his family and the Forum Gallery; oils and sculptures by prize-winning artists Francine Barken, Babs Kent and Martin Schreiber; Ruth Leaf's intaglio prints; Estaban Vicente; lithographs and sculptures of Leonard Baskin, winner of Louis Tiffany and Guggenheim Fellowships. The world-renowned painter, Frank Stella, was unquestionably one of the most prestigious of all those exhibited in the Art Gallery.

Early in 1971 Norman Laliberte became a firm friend of Port Washington art patrons when his exhibit of brilliantly colored banners graced the gallery walls for a month. He and his banners returned many times right up to the 1992 Centennial.

"Youth Art Months" sponsored jointly by the Port Washington Schools and the Art Council brought together in the Gallery paintings, ceramics, sculpture and crafts produced by students in kindergarten through 12th grade. Blossoming in an adult arena far from the classroom, young artists and their friends tasted the rewards of public recognition.

In later years distinguished artists who exhibited at the gallery included Jane Wilson, Isabel Bishop, the leading Japanese artists in the metropolitan area, Stuart Davis, Paul Jenkins, Milton Avery and Guy Pene duBois.

In June of 1992, as part of the gala Centennial Celebration, members of the Art Advisory Council exhibited their own works—paintings, photographs, sculpture, and works created exclusively for the Centennial.

MUSIC ADVISORY COUNCIL

With a Meeting Room, now *concert hall*, just waiting for music to fill the air, the trustees in 1971 approached Ruth Feingold, an accomplished musician in the community, to help "organize some music for the library." Promptly a Music Advisory Council came into being and has been a major moving force behind good music—Bach to rock—in Port Washington for over twenty years.

Insisting that "good music requires good instruments" the Council set about getting a concert grand piano for the Meeting Room. In less than four years through benefit concerts and generous patrons who joined as members, the Music Advisory Council was able to purchase a seven-foot Steinway, the mainstay of most concerts.

The Council prides itself on the quality of the hundreds of concerts booked into the library, striving for both variety and excellence.

Art Advisory Council 1992

Fred Blumlein, Catchi, Arthur Conescu, Barbara Fishman, Betty Gimbel, Marian Goodman, Mark Graham, William Haussler, Rita Katz, Marion Klein, Madeleine Lane, Viggo Holm Madsen, Jean-Marie Martin, Marion McManus, Ann Pellaton, Eric Pick, Catherine Sandy, Shellie Schneider, Lynda Schwartz, Myrna Turtletaub, Kensuki Wakeshima, Aida Whedon, Clem Wrenn

Typical postcard promoting an AAC exhibit: artist Abe Ajay's The Portal Series, December, 1991. Artist Abe Ajay, The Portal Series, *December, 1991*

John Browning, distinguished pianist,
frequent guest on the library's concert stage.

Music Advisory Council—1972

Ruth Feingold	Susan Aberbach
Suzette Halasz	Lucretia Harrison
Jean Ritchie	Jerald Stone

Music Advisory Council—1992

Arthur Conescu	Ruth Feingold
Sterling Gorrill	Richard Moore
Jean Ritchie	Marlene Schiller
Bernard Wasser	Jacqueline Wood

library coordinator: Amy Pett

A particular coup of the MAC was the appearance of Pamella Ross, pianist, in "I Clara: An Evening of Words and Music" reflecting on the life of Clara Schumann in the first half of the 19th century using her diaries and the music of her husband and of Beethoven, Chopin, Brahms and others to enhance the story.

Port Washington has been the home of many well-known musicians who have graced the Lapham Meeting Room with their performances: Susan Quittmeyer Morris, now with the Metropolitan Opera; Howard Dietz, lyric writer and his colleague, composer Arthur Schwartz; Jean Ritchie, scholar, folk singer, library neighbor; pianist Marian McPartland; and the Wood family whose members excel at so many musical instruments.

Among other outstanding musicians who have appeared at the library are Soprano Dawn Upshaw, violinist Daniel Phillips, Stephanie Chase and Judith Alstadter in a concert of violin and piano sonatas, Orpheus Chamber Ensemble, Primavera Quartet, and pianist Robert Taub.

Some unusually distinguished pianists such as John Browning and Anne Marie McDermott have returned to the library many times.

Jazz programs offered by the Music Advisory Council rank with the best in New York City or elsewhere:

Tenor sax stylist Billy Mitchell...Pianist Dill Jones...Barbara Carroll, singing jazz pianist...Bob Rosengarden and trio...Maxine Sullivan with Dill Jones Trio...Hal Schaefer, Port Washington resident and extraordinary jazz pianist...George Shearing...Billy Taylor. After Dill Jones death in 1984 a Jazz Fund in his name was founded at the library and used to sponsor annual concerts each spring.

Summer concerts featuring chamber orchestras with soloists, American Song and Poetry, piano recitals, songs and music of the "swing-era," opera and folk singers, vocal quartets, in short the entire spectrum of music on the light side for summer audiences.

MEDIA PORT

Cultural Program Specialist, Lillian Katz, later director of Media Port, explained the purpose of the VTR (Video Transcription Recording) Program which in 1971 was the first of the New York State Council on the Arts funded projects:

to aid communication *within* Port Washington...to bring diverse sections of the community together...to get a video portrait of Port Washington.

A year later more than 350 residents had been trained in use of the VTR, filming such diverse events as North Hempstead Town

Meetings, school classrooms, both formal and sidewalk interviews.

Video workshops and training programs for all interested library patrons—junior high students to senior citizens and local agencies—became a regular feature of Media Port scheduling throughout the twenty years following the first New York State Council on the Arts grant.

In addition to the public, representatives of local agencies were trained in the use of video in fund-raising, staff training and counseling techniques.

Cable television, in its infancy, was explored by Media Port in an open panel discussion (1977). The proceedings were taped by "video volunteers" and made available to anyone seeking help in making a decision about cable TV.

The sandpits, Port Washington's shrinking past, have fascinated photographers and writers for generations. In the mid-70's Marcia (Dickerson) Hawthorne and her crew trained their VTR's on that vast area in order to examine the sand pits as they are and as they once were.

Media Port's home today is the entire fourth level of the library building where movable storage facilities house over 4,200 VHS videotapes for all ages and interests: feature films for adults and children, documentaries, instructional films; 5,200 compact discs; 3,500 LP records; and 2,700 spoken word audio cassettes. A well-lighted gallery specializing in photography exhibits is a focal point of Media Port throughout the year.

Encouraging the growth and wide use of video and film as teaching and enrichment media, the New York State Council on the Arts, the New York State Council for the Humanities and the National Endowment for the Arts have provided many thousands of dollars in grants to the library, recognition for which constantly appears on programs, news releases and the monthly newsletter and calendar as "funded (in part) by" one or more of these enlightened organizations.

A GALA CENTENNIAL CELEBRATION

Just twenty-two years after proudly opening the doors on a new Port Washington Library the time had arrived for the Trustees and staff to celebrate the century-long existence of the library. Members of the community, including a Centennial Celebration coordinator, Susan Shattuck, joined the committee at the library bringing ideas, inspiration and hard work to scheduling a full year of events.

As this is written, one half of the Centennial Year Celebrations have passed. A capsule review of some of those events includes:

"The most wonderful party I've ever been to" were the words one

Gala Celebration

Aida Whedon

Gala Celebration, a painting by Aida Whedon, the centerpiece of the Anniversary.

lady used to describe the elegant Costume Ball held in the library to inaugurate Centennial Year. The following day Daniel Boorstin, Librarian of Congress Emeritus, addressed an audience of 400, toured the library, and on leaving said, "This is the best library of its size in the U.S."

The first half of the year brought one of the most beautiful art exhibits seen in Port Washington, forty-two magnificent works from the Colby College Museum of Art. The exhibit, titled "100 Years of American Art," filled the library's Art Gallery, the Media Gallery and the lobby with masterpieces by Alexander Calder, Mary Cassatt, Gertrude Fiske, Walter Gay, Rockwell Kent, Bernard Langlais, Reginald Marsh, Louise Nevelson, Georgia O'Keefe and N.C. Wyeth and many others.

Norman Laliberte's banner art enhanced the Reading Room Walkway for two months, followed by exhibits of paintings by Karen Weinberger and Robert Cariola in the Gallery.

Maggie Kuhn of the Gray Panthers regaled her audience with her wit and wisdom in her third visit to the library.

In June members of the library's Art Advisory Council continued with an exhibit of their own works. Many of the artists on the Council achieved not only local fame but were known throughout the U.S.

Music filled the air in the library throughout the spring. John Browning opened the Centennial year with his piano concert in January, followed by Anne-Marie McDermott, another of the popular pianists whose concerts had "sold out" in previous years.

Four concerts for young people featured flutist Eugenia Zuckerman, The Bill Taylor Trio, The Little Orchestra Society of Lincoln Center, and Festival Brass.

During April and May two outstanding exhibits, *Cross Currents: Baymen, Yachtsmen and Long Island Waters* and *Changing Channels: Maritime Folk Artists* reflected on the changing world of Manhasset Bay adjacent to Port Washington.

AWARDS

Shortly after the successful bond issue vote in 1965 the library received the John Cotton Dana Publicity Award for outstanding publicity (See page 159).

From the time the Port Washington Public Library moved into its new home in 1970, the library has been singled out by national and local organizations for merit awards in many areas.

Right after it opened the new library was selected for the 1970 Concrete Industry Board, Inc. award
"as representing the best in conception, originality and applicability of concrete both in design and construction."

Also in 1970 the library was honored with a citation from Residents For A More Beautiful Port Washington:

1970 Citation
to
The Port Washington Public Library

More than a center of learning
More than a structure of beauty
It has become the center of
cultural life for this community

Italian-American Festivals at the library brought many people from diverse backgrounds together and in 1983 the library received a Certificate of Appreciation from the John Michael Marino Lodge of Order of Sons of Italy.

The newsletters and calendars sent to every residence in Port Washington have been the major source of communication between the library and the community. Taking many forms, from one-page sheets to colorful folders, the newsletter finally hit its prize-winning stride in September, 1987, with the publication of Volume 1 of a tabloid-size newspaper, "The Port Washington Library. A monthly guide to your community library, its programs and services." This publication has now won the following award in 1988, 1990 and 1991:

The Library Public Relations Council Award
For outstanding achievement in
Library Public Relations Promotion

The Helen Keller National Center for Deaf-Blind Youths and Adults and the Town of North Hempstead each recognized the library for *providing work experience to the clients of the Helen Keller National Center.*

EPILOGUE

This gracious community called Port Washington—"one of the most delightful hamlets of the entire world"—has helped nurture, support and enrich "the best library of its size in the U.S."

The preceding pages hopefully have conveyed the sense of history which surrounds this institution, but more importantly an awareness of the service which abounds there. Changes in Port Washington and in the world have brought changes in book collections, in art, in music and in all the facets of learning which lure people to libraries.

Looking to the the 21st century where untold electronic gadgetry will manage, or at least help us to manage, our lives, no matter how information, knowledge, and entertainment are packaged, there will always be books, else why bother with the word *library.*

Appendix

THE UNIVERSITY OF THE STATE OF NEW YORK

CHARTER OF
PORT WASHINGTON PUBLIC LIBRARY*

This instrument witnesseth that the Regents of the University of the State of New York have granted this charter incorporating

John S. Witmer, Jr. Walter S. McGrane Karl W. Kirchwey
Frank G. Lippert and Helen Sands

and their successors as a free public library, in accordance with the vote establishing the same, under the corporate name of Port Washington Public Library, to be located at Port Washington, Nassau County, New York, the library to have, as provided by law, five trustees, to be at first the persons named herein as incorporators, who are the duly elected library trustees of union free school district no. 4, town of North Hempstead, Nassau county, New York, to hold, respectively, in the order of their naming, as they have determined by lot, one, each for the term which shall expire with the official school year in each of the years 1925, 1926, 1927, 1928 and 1929; and their successors to hold for terms of five years, beginning with the official school year next following the ending of the term to which each, respectively, is to succeed, to be chosen, in conformity to law, one in each year, by the electors of said union free school district no. 4, town of North Hempstead, Nassau County, New York, at the annual school meeting. (The above paragraph is written by hand.)

Granted, January 1, 1925, by the Regents of the University of the State of New York executed under their seal and recorded in their office. Number 3406

*The original charter of the Port Washington Public Library is on view at the library.

HEAD LIBRARIANS
PORT WASHINGTON PUBLIC LIBRARY

Wilhelmina M. Mitchell	1892–1926
Helen B. Curtice	1926–1958
Edward de Sciora	1958–

BOARD OF TRUSTEES
PORT WASHINGTON PUBLIC LIBRARY

Notes:

1. Trustees before 1913, the year the library received the Department of Education Certificate, were all members of the Port Washington Woman's Club.

2. 1922 is the last year *complete* minutes of Board Meetings are available until January 1944. Members listed between those years were found in other documents or in the *Port Washington News.*

3. *Asterisk indicates member served as President of the Board of Trustees.

Miss Wilhelmina M. Mitchell   1892–1926
Mrs. Ellen B. Stannard   1894–1916
Mrs. A. Valentine Fraser   1903–? and 1942
*Mrs. Mary Elizabeth McLean   1900–1921
*E.W. Gaillard   1913–1914
Mrs. Mary E. Baxter   1913–1914
Miss Florence I. McKee   1913–1916
*Charles N. Wysong   1913–1917
*John S. Witmer   1914–1922
Burges Johnson   1914–1916
Miss M. A. Baxter   1914–1922
Mason Trowbridge   1914–1916
Joseph H. Aston   1915–?
Miss Helen Sands   1916-1923
Miss Phoebe A. Underhill   1916–1919
J. E. Bullard   1915–1919
*Charles W. Weeks   1918–1919
W. H. Kellogg   1918–?
Mrs. Charles E. Tuxhill   1918–1919
Mr. A. C. Wysong   1919–?
Samuel J. Gutelius   1920–1921
Paul D. Schreiber   1920–?
H. R. Woltman   1921–?
Mrs. Olive Singer   1922–1923
Frank G. Lippert   1922–?
Walter S. McGrane   1924–?
Karl W. Kirchwey   1924–?
*Cedric R. Crowell   1926–1944, 1947–1952
Herbert E. Rose   1926–?
Miss E. J. Brown   1927–1932
*Dr. Everett N. Whitcomb   ?–1946
Mrs. Ruth Hartell   1944–1955
*John C. Crawley   ?–1959
*Linus E. Kittredge   1945–1959
Mrs. Evelyn Kelley   1948–1953

*Thomas W. Lapham   1952–1972
Mrs. Marie Dunnells   1953–1962
Mrs. LuEsther T. Mertz   1955–1964
Benjamin E. Haller   1959–1969
Hedley Donovan   1960–1963
Mrs. Lena Ruppert   1962 (served one month)
Theodore W. Davis   1962–1973
Robert Fried   1963–1968
Mrs. Muriel Neville   1964–1971
*Donald Christ   1968–1976
*Richard D. Whittemore   1969–1979
William I. Stoddard   1971–1975
Mrs. Esther Margolius   1972–1991
*Henry A. Salomon   1973–1984
*Mrs. Joan G. Kent   1975–present
Farrell Jones   1976–present
Mrs. Janet Reinhardt   1979–1982
Daniel Kurshan   1982–present
Mrs. Eileen Hickson   1984–present
Frederick W. Kramer   1991–present

BIBLIOGRAPHY

Archives of the Port Washington Public Library
Curl, D.W., *Mizner's Florida,* MIT Press, Cambridge, Mass. 1984
Hallowell, Anna Davis, *James and Lucretia Mott,* Houghton Mifflin, Boston, 1885
Lewis, Grace H., *With Love From Gracie,* Harcourt Brace, N.Y. 1951
Map: Beers, Comstock, Cline, *Atlas of Long Island*
Norris, Kathleen, *Family Gathering,* Doubleday & Co., Garden City, NY 1959
PLAIN TALK, 1911–1914
PORT WASHINGTON MAIL, 1965–1970
PORT WASHINGTON NEWS, 1903–1990
PORT WASHINGTON REPORTER, 1968

PHOTOGRAPH CREDITS

Archives of the Port Washington Public Library
Linda Cohen
Cow Neck Peninsula Historical Society
William Haussler
Hugh Malone Collection, Port Washington Public Library
Frank Pavlak
George Pickow
Leo Stoecker
David Williams (Crawley family)

Cover rendering by Richard C. Baehr A.I.A
Composition by TypeLink, Inc.
Halftone production by Leebolt, Inc.
Printed by Eclipse Press, Inc.